World Mythology

ISBN 1-84084-451-5 (Hardback)

This is a Dempsey Parr Book
This edition published in 2000
Parragon
Queen Street House
4 Queen Street
Bath BA1 1HE ,UK
Copyright © Dempsey Parr 1999

Printed in Indonesia
Produced for Dempsey Parr by
Foundry Design & Production, a part of
The Foundry Creative Media Company Ltd,
Crabtree Hall, Crabtree Lane,
Fulham, London, SW6 6TY

A copy of the CIP data for this book is
available from the British Library.

World Mythology

GENERAL EDITOR:
Arthur Cotterell

DP

DEMPSEY
PARR

Contents

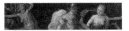

Introduction

W E OWE THE WORD myth, like many others in common use today, to the ancient Greeks. No modern language has a substitute, and there can be no better way of understanding what mythology is about than by taking a look at the original meaning of the word.

Descended from the idea of speech itself, myth had by the fifth century BC come to mean a story, a narrative of events. The historian Herodatus, who wrote an account of the wars between the Greeks and the Persians, was anxious to record everything he could about this great struggle, even if some of the tales might be regarded as myths or legends. He admitted that he was unsure of their factual accuracy, but such was their interest they simply could not be ignored. It was for his reader to decide what could or could not be believed. This suggestion of a myth being a tall story, something fictitious rather than a statement of fact, was pushed even further by the philosopher Plato, who was concerned to distinguish between those things we can accept as being true and those we cannot.

▲ *Iranian statue of a bull, the central symbol in Mithraism.*

But the rise of reasoning in Ancient Greece did not immediately undermine the importance of mythology. For it was realised how myths were traditional stories which embodied the heritage of the Greek-speaking world. They contain, a mythologer would say today, the basic thought-patterns by which the ancient Greeks knew themselves as a separate people. He might add that the strength of Greek mythology, like other notable traditions, lay in its collective narrative. Unlike a story composed by a single author, a myth always stands on its own, with a plot and a set of characters easily recognised by those who listen to the story-teller, poet or dramatist making use of it. When for instance, the Athenians watched plays performed every year at their religious festivals, they were already aware of the events a playwright like Aeschylus or Sophocles would so often choose to tell. The aftermath of the Trojan War never ceased to fascinate them, nor did the

▲ *San-shin accompanied by his messenger tiger.*

tragedy of Oedipus ever fail to hold their attention. That after becoming aware of his terrible deeds of patricide and incest, Oedipus should have chosen to die in the grove of Colonus near Athens made his tragedy a subject of intense local interest. Sophocles's play *Oedipus at Colonus* can indeed be said to draw together the deepest feelings of the ancient Greeks about crime, punishment and fate in the final release of the blind Theban ex-king.

In the fourth century BC, Euhemerus, a philosopher resident at the Macedonian court, went as far as to argue that all myths and legends related to historical events, and that the gods were originally men who had achieved great success and who, after their death, received divine honours from a grateful people. Such a rational point of view might not seem far off the mark for the Trojan War, since the ruins of a major city were located during the nineteenth century in Asia Minor, where Troy was once supposed to have flourished. Agamemnon, Ajax, Menelaus, Helen, Paris, Achilles, Hector, Nestor, Odysseus, Priam – the great names of Homer's two epic poems, the *Iliad* and the *Odyssey* – could have been part of an historic conflict which had occurred there. The problem is that this is too obvious an explanation. Study of Indian epics has revealed unexpected parallels with Homer, especially between the *Iliad*, the account of Troy's downfall and the *Ramayana*, Rama's expedition to Sri Lanka in order to recover his abducted wife Sita. Both Greek and Indian story-tellers must have drawn upon a shared Indo-European heritage, albeit later changed to suit the different historical experiences involved in migration and settlement of Greece and India. Even though he may really have been a Mycenaean king, the account of Agamemnon's leadership of the Greek expeditionary force has been absorbed into a story of divine rivalry, of gods and goddesses settling their personal disputes by backing either the Trojans or the Greeks. Yet a close reading of the text shows that in Helen herself (who was the cause of the conflict), we are dealing with a goddess rather than a wayward queen. Hatched from an egg, this daughter of Zeus was undoubtedly a pre-Greek tree goddess, whose cult involved both abduction and recovery. Her husband Menelaus, the Spartan ruler, is also known to have had a shrine of his own in historical times. In all likelihood he was made King Agamemnon's brother in the course of the innumerable retellings of the story which Homer finally recast as the *Iliad*.

What this more complex view of Homer should remind us of is the variety of forms in which myth actually survives. It can be handed down almost unchanged, as sacred narrative associated with theology and ritual or in an altered form, as historical narrative that has lost contact with purely sacred events and instead deals with extraordinary secular happenings. Epics, sagas, puranas – these are perhaps the grandest expressions of mythology: but a great deal of our own knowledge comes from the writings of past mythologers. Much of Germanic mythology would have been lost without the efforts of the Icelandic scholar and statesman Snorri Sturluson. He wrote, in the early thirteenth century, a handbook for poets on the world of the pre-Christian gods, providing detailed explanations of their myths. He was recalling the sagas of the Viking period, approximately AD 750–1050. when a vigorous tradition formed around the wisdom and deeds of one-eyed Odin and giant-slayer Thor.

Myths bring divinity into focus. And their

▲ *Aboriginal female figure.*

subject matter inevitably touches upon the nature of existence, the world over which the gods rule. In ancient Sumer, present-day southern Iraq, the oldest surviving myths tell us that kingship 'came down from heaven', the ruler being chosen and invested by the assembly of the gods. During the third millennium BC the local deity was imagined to be the actual owner of each Sumerian city, and his or her temple possessed and worked most of the irrigated land, with the result that the king was rather like a steward managing the god's estates. The temple, placed on a high brick-built platform, served as the house in which the deity was fed and clothed, and received worshippers. In the city Eridu the temple was actually called Apsu, after the freshwater ocean that was believed to lie under the earth. Because the climate of Sumer was semi-arid with insufficient rainfall for sustaining a crop of cereals or an orchard or garden, agriculture was only possible through irrigation. Small schemes of canalisation gradually grew into a large interdependent system needing constant supervision, dredging and repair of breaches in the dykes to keep it functioning. Hardly surprising, therefore, is the circumstance that the divine owner of the Apsu temple was named Enki, or 'Productive Manager of the Soil'. Characteristic of Enki was his craftiness, for in conflicts with other, usually more powerful deities such as the wind god Enlil or Ninhursaga, goddess of fertility, he won by means of his wits, never by the use of force.

In the subsequent Babylonian and Assyrian periods, following the decline of Sumer after 2004 BC, the gods in the region became more like national gods and were identified with the political aspirations of their nations, so that their relation to Nature came to seem more acciden-tal, and their share of managing the world dwindled.

Thus, Marduk of Babylon and Ashur of Assyria assumed in turn a dominating position over the entire pantheon. The exploits of the older gods continued to be retold, however. In a parallel of the biblical story of the Flood, Enlil is credited with a series of assaults upon mankind. The popu-lation of the cities had grown so large that the din kept Enlil awake at night. Thoroughly annoyed, he persuaded the assembly of the gods that a plague should be sent down to thin out the people and reduce the noise. But a wise man named Atrahasis (sometimes Utnapishtim or Ziusudra) consulted Enki (or Ea) and learned of this terrible threat.

Mankind was told to be quiet, and so many offerings were made to Namtar, the plague god, that he did not dare to appear. When the crisis had passed and Enlil once again noticed the rising level of noise, he sent a drought which brought mankind to the verge of starvation. Only

▲ *Greek amphora showing Herakles capturing Cerberus.*

shoals of fish sent along the rivers and canals by Enki saved the situation. But he realised that this was only a temporary reprieve, since Enlil would next employ the combined power of heaven against mankind. So he warned Atrahasis to build a ship in order to escape a flood which lasted for seven days and seven nights. When the storm passed, the only survivors were Atrahasis, his family and the animals he had taken on board. Other than Enlil, the gods were horrified by the extent of the destruction, until the devout Atrahasis landed on dry

▲ *A head-dress in the form of the Thunderbird.*

land and sacrificed to them. Then, smelling the goodness of the offering, they gathered 'like flies around the priest and his sacrifice'.

These two myths from the Ancient Near East could be termed cosmological, because they deal with such major happenings as the creation of mankind and its destruction, with the exception of a single family. Most traditions of mythology have stories dealing with events of similar importance, but the majority of myths tend to be more mundane. They usually deal with human conflicts and uncertainties, behind which divine activity is nonetheless apparent. Among other themes treated by myths are misfortune, success, cruelty, love, death, family relations, betrayal, old versus new, youth versus age, magic, power, fate, war, chance, accident, madness, quests and voyages. The richness of incident and description in mythology suggests a very deep origin in the human mind.

Such a rich source of stories is bound to fascinate every generation, and especially our own which is so fortunate in enjoying access to the traditions of the whole world. This book invites you to explore the links and contrasts between these traditions with a fully global approach that provides the best possible introduction to the still unfathomed depths of mythology in all its diversity.

ARTHUR COTTERELL

CHAPTER 1
Ancient Near East

Sumerian Mythology

THE SUMERIANS INHABITED the southern part of the alluvial basin formed by the Rivers Tigris and Euphrates (in present-day Iraq). Their language was written on clay tablets in wedge-shaped (cuneiform) characters in a complicated system comprising signs for words, syllables and vowels. On linguistic grounds it cannot be linked to any other known language.

THE BEGINNINGS OF SUMERIAN civilisation go back to the fourth millennium BCE when the first cities with monumental mud-brick architecture appeared. The economic basis for this civilisation was agriculture, mainly producing grain on irrigated land, as well as livestock. The surplus was exchanged for materials lacking in the region, most notably metal, timber and precious stones, which stimulated long distance trade. The characteristic political unit was the city with its surrounding arable land. In the second half of the third millennium attempts were made to unify the country and impose a centralised political and administrative control. The most successful Sumerian state was that ruled by the Third Dynasty of Ur (c. 2113–04 BCE). In the

▲ *Cuneiform writing dating back to the Ur Dynasty*

eighteenth century BCE Semitic-speaking groups (known as the Amorites) formed a new state, Babylonia, and Sumerian ceased to be a spoken language, though written Sumerian continued to be used for religious purposes for more than a thousand years after that.

THE SUMERIANS

MOST SUMERIAN MYTHS are known from cuneiform tablets dating to the beginning of the second millennium BCE, although some compositions can be traced back some 700 years earlier. The tablets were discovered among the remains of temple archives, and most of the myths feature the deities worshipped in these temples. Their purpose remains unclear; there are elements of popular narratives, some passages seem to refer to cult rituals, others contain dialogue that may have been recited at a festival. The general background of the texts is a centralised urban bureaucratic state (the Sumerian empire of the Third Dynasty of Ur) which imposed centralised control over smaller city-state-like political units.

The reconstruction and translation of Sumerian myths is fraught with difficulties. Tablets are often fragmentary, with crucial passages missing. Furthermore, linguistic

▲ *Portion of a cuneiform tablet inscribed with the myth of Marduk and Tiamat.*

knowledge of the language is still developing and there is as yet no general consensus on the workings of Sumerian grammar. Hence all translations are at best provisional, while many older published versions are unreliable and out of date. Similarly, interpretations as to the meaning, function, and even context of individual compositions, are often subjective and quickly superseded.

 **Myths Retold**

GILGAMESH, ENKIDU AND THE NETHERWORLD

INANNA GROWS A HULUPPU TREE at the banks of the Euphrates and later has it transplanted to her shrine at Uruk, planning to fashion a bed and chair from its wood. However, she discovers that she is unable to cut it down because it is inhabited by three demonic creatures, a serpent, a raptor bird and a female demon. Gilgamesh volunteers to help her and with his mighty battle-axe fells the tree and kills the snake, whereupon the demon and bird fly away. Apart from the furniture, Inanna makes two objects from the timber, which she presents to Gilgamesh as a reward – but for some reason they fall into the Underworld. His servant Enkidu volunteers to retrieve them. Gilgamesh gives him careful instructions as to how to behave there, as all the normal rules of behaviour are inverted. Enkidu goes down to the Underworld, but promptly forgets all his warnings and breaks every single taboo. Through the mediation of Enki, Gilgamesh summons the spirit of Enkidu through a hole in the ground and is told of the conditions in the Land of the Dead, where one with three sons has water to drink, one with seven sons is close to the gods, but those whose bodies are never buried are destined to roam forever without rest.

▲ *Stone relief of the hero Gilgamesh with captured lion.*

NINURTA

ORIGINALLY AN AGRICULTURAL and rain deity, he became a 'young god', associated with violent storms and martial prowess. In one mythological text known as the *Splendid Storm King*, in the beginning of time, when there was no agriculture to feed the people, Ninurta defeated a demon and then made a giant stone dyke to stop the waters of the Tigris from flowing eastwards on top of the remains of his slain enemy.

THEMES OF SUMERIAN MYTHS

THE SUMERIAN THEOLOGICAL works (such as hymns, prayers, incantations) and the extant myths, reflect the emergence of a coherent cosmic order, represented by various deities, each fulfilling an essential role in the realisation of divine harmony in heaven and on earth. This parallels the emergence of the Third Dynasty of Ur, when

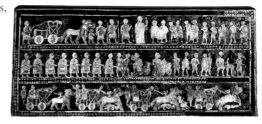

▲ *A mosaic Royal Standard from royal graves of Ur.*

previously independent Sumerian cities were subsumed in one political body ruled by kings who assumed quasi-divine status. The creation and maintenance of such order, and its protection against forces of chaos or rival claims amongst equal contenders, are a characteristic theme in Sumerian mythology. Various myths of origin propose accounts for the creation of Sumerian institutions, practices and rituals. However, successful myths function on several levels at once; they may reflect the socio-political background of a bureaucratic and hierarchical society and project the image of well-managed universe, and at the same time address general human concerns and the ambiguities of life and death within a particular historical setting. Similarly, the style of Sumerian myths ranges from liturgical solemnity to raunchy dialogue, often within the same text.

Myths Retold

ENKI ON DILMUN (OR ENKI AND NINHURSAG)

DILMUN IS INTRODUCED as a place which has potential but because of the absence of fresh water does not as yet function fully. The mother goddess complains about this state of affairs to the god of water, Enki, who produces rivers, canals and cisterns. The fields are now ready to produce grain, and the waterways allow profitable trade to be established. Enki then copulates with a goddess in the marshland beyond the city. She conceives straight away and gives birth to another goddess after a pregnancy of nine days, who is eventually inseminated by Enki in turn. This happens several times until Ninhursaga intervenes and advises the nubile girl Uttu to avoid the advances of Enki by demanding fruits and vegetables which he produces by extending the water into the dry zones around the city. When Enki arrives laden with cucumbers and apples, Uttu lets him into her house and they embrace. Ninhursaga removes Enki's seed from Uttu's womb to create eight plants. Enki desires these plants and eats them as soon as they have grown, which infuriates Ninhursaga so much that she curses Enki to become afflicted in eight parts of his body. Near death, he is only saved by the intervention of a fox who persuades the goddess to restore Enki to health. She takes him on her lap and gives birth to eight divine beings, one for each ailing part.

▼ *The Sumerian goddess of fertility.*

SUMERIAN PROTAGONISTS

ATTEMPTS TO ENUMERATE the many local gods and list them according to rank were made early in the third millennium BCE. These lists of deities are invariably headed by the supreme sky god An. The most important gods were those of major shrines, such as Enlil of Nippur, Enki of Eridu and Inanna of Uruk. Astral deities were Utu (Sun), Nannar (Moon) and Inanna (Venus). Female deities, often tutelary goddesses of cities, such as Baba of Lagash, Nammu of Eridu and Ninhursaga of Kesh, were mother-goddesses, while others had specific functions: Nisaba: patroness of scribes, Nanshe: goddess of fish and magic, Ninisina: goddess of healing. Enlil was a major Mesopotamian god, whose cult centre was Nippur. He was the son of An, the leader of gods, and he bestowed kingship. He had the characteristics of a weather-god whose rains ensure good harvests but who also has an unpredictable temperament which causes him to punish a troublesome earth with plagues and floods. Gods were invisaged to reside within their temple estates, represented by their image or statue. The divine household consisted of the god and his wife, their children and numerous servants. The pantheon also included demons and evil spirits: offspring of An, who to some extent were susceptible to magic spells and rituals of banishment.

▶ *Goddess Ninsun, mother of Gilgamesh.*

ENKI

ENKI IS THE SON of the sky god An and his mother is Nammu, a goddess of water and creation. He lives in the Apsu, the watery depths below the earth, the source of all fertility and organic life. Since water in Mesopotamia also had an important magical role, Enki was invoked in magic spells and rituals and hence was regarded as wise among the gods, and the one called upon to find solutions to difficult problems. On the other hand his sexual appetite and his weakness for drink account for less than perfect conditions of life on earth. He is not a war-like god and his major adversaries are various goddesses, most notably Inanna who tricks him into giving away divine prerogatives and powers.

▲ *Terracotta relief of the goddess Inanna.*

INANNA'S DESCENT TO THE UNDERWORLD

INANNA, 'queen of heaven and earth', decides to go down to the Underworld. Realising the danger that such undertaking involves, even for a goddess of her power, she makes contingency plans. She not only dresses in all her regalia and magic amulets, but instructs her vizier, Ninshubur, on emergency procedures. At the gate of the Underworld she demands to be admitted in order to attend the funeral of her brother-in-law. When the gate-keeper informs his mistress, Ereshkigal, Inanna's sister and queen of the Underworld, of this request, she is furious and instructs him to lock all the seven gates. At each of these gates Inanna has to divest herself of one of her regalia. Naked and defenceless she finally appears before Ereshikigal, and her desperate attempts to seize the throne are swiftly thwarted. The summoned judges of the Underworld condemn her to die, and her corpse is hung upon a peg on the wall.

When, after the appointed time, Inanna fails to appear, Ninshubur follows her instructions to the letter. She dons mourning and makes an appeal to other gods to help her secure Inanna's release. Both Enlil and Nannar refuse, saying that Inanna's unbridled ambition had got her where she was. Only Enki is prepared to assist. From the dirt under his fingernails he fashions two beings (their names reflect those of cult actors or transvestites associated with Inanna's rituals), who gain admission to Ereshkigal by pretending to be sympathetic to her suffering. Flattered by such attention she offers a reward, and, instructed by Enki, they demand the corpse of Inanna, which they then sprinkle with the Water of Life, provided by Enki. However, the judges of the Underworld demand that Inanna must provide a substitute for herself.

A host of demons accompany her on the way back, as she pauses at each gate to clothe herself once more in her apparel. Emerging from the Underworld she finds Ninshubur. When the demons try to seize her, Inanna refuses, nor does she allow them to take other gods of Uruk who had all been mourning her. Only when she sees her husband Dumuzi in splendid robes on a splendid throne, does she indicate in anger that he is the one who will have to die for her, in punishment for his faithlessness. In the end Dumuzi's sister Geshtinanna shares in his fate, so that they each spend half the year in the Underworld and half the year on earth.

◀ *Sumerian harp decorated with a bull's head.*

INANNA

A SUMERIAN GODDESS with a complex mythological persona, perhaps the result of a theological/philosophical combination between a local Sumerian deity associated with Uruk and the west-Semitic Venus-star deity Ishtar, introduced by the Akkadian ruling dynasty in the middle of the second millennium BCE. The former was regarded as the daughter of the supreme sky god An, the latter as the daughter of the moon god Nannar. The dual nature of the planet Venus was conceptualised as a bisexual deity, and this accounts for Inanna's association with warfare, aggression and lust for power, as well as childbirth and erotic attraction. The myths about Inanna either stress her irascible nature and the fatal consequences of her anger, and/or her sexuality.

Babylonian Mythology

IN THE BEGINNING OF the second millennium BCE Semitic-speaking Amorite tribes established themselves in southern Syria and the middle Euphrates region, and formed a state under the leadership of Hammurabi, who in the eighteenth century BCE made the city of Babylon his capital.

L IKE THE PRECEDING SUMERIAN civilisation it continued to be urban and bureaucratic, based on irrigation agriculture and commerce. Most of the earlier Sumerian institutions, especially temples, were maintained. Babylonian, written in the cuneiform system, became the medium of international communication in the mid-second millennium BCE, and Babylonian scribes were employed in all the major urban centres of the Ancient Near East, from Egypt to Anatolia. This disseminated Mesopotamian literary culture across a large area. Following the defeat of the Assyrian empire, Babylonia became one of the great powers in the first millennium BCE, especially during the reign of Nebuchadnezzar II.

THE BABYLONIANS

WHILE THE BABYLONIANS inherited the culture and religious institutions of Sumeria and translated a number of Sumerian myths, they introduced a number of new deities, and their religious sensibilities owe much to their pastoralist origin. While the important Sumerian gods were simply renamed with a Semitic appellative (An: Anu; Enki: Ea; Enlil: Ellil; Inanna: Ishtar; Utu: Shamash; Nannar: Sin) new deities were also introduced. Important themes were justice, morality and personal piety, as well as concerns with death and the Underworld. While a number of Sumerian myths were translated into Babylonian, their emphasis was changed to reflect a more pessimistic outlook, in keeping with the social and political instability of the second and early first millennium BCE. Their myths are set in a more unpredictable world in which capricious gods at once uphold and threaten universal order. There is also a new consciousness of national identity and ideology, as exemplified by the rise of god Marduk.

▲ *Part of a cylinder seal depicting Zu being judged by Ea.*

Myths Retold

THE FLOOD STORY FROM NINEVEH
(ELEVENTH TABLET OF THE GILGAMESH EDITION)

THE STORY IS TOLD to Gilgamesh by the flood-hero Utnapishtim. The parallels with the Biblical Flood story are striking.

Utnapishtim is a citizen of the Babylonian town Shurrupak when he receives a message from the god Ea (through the brick–wall) that the gods are about to bring on a deluge. Ea instructs him to build a boat, gives him the exact measurements and warns him to tell his inquisitive fellow citizens that he is preparing to live with Ea in his watery abode below the earth. When the vessel is finished, Utnapishtim loads it with his family, silver and gold, and all species of living creatures. At the appointed time the dams burst, ground-waters swell up and the rains come down. The storm is so fierce that even the gods 'cower like dogs'.

On the seventh day the floods subside and when Utnapishtim opens a vent to look out, he realises that the ship has run aground. He lets out a dove

▲ *Utnapishtim, the flood-hero, and his boat.*

which, finding no resting place, returns to the vessel. The swallow fares no better, and eventually he lets fly a raven, who eats and flies about and does not return to the boat. Utnapishtim disembarks with his family and makes a sacrifice, pouring out libations and burning incense. 'The gods smelling the sweet savour gathered like flies about the priest and his offering.' The mother-goddess arrives and, grieving over the destruction of her creatures, vows never to forget what has happened. She blames Enlil for the almost total annihilation of mankind. Although Enlil is furious that one human family escaped, Ea soothes his anger and confesses that it was he who engineered Utnapishtim's escape. Enlil, assuaged, blesses the flood-hero and his wife and grants them eternal life.

GILGAMESH

THE STORY OF Gilgamesh has survived in several different versions from different period, beginning with the Sumerian tales. It was known throughout the Ancient Near East and combines the theme of Mesopotamian hubris – the cutting of valuable timber in foreign territory – with a dragon-slaying motif (the trees are protected by a demonic creature). Added on to this core were other popular narratives, such as the Flood

▲ *Gilgamesh avoids seduction by the goddess Ishtar.*

story, the rebuttal of the love-goddess' advances, and speculation about the Underworld. The framework of the most coherent version, the so-called Twelve Tablet edition, probably dating to the late second millennium BCE, but best known from the revision discovered in the library at Nineveh from the seventh century BCE, revolves around male friendship and the question of man's mortality. The Ninevite edition adds the Babylonian version of the old Sumerian narrative about Gilgamesh, Enkidu and the Netherworld.

ETERNAL LIFE

ADAPA IS ONE OF THE SEVEN Sages, created by Ea (the Sumerian Enki) as an exemplary man with superhuman wisdom. He serves the god as a priest in Eridu. The myths surrounding him reinforce the Mesopotamian view that eternal life is for the gods; even when offered the chance of immortality, Adapa is unable to take advantage. One day he is out fishing when the south wind overturns his boat. In anger he curses the wind to 'break his wings', with the result that no south wind blows for a long time. The great god Anu hears of the matter and has Adapa summoned to heaven so that he can be made responsible. Ea, anxious for his protegé, instructs him how to prepare for his journey. He must don mourning and express his sympathies to two gods, Dumuzi and Ningishzida, stationed before the gate, in order to win their support. The plan works, as Anu is mollified by the gods' intercession. When he hears that Adapa had acquired his wisdom (and magic) from Ea, he offers him the Water and Bread of Life which would make him like the gods. However, forwarned by Ea not to accept the proffered Water and Bread of Death, Adapa rejects the offer. Anu breaks into laughter at his folly and sends him back to earth.

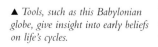

▲ *Tools, such as this Babylonian globe, give insight into early beliefs on life's cycles.*

 **Myths Retold**

ERRA

ERRA, GOD OF PESTILENCE and rebellion, is asleep in his underground abode when he is woken up by the dangerous, demonic 'Seven'. They remind him of the glories of war and taunt him that his weapons have rusted from inertia. Unless he takes up his former ways, they say, he will become the butt of jokes, and furthermore, mankind has become too noisy. Erra decides to comply with their suggestion and goes to find the god Marduk. Erra criticises the lacklustre state of the god's regalia and Marduk tells him that he cannot leave his palace untended while he goes to procure the necessary precious stones and metals, since last time he absented himself terrible calamities befell the earth. Erra persuades Marduk to let him be his temporary representative but at the same time makes efforts to delay Marduk's quest. He vents his anger upon the earth, causing civil war, terrible violence and anarchy. Ishum, his vizier, feels compassion for the suffering of the people. By flattery, he manages to direct Erra's destructive energy towards the enemies of Babylonia until his fury is spent and he is ready for a period of rest. Before his retirement Erra utters a blessing over the devastated lands to make them populous and fertile once again.

MARDUK

THE NATIONAL BABYLONIAN god rose to importance during the 1st Dynasty of Babylon. He was the son of Ea and like him had associations with magic. He also shared aspects of the solar deity Shamash, especially in terms of justice, impartiality and compassion. His mythological persona is that of a young warrior and dragon slayer, combined with executive functions (the order of the universe and the division of offices among the gods). His symbol was the horned and winged dragon, known as Mushhushu.

Warrior Marduk sets out to attack Tiamat.▲

Myths Retold

ENUMA ELISH (THE BABYLONIAN CREATION)

THE BULK OF THIS LONG TEXT, recited on the occasion of the
Babylonian Near Festival, is taken up with the recitation of Marduk's names,
his glorification, and a praise of Babylon. The cosmogonic myth, reworking
older creation accounts concerning other deities, such as Enlil and Ninurta,
introduces the litanies.

In the beginning, before Heaven and Earth were named, the primeval
waters were mingled together. From this creative source three generations of
gods emerge, leading to Anu and Ea (the Sumerian Enki). The young gods
are restless and disturb the quiet of Apsu, their ancestor, who decides to
destroy them. His plan is thwarted by Ea who puts a spell on Apsu to make
him fall into a deep sleep, while Ea takes over the watery depth as his own
domain, where he lives with his wife Damkina. She gives birth to Marduk

▲ *Ancient Babylonian ceramic art depicting a lion.*

whose vigour disturbs Apsu's consort Tiamat. Urged on by the other old gods she prepares to do battle against Marduk, and assembles a host of monsters and serpents, headed by her son Kingu. When Ea's magic fails to prevail against her host, he calls on Marduk to take on the fight. Marduk accepts on condition that should he win he would have supreme command among the gods. This is

▲ *Marduk defeats Tiamat, goddess of the Deep, personification of evil.*

accepted and he is armed with irresistible weapons, including the seven winds.

He raises a storm and charges against Tiamat, whom he catches in his net and immobilises with winds. He then rounds up the fleeing army and seizes Kingu, from whom he takes the Tablets of Destiny. He splits open the prostrate body of Tiamat whose upper part he fixes above to form the sky, complete with stars and planets. The lower part becomes the earth, and the Tigris and Euphrates flow from her eye-sockets. Her knotted tail serves as a plug to keep the waters of the Apsu from flooding the land. Solid pillars separate Heaven and earth. The Tablets of Destiny he hands over to Anu for safe-keeping, and then he is officially installed by the assembled gods. Kingu, blamed for causing the revolt, is executed and from his blood and clay Ea creates Man, imposing the services of the gods upon him which frees the Annunnaki gods from labour. In gratitude they build a sanctuary for Marduk which he names Babylon. Then all the gods sat down to celebrate.

The text goes on to continue the exultation of Marduk.

Ugaritic Mythology

UGARIT IS THE NAME of the an ancient city on the Syrian coast (the modern Ras Shamra near Lattakia). In the mid-second millennium BCE it became the centre of a small but influential and wealthy state, based on agricultural exploitation of a fertile soil and benefitting from the international trade between Egypt, Mesopotamia and the Hittite empire to the north.

THE INHABITANTS, like the other Canaanite peoples in Syro-Palestine, spoke a west-Semitic dialect. They used Babylonian cuneiform for official record-keeping and correspondence, but invented an alphabetic system, also written on clay, for their ritual and mythological compositions. Ugarit was destroyed in the thirteenth century BCE. Most of their gods were weather-gods and were associated with rainfall, crucial for the agriculture of the Fertile Crescent that depends on natural precipitation.

◄ *Cuneiform symbols carved into stone.*

UGARITIC TEXTS

MOST OF THE MYTHS of Ugarit are known from the tablets discovered in the ruins of a priests' house in the city. The texts written in the Ugaritic alphabetic system still pose considerable problems in terms of vocabulary, syntax and grammar. Even the sequence of the tablets is disputed, and new translations and editions keep appearing to replace existing versions. The main deities featured in the myths of Ugarit were creator-god Èl, his son, the storm-god Baal, who was thought to reside on Mount Zaphon, the peak that towers above the city, and the goddesses Astart and Anat, an Ishtar-like deity of war and sexual love.

UGARITIC PROTAGONISTS: BAAL

THE NAME SIMPLY MEANS 'lord, master'. It was a common appellative of West Semitic deities. There are local manifestations of this weather-god, usually named after a mountain peak which is their habitual domain of storm deities. The Baal featured in the Ugaritic texts was Baal-Zaphon (present day Jebel el-Aqra). He was identified with the ancient Syrian deity Hadad. He was called 'Rider of the Cloud', manifest in the storms that herald the autumn season with thunder and lightning. In the myths he battles against the unruly waters of the sea (personified as the god Yam or 'Sea') – Ugarit depended on maritime traffic for its prosperity and against the scorching heat of the summer. He is regularly overcome by his foes but destined to rise again in a cyclical waning and waxing of power. As he represents fertility and the renewal of life, he is often associated with the Bull, an ancient symbol of vitality and sexual vigour.

▶ *Bronze statue of the Ugaritic god Baal.*

 **Myths Retold**

BAAL-MYTHS: PART ONE

THE GODDESS ANAT is bathing and anointing herself before she goes down to the seashore where she causes a blood-bath among the people. Hung with the severed heads and hands of her victims, she wants still more violence and turns her household furniture into an army, until she wades knee-deep in blood and gore. Then she returns to normality and washes herself with dew and rain. Meanwhile Baal has sent a messenger from Mount Zaphon, asking her to join him there. He complains that he alone of all the gods has no house or court. Anat promises to take up his case and goes to visit her father El who seems to prevaricate. Somebody suggests he send for Kothar-and-Hasis, the Clever-Craftsman, who leaves Egypt to take up the commission. Because of a plot against Baal, El is swayed to offer the palace to Yam.

▶ *Stele or funeral stone, depicting the god Baal.*

Baal has a premonition that he is soon to be 'bound between the stones of the stream'. Yam sends words to El to deliver Baal up to him, and although Baal defends himself he is overcome. Yam tries to take up residence in the unfinished palace originally built for Baal. However, he is too big for it and Kothar-and-Hasis is told to make another, larger palace for him. The craftsman god goes to find Baal, who 'cowers under the chair of Prince Yam' and tells him that now the time has come to challenge Yam and claim his kingdom. Kothar-and-Hasis gives him two magical weapons which Baal uses to defeat Yam who is taken captive. Baal departs with Anat to visit the Astart, the 'Lady Asherah of the Sea', El's estranged wife, in order to persuade El to allow the building of Baal's palace to proceed. Astart, pleased by the rich gifts they bring, agree to plead with El who is so pleasantly surprised by her visit that he finally consents to the building of the palace. Kothar-and-Hasis is called and Baal tells him not to put any windows in. When all is finished he prepares a banquet to celebrate. Baal returns, having sacked ninety cities, and revoked his earlier decision not to have windows. He raises his voice until the earth shakes and is enthroned in the palace. But at the height of his power he knows that his destiny is to 'descend into the gullet of Mot' (Death).

EL

THE ETYMOLOGICAL ORIGIN of this word is still unclear. It was the common designation for god in all Semitic languages, from the Old Sumerian period to the Arabic (Allah). In the Ugaritic myths, El, like the Sumerian god An, represents divine authority and cosmic order. He is the father of all gods (with the exception of Baal who is always called 'son of Dagan') and, like Enlil in Mesopotamia, the source of royal power. He is seen as the 'Father of Mankind' and has some connection with human fertility and childbirth. His relationship with Baal is ambiguous, and the Baal-myths in particular show that there is tension between them.

Myths Retold

BAAL-MYTHS: PART TWO

BAAL SEES THE DUST STORMS (envoys of Mot) and sends an invitation to Mot to come to his palace. Mot refuses the request and threatens to swallow Baal in two gulps. Baal has to obey his summons to go down to the Underworld and receives instructions on how to get there. On the way he sees a heifer and copulates with her, which results in the birth of an ox, called his 'twin-brother'. Messengers arrive at El's palace and announce the death of Baal. They lament him and Anat goes in search of his body to bury him with all honours on Mount Zaphon. El calls for Astar, one of the sons of Astart's, who is eager to promote her own offspring, to mount the throne of Baal. He proves too small to occupy Baal's enormous seat.

When Mot admits that he has indeed eaten the young god, she is seized with fury and grabs Mot, splitting and sieving, burning, grinding and milling him. El meanwhile is asked to perform a dream oracle which would reveal whether Baal was still alive. Should he dream the heavens rained oil and the valleys run with honey, then Baal is not fully dead. El does indeed

◀ *El, the paramount deity, father of all gods and men.*

dream in this manner and sends Anat, accompanied by the sun goddess Shapash, to look for Baal. El describes the sun-parched fields that await the harrowing (wetting) by Baal. Shapash instructs Anat to pour 'sparkling wine into the wine skins' and to bring wreaths, and presumably Baal returns, since after seven years Mot, now also revived, sends another challenge. He orders one of Baal's brothers to be killed in order to atone for the wrongs done to him by Anat.

ANAT

ANAT, WHOSE NAME may be related to the Akkadian word *ettu* ('active will'), was a goddess popular throughout the western areas of the Near East, including Egypt. In the Ugaritic myths her epithets are 'Virgin Anat' and 'Destroyer'. Like the Babylonian Ishtar, she was portrayed as a beautiful woman, a passionate lover, as well as a ferocious and blood-thirsty warrior. She has an intimate relation with Baal, her beloved 'brother' (a term of endearment rather than kinship in the context). She is always ready to fight with and sometimes for him, and there is also a strong erotic bond between them which is consummated in the guise of cattle, Baal the Bull mounts Anat the Heifer.

Baal pretends to comply, but he intends to outwit Mot by offering him 'brothers of Mot' (perhaps wild boars, the usual sacrifice in Ugarit to gods of the Underworld). When Mot discovers that he has eaten his own kin he goes to Zaphon and attacks Baal. They fight bitterly but neither can defeat the other. Shapash intervenes and warns Mot that El will take away his kingship over the Underworld if he continues to fight Baal. Mot retreats.

The final passages contain a hymn-like conclusion, celebrating Baal's 'eternal kingship'. The gods sit down to a banquet and the sun goddess is asked to rule over the spirits of the dead with Kothar-and-Hasis' assistance.

Persian Mythology

THE PERSIANS ARE A branch of the Aryan family of races as defined by language; more specifically they belong to the Indo-Iranian branch. Originally horse- and cattle-nomads on the steppes of Central Asia, they migrated on to the Iranian plateau around 1000 BCE. Other Iranian tribes, Medes, Parthians, Scythians, were migrating at the same time. Some Persian tribes settled, others remained nomads. Those that settled took over many customs of the older urban cultures of West Asia, especially when Cyrus (559–30 BCE) began to conquer Elam, Assyria and Babylon. The erstwhile nomads became rulers of a multi-ethnic cosmopolitan empire stretching from the Mediterranean east to the Oxus and the Indus rivers.

AT SOME PERIOD before Cyrus (scholars do not agree when), the traditional religion of the Iranians was reformed, probably in the north-east of Greater Iran, by a priest (*zaotar*), the Prophet Zarat-hushtra (variously translated as gold or old camel), known to the Greeks as Zoroaster. Zoroaster approached monotheism: Ahura Mazda, constantly invoked in the

▶ *The prophet-teacher, Zoroaster.*

inscriptions of Darius the Achaemenid (521–486 BCE) and subsequent rulers of the Achaemenid dynasty (550–330 BCE) descended from the clan-ancestor Hakhamenesh (Achaemenes in Greek), is the supreme Wise Lord of Zoroastrianism, even though the faith emphasised the utter separation and conflict of the Holy Thought and Evil Thought.

GUARDIAN SPIRIT AT PASARGADAE

CYRUS, WHO RULED 559–30 BCE, and the founder of the Persian empire, built the palace and tomb at Pasargadae near Anshan, his family's fief in Pars. His extant inscriptions in Old Persian, Elamite and Babylonian merely state: 'I am Cyrus, the King, the Achaemenid.' The figure on the remaining door-jamb of the ruined palace has been interpreted as a protective spirit, comparable to the four-winged figure in the Assyrian Palace at Khorsabad; here it wears an Egyptian-style triple-crown resting on rams' horns. This is characteristic of the eclectic court-style of the early Achaemenids, where elements from Media, Elam, Babylon, Assyria, Egypt and Asia Minor were borrowed and blended.

▲ *This door relief is all that remains to indicate the palace's former splendour.*

CULT OF FIRE

THE CULT OF FIRE goes back to the earliest phase of Aryan nomad religion. The five daily offerings to the fire, accompanied by the short prayer Atash Niyayesh, remain typical of Zoroastrian worship. Atar (later known as Adhur) was categorised into five types by the Sasanian clergy:

1. Atash Bahram, the fire in temple and hearth
2. Vohufryana, the fire life-principle in men
3. Urvazista, the fire life-principle in plants
4. Vazista, the fire or lightning in clouds
5. Spanishta, the pure fire that burns in paradise before Ohrmazd, with the royal glory, Khwarna (later forms, Khorra or Farr).

Fire-altars were emblems of religious legitimacy, as can be seen on the tomb of Darius the Achaemenid and on the coins of Ardeshir the Sasanid, where their regnal fires are represented. The major fire temples were Adhar Farn-Bag at Karyan in Fars, Adhar Gushn-Asp at Shiz in Adharbaijan and Adhar Burzin-Mehr on Mount Revand in Khorasan; they were associated respectively with the three classes of society, the priests, the warrior-nobility and the farmers.

TOMB OF DARIUS I AT NAQSH RUSTAM

IN 522 BCE, Darius overthrew a magician posing as Cyrus's grandson. He prepared his own tomb cut into the rock-face at Naqsh Rustam, where he is shown on a dais supported by the subject peoples of the empire, standing with hand upraised in salutation of the regnal fire burning on the stepped fire-altar before him. With his other hand he holds a bow, a motif that reappears on his gold coins. Above hovers the solar winged disk, which has been taken as representing Ahura Mazda the supreme god, or the Khwarna, royal glory of divine rule.

▲ *Intricately deco-
rated pillar relief
from the Palace of
Darius.*

 **Myths Retold**

THE GOOD CREATION (FROM THE BUNDAHISHN)

THE HISTORY OF THE UNIVERSE lasts 12,000 years: at first Ohrmazd's world of light co-existed with Ahriman's world of darkness. Ahriman (earlier known as Angra Mainyu) saw the light and heard Ohrmazd's proposed 9,000-year war between light and dark, and fell back into the abyss. After another 3,000 years, Ohrmazd (earlier known as Ahura Mazda) created the physical world (*getig*), the primal bull Gosh and the first living mortal Gayomard.

Ahriman determined to destroy the good creation. He smashed his way through the crystal vault of the sky, sped through the waters which turned bitter and salt, turned the earth into desert and mountains and sullied everything, killing the plants, the primal bull and living mortal. Gayomard's sperm was taken to the sun and Gosh's to the moon. From the moon-preserved seed came new plants and life, renewed by the rains of Tir, and from the sun-preserved seed grew, after 40 years underground, an androgynous rhubarb (*rivas*) out of which stepped the first human couple Mashyagh and his mate Mashyanagh.

GOOD AND EVIL

ZOROASTRIANISM, like the monotheistic religions, is not rich in mythical narratives; it has basically just one myth, the fight of good against evil, re-enacted until the end of the world; evil is seen in filth, vermin, disease and death as well as moral impurity such as lying. Man and the natural creation, being basically good, must be kept pure or returned to a state of purity and order. Observance of the purity laws in life and death, avoiding pollution of Fire, Water or Earth, prayer in the presence of the bright flaming fire that recalls divine energy and life force – these have been features of Zoroastrianism since earliest days.

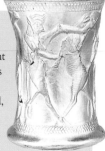

▲ *Persian vase depicting a battle between mythological creatures.*

MITHRA

THE INDO-IRANIAN tribes of the Hittites moved into Asia Minor, and in one of their treaties, dated to 1350 BCE, they invoke, among other gods, Mitra, Varuna and Indra, the earliest mention of these gods more familiar from the Indian pantheon. In the commentary on the earliest religious composition of the Indo-Iranians in India, the *Rig Veda*, the name Mitra is translated as friend; in Iran, he is associated with agreements, like his Babylonian counterpart Shamash, the all-seeing sun who guards legal

contracts. In the Mihr Yasht, Mithra is described watching over the land of the Iranians from the high Alborz mountains, marching out to support their fight against cattle-raiders, aided by Sraosha (later known as Sorush), Verethraghna (later known as Bahram) and Rashnu.

Mithra's popularity is attested by the wealth of personal names derived from his name, eg. Mithra-dates (later form Mihr-dad) given by Mithra. The feast of Mithra in the month of Mithra, the Mihrgan at the beginning of autumn, was a great feast with wine-drinking and royal gifts.

▲ *Iranian statue of a bull, the central symbol in Mithraism.*

The initiatic mysteries of Mithraism spread with the Roman legions throughout the Roman empire. The central symbol of Mithraism is the rejuvenating sacrifice by the young god of the bull, which parallels the killing of the primal bull Gosh by Ahriman in the Zoroastrian tradition. Associated with the unconquerable power of the sun, the Roman Mithraic feast of 'sol invictus' gave the traditional birthdate of Christ, 25 December.

THE WARRIOR

THE WARRIOR who fights for his king and his religion against monsters, demons and foreigners recurs throughout Persian mythology: Fereydun who defeats the tyrant Zuhhak and finally chains him in a cave under Mount Damavand; Isfandyar who is only defeated when the magic bird aids Rustam with one of its feathers; and Garshasp who will come at the end of the world to help in the final defeat of evil. Later heroes of epic, Ali and Hamza are depicted in the style of the great pre-Islamic heroes.

▶ *Frieze of an archer of the Persian king's guard.*

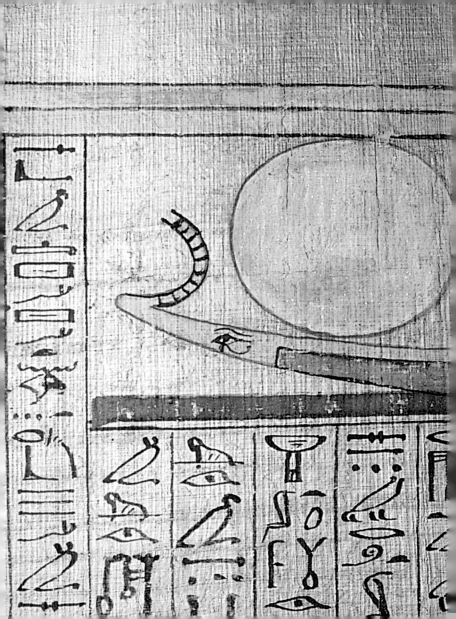

CHAPTER 2

Egypt

Egypt

EGYPT, AS THE GREEK historian Herodotus wrote on visiting the country in c. 450 BC, was 'the gift of the Nile'. It was by virtue of the annual inundation, the rising of the waters of the Nile in July which then spread the fertile mud across the landscape, that gave Egypt life – without the Nile and its flood Egypt could not have existed. It was this regularity, although there were times of low Nile – famine, and of high Nile – disaster, the gods being benefi-cent or angry, that gave a stability to the ancient Egyptian ideas about life and death. The concept of Ma'at, the goddess who embodied stability and law, therefore governed all aspects of Egyptian life and religion.

THE EGYPTIANS envisaged a hereafter, *Kherneter* or the *Fields of Iahru* (the Elysian Fields in Greek mythology) located not in the heavens above but in the west, the land of the setting sun. One of the titles of Osiris, the god of the dead, was 'First Lord of the Westerners'. In order to achieve entry into that Afterworld it was first necessary to preserve the body – which gave rise to the process of mummification, and also to have been judged a righteous person, *mq'at heru*, 'True of Voice', by the 42 gods in the Hall of Judgement, each of whom

▲ *Wall painting in the tomb of Sennedjem in Thebes, depicting the Fields of Iahru, the Egyptian equivalent to the Blessed Afterworld.*

◀ *Gold and lapis lazuli trinity of Osorkan II, Osiris flanked by Isis and Horus.*

asked the deceased a direct question to which the truthful answer had to be 'No' – it was known as the Negative Confession. A green hard stone heart scarab within the bandages of the mummy was inscribed with Chapter 30A or B of the *Book of the Dead*, 'Whereby my heart shall not speak falsehood against me in the Hall of Judgement.' Other gods and goddesses appear in some of the myths but have no individual mythical background.

Since the Classical times of Greece and Rome the religion of ancient Egypt has been a source of wonderment and incredulity, even down to the modern day. Although the Classical world had a large pantheon of gods with Zeus (Jupiter in the Roman world) at its head, as did ancient Egypt (with Amun-Re as chief of the gods), it was the theriomorphic (animal) forms of the Egyptian gods that caused concern. Herodotus also wrote that in Egypt the animals 'are without exception held to be sacred', and he declined to discuss the religious principles involved.

Egyptian mythology is, in fact, quite tightly focused – there are not as many myths when compared with the ancient Near East and the later Mediterranean civilisations. Essentially the Egyptian myths are concerned with the Creation, the Destruction of Mankind, the story of Isis and Osiris, the Contendings of Horus and Seth, and the sun god Re's journey across the daytime sky and then through the 12 terrible dark hours of the night to be safely reborn at dawn in the east.

HELIOPOLIS (THE CREATION)

AT HELIOPOLIS, 'the City of the Sun', Atum was alone on a muddy bank that had emerged from the primeval Waters of Nun that covered the world (like the inundation of the Nile). Realising that he needed other gods to assist in the creation he masturbated himself and from his semen emerged two other gods: Shu, god of the sky and Tefnut, his sister, goddess of moisture. Their children were Geb, god of the earth, and Nut, goddess of the sky (such relationships, consanguineous marriages, usually abhorred as incest in the modern world, were not uncommon in ancient mythology). In papyri illustrations Nut appears arched over Geb and being separated to their respective spheres by Shu. Geb and Nut had five children: Osiris, Isis, Horus the Elder, Set and Nephthys – born on five consecutive days, outside the normal calendar of 360 days. This was (and has reflections in Classical mythology) because of a prophecy that Nut's children would surpass the power of Atum-Re (as the children of Kronos by Rhea would surpass their father). Being born on non-calendar (epagnol) days overcame the problem of the curse that Nut could not give birth on any day of the year.

◀ *Bronze statuette of the god of Creation and craftsmen, Ptah.*

MEMPHIS AND HERMOPOLIS (THE CREATION)

AT MEMPHIS, the secular capital of Egypt from the 1st Dynasty, c. 3100 BCE, the major deity was the creator god Ptah. According to the legend, Ptah took precedence over Atum because he had created the heart and tongue of Atum. Ptah was particularly revered as the god of craftsmen and workers and amongst his many titles was that of 'the father and mother of all gods'.

A third creation legend was identified at Hermopolis, a revered cult centre of the god Thoth. He was often represented with the head of an ibis bird, and the baboon was an animal particularly regarded as sacred and associated with him. He was the god of wisdom and learning who had invented hieroglyphs, literally 'the sacred writings'. Of special importance, he was the patron god of scribes and was also associated with the moon.

The variation on the creation legend here said that it was at Hermopolis and not Heliopolis where the primeval mound had emerged from the Waters of Nun. From an egg lying on the

▶ *The ibis-headed Thoth, god of wisdom, before a bronze obelisk.*

mound emerged the sun god or, in an alternative version, a lotus flower grew from the mound and its leaves opened to reveal the young god of creation, Nefertum.

ESNA (THE CREATION)

AT ESNA THE TEMPLE was dedicated to the ram-headed god Khnum. He, it was believed, fashioned man on his potter's wheel, but in duplicate because everyone had a *ka*, or

▲ *The temple at Esna, dedicated to the creator god Khnum.*

double. This was the spirit that remained near the dead man's tomb whilst his *ba*, his soul, in the shape of a human-headed bird, flew away at death to the next world. The fullest version of the creation is carved on the walls of the temple at Esna and that tells of a goddess called Neith, who was associated with the city of Sais in the Nile Delta, who came into being before the primeval mound, emerging from the Waters of Nun to create the world.

Whilst to the modern religious mind four basic versions of the story of creation would cause concern and question, to the ancient Egyptian this posed no problems. Each creation legend took precedence at its appropriate place, although overall it was the Heliopolitan version that held prime position because of its association with the sun and the chief of the gods, Re who was later assimilated with Amun of Thebes to become the great god Amun-Re.

THE CREATION

WHILST CHRISTIAN THEOLOGY has a single creation story there were four accounts in ancient Egypt, each connected with a major city: Heliopolis; Memphis; Hermopolis, and Esna, and each with a major god – Atum (later assimilated with Re); Ptah; Thoth, and Khnum respectively.

Myths Retold

THE DESTRUCTION

THE WORLD AND MAN having been created, the gods then proliferated, most being closely related to each other (as with the 12 gods of Mount Olympus in Greek mythology). However, as in the Christian tradition, there is a story of destruction. Man had become too full of himself and was ignoring the gods and not making the proper offerings to them. Re, as chief of the gods, took council with the rest to see how best to punish man and make him continue the proper religious observances. It was agreed that the goddess Sekhmet, a lion-headed goddess who represented the power of the sun at midday, and hence was the personification of evil, being able to kill man, would be sent down to earth. There she began an indiscriminate slaughter, delighting in the taste of blood. The gods were appalled as they realised the eventual outcome, the extinction of mankind, but Sekhmet had a blood lust and would not stop. She was eventually brought to heel by a trick of the gods who flooded a field with a red drink (khakadi) that looked like blood but was mixed with strong beer. Sekhmet gorged

▲ *Granite seated statue of the lion-headed goddess Sekhmet in the temple of Mut in Karnak.*

herself on it and fell into a drunken stupor. When she awoke the killing had stopped and man had learnt his lesson not to disregard the gods.

Myths Retold

OSIRIS AND ISIS

THE MOST IMPORTANT MYTH of which the Egyptians took note and had the greatest affinity with was that of Osiris and his wife and sister Isis. Osiris, the good king, had a jealous brother Set who, by a trick, contrived to have him killed and his body floated out to sea to end up on the shore at the city of Byblos in the Lebanon. The grieving widow, Isis, eventually located the body and brought it back to Egypt, hiding with it in the marshes. Hovering over it in the form of a hawk she became prgenant with their son, Horus. However, evil Set discovered the body in the marshes one day and tore it into 14 pieces that were scattered far and wide throughout Egypt. Once more Isis set off to retrieve her husband's body, now in fragments.

▼ *A bronze statue of the oxyrhyncus fish, sacred in the city of that name in the fertile area of the Fayum.*

One version of the myth said that Isis buried each portion where she found it and there founded a temple. Another said that she brought all the pieces together, save for one, his phallus, that could not be retrieved because the oxyrhyncus fish had swallowed it. Thereafter the fish was abhorred, except in the city of Oxyrhyncus in the Fayum, where it was held to be sacred. The body (or only the head according to another version) was buried at Abydos which became the most sacred site of ancient Egypt, and where one of the most beautifully decorated temples was built.

HORUS AND SET

SET DECLARED HIMSELF to be king and Isis, with her small son Horus, went into hiding. When Horus reached young manhood he challenged his evil uncle Set for his father Osiris's throne. Their various battles, known as the Contendings of Horus and Set, are inscribed and illustrated in long texts and reliefs on the walls of the temple of Horus at Edfu. Eventually the gods tired of the continual conflict and Horus and Set were brought before the Council of Gods to state their case. The court case dragged on for several years, but after various reverses of decision, the gods eventually decided in favour of Horus as the rightful king. His father Osiris, whose shattered body had been embalmed by the jackal-headed god Anubis, was confirmed as the god of the dead and Set banished to the desert, a place of evil, and was also made the god of storms. Thereafter, the ruling pharaoh was recognised as the god Horus on earth, and to become a god amongst the gods at his death.

▲ *Horus, the hawk-headed sky god.*

ISIS

ISIS WAS THE MOST important deity of the Egyptian pantheon. She was the embodiment of all that Osiris's life stood for and was governed by. She was the 'Great Mother', the ever-loving wife, the 'Queen of Heaven' (a title she shared with the Virgin Mary in Christianity), and fierce protector of the family and family values. Her most frequent representation is as a seated mother suckling her small son Horus on her lap. The iconography is very similar to that of Mary and the Christ Child and caused many violent religious arguments amongst the early Christian church fathers.

THE DARK HOURS OF THE NIGHT

WHEN THE SUN DIED in the west each day it was imperative that it should be reborn the next dawn. To do this, the god Re had to travel underground through the dark hours of the night, each hour's doorway being guarded by frightening and obnoxious demons which the god had to succeed in passing. There were three major compositions that acted as safeguards to make the journey possible: the *Book of Am-Duat* (also known as the *Book of That Which is in the Underworld)*; the *Book of Gates*, and the *Book of Caverns*. Another well-known Egyptian composition was the *Book of the Dead* which consisted of a series of some 200 chapters, 'spells' or 'utterances', designed to help the deceased on his journey from this life to the next. The most important chapters were Chapter 125 relating to the weighing of the heart in the Hall of Judgement; Chapter 30B, whereby the deceased's heart would not speak evil against him at the Judgement; and Chapter 6, the 'Ushabti chapter', also to be found as a text on the ushabti figures provided in burial, since they were intended to answer the summons and stand in place of the deceased if he was called upon to carry out any tasks in the Afterworld.

▼ *The sun-god Re travels through the Underworld in his sacred barque; a vignette from the* Book of the Dead *of the Royal scribe Ani.*

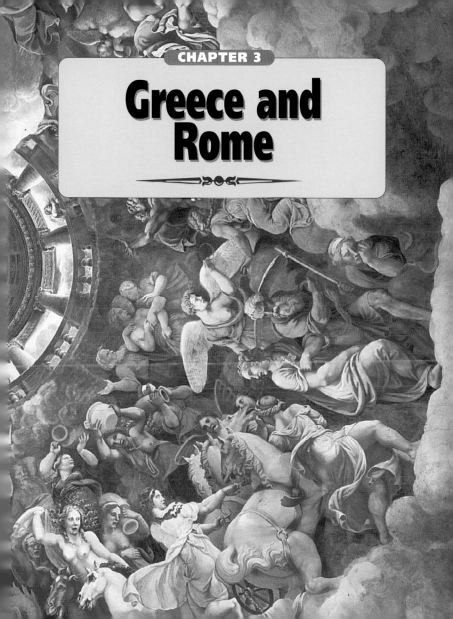

CHAPTER 3

Greece and Rome

Greece

GREEK MYTHOLOGY HAS exercised a profound and unparalled influence upon Western culture. Dramatists, artists and philosophers from Roman times, through the great revival of interest in antiquity in the Renaissance, up to the present day, have been inspired by the thrilling legacy of ancient Greece. The origins of these myths are impossible to determine and there is no one true version of any myth. Instead, every city in the ancient Greek world, from southern Italy across the Aegean and Adriatic islands to the coast of Asia Minor, created its own myths. This can result in confusion, as many different, and often contradictory, versions of the myths exist.

ORIGINALLY PASSED on, adapted and developed by an oral tradition of storytelling, the basic canon of gods and heroes was well established by the time the myths came to be written down, from about 750 BCE. The literature from this period, in particular Homer's epic poems the *Iliad* and the *Odyssey*, and the works of the writer Hesiod, are one of our major sources for Greek myths. The *Iliad* dramatises a few days at the end of the myth of the Trojan War, while the *Odyssey* tells of the adventures of the hero Odysseus as he returns home after fighting at Troy. Hesiod's *Theogony* is a poem concerned with the origins of the world and the gods who rule it.

◀ *The magnificent remains of the Acropolis, Athens.*

THE ROLE OF THE MYTH

AROUND 200 YEARS LATER, Athens had become one of the most powerful cities in Greece and had made the radical political innovation of instituting a democracy. Classical Athens was a time of enormous creativity; politically, culturally and artistically. Mythology permeated every area of life, public and private. It was an essential part of education, as children would be required to learn and recite the stories recounted in Homer and Hesiod. Myths played an important role in the philosophy and science of the period and were portrayed in art, from images of vase paintings and jewellery to the great sculptures and statues seen adorning temples. The *Iliad* and the *Odyssey* were recited in full at the Great Panathenaia, the most important religious festival in Athens, when worshippers came from all over Greece to honour Athens' patron goddess, Athene. The Greek myths commonly involved extreme circumstances, in which human beings transgressed established norms (for example, Oedipus killing his father and marrying his mother). In doing so, they repeatedly debated, challenged and reaffirmed the traditional values of the societies which produced them.

▲ *The goddess Athene in a classical pose portraying contemplation.*

Myths Retold

ATHENE AND THE NAMING OF ATHENS

THE GODDESS ATHENE sprang into the world fully armed and ready to do battle. She was conceived by Zeus, the king of the gods and Metis (meaning 'Cunning Wisdom'), but Zeus heard a prophecy that said any child born of Metis would be greater than its father and to prevent this he swallowed Metis up whole. Soon after he suffered a terrible headache, his head split open and the fully grown Athene appeared. Athene inherited her mother's wisdom and was patron goddess of skilled crafts, such as ship building and weaving. The owl, the wisest of birds, was one of her special symbols.

Myth had it that Athene and Poseidon quarrelled over who should be patron of Athens and it was decided that whoever provided the best gift for the city would win. Poseidon made saltwater spring from the Acropolis (the hill above Athens), thus giving Athens access to the sea. Athene created the olive tree, whose oil is important for lighting, cooking and trade. This was judged the better invention and the people named their city after Athene. They built a shrine to her on the Acropolis, called the Parthenon, a name taken from one of Athene's epithets 'parthenos', which means 'virgin'.

▶ *The mighty Zeus, king of the gods.*

THE OLYMPIC PANTHEON

THE PRINCIPAL DEITIES were thought to live on Mount Olympus, which was the highest mountain in Greece, and which lay in the north of the country. The gods there were represented as anthropomorphic and often quarrelsome. Supreme among the gods was Zeus, whose dominion was the sky. One of his brothers, Poseidon, ruled over the sea and the other, Hades, was sovereign of the Underworld, the realm of the dead. His sister Hestia was goddess of the hearth and home, and Demeter, whose name means 'Grain Mother', was goddess of agriculture. Zeus's sister Hera also became his wife. They gave birth to Ares, the god of war, Hephaestus, the god of fire and metal-working, Hebe, goddess of youth and Eileithyia, goddess of childbirth.

With Metis, Zeus fathered Athene, and with Demeter he fathered Persephone who became goddess of the Underworld. The virgin huntress, the goddess Artemis, and her brother Apollo, god of music and poetry, resulted from an affair between Zeus and the Titaness Leto. With the divine Maia, Zeus had Hermes, the messenger of the gods, and with a mortal woman, Semele, he fathered Dionysus, god of wine and religious ecstasy. Zeus's daughter Aphrodite, goddess of desire, sprang from the foaming sea.

▶ Trompe l'oeil *from the Sala dei Giganti, showing the gods of Olympus.*

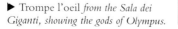

POSEIDON, LORD OF THE SEA

POSEIDON IS AS FEARSOME as his brother Zeus. He holds sway over the sea and forces of nature, particularly tempests. One of his cult titles is Enosichthon which means 'Earth-shaker'. His symbols include the trident, with which he could split open the earth, the bull (possibly representing his aggressiveness) and the horse, since he was supposed to have created the first horse. Poseidon was often warring with Athene. He is ancestor of some of the most awesome monsters in Greek myth: the Echidna, Cerberus, the Hydra and the Sphinx.

◀ *Statue of Poseidon, god of the Sea.*

BIRTH FROM THE SOIL

OF THE MANY DIFFERENT accounts of the birth of humanity perhaps the most important is the idea of birth from the earth itself, *autochthony*. Zeus, enraged with mankind, sent a flood to destroy them. Prometheus managed to warn his son Deucalion and Deucalion's wife Pyrrha who survived by building an ark. When the waters had subsided, they made sacrifices to Zeus who sent the Titan Themis to help them. She advised them to walk along, throwing stones over their shoulders. The stones thrown by Deucalion turned into men and those thrown by Pyrrha, into women. The human race was thus created from the earth.

Myths of autochthony were particularly important to the Athenians, who emphasised their ancestry from the earth to show their superiority over other Greeks and 'barbarians', who, they claimed, did not have such a special relationship with the land. In Euripides' play *Erechtheus* the wife of the king of Athens talks about her people: 'Our people did not immigrate from some other place; we are born of the earth. Other cities, founded on the whim of the dice, are imported from other cities. Whoever inhabits a city derived from another, like a joint fitted poorly in wood, is a citizen in name, not in fact' (fragment 50).

 **Myths Retold**

FROM CHAOS TO CREATION

FIRST THERE ONLY EXISTED Chaos, 'the void', from which Gaia 'earth' was formed (exactly how remains ambiguous) together with Tartaros (the Underworld), Eros (desire), Erebos (the darkness of the Underworld) and Night (the darkness of the earth). Night joined with Erebos to produce Aither (the ether, or bright air) and Day. Gaia gave birth to Uranos (the sky) and togther they produced the first divinities: 12 Titans (human-shaped giants), three Cyclopes ('wheel-eyed' creatures) and three Hekatonchires (monsters with 100 hands). Disgusted with his children, Uranos banished them to the underworld. In anger, Gaia persuaded the youngest Titan, Kronos, to castrate his father and take power.

Kronos married his sister Rhea and had five children. He had been warned that one of them would kill him and so swallowed each of them as they were born. To protect her sixth child, Rhea tricked Kronos into swallowing a stone and hid the baby who was brought up safely by the nymphs. This child was Zeus who returned as an adult and fought a mighty battle against the Titans, the Titanomachy. With the help of the freed Cyclopes and Hekatonchires, Zeus was victorious. He made Kronos vomit up his sisters and brothers, and became king of the gods.

▶ The Banquet of the Gods,
portraying a hedonistic lifestyle.

PROPAGANDA MYTHS IN ART

GREEK ART OFTEN featured mythology which reinforced the Greeks' superiority over non-Greeks. Athenians, in particular, used mythological scenes as propaganda. Many friezes, in particular the one from that monument to Athenian supremacy, the Parthenon, show the Athenians fighting and vanquishing the Amazons, a mythical race of warrior women who were

unlike Athenians in every way. Other 'foreign' enemies whom art shows Athenians fighting include the Persians (Athens' non-mythical foe) and the centaurs, the fabulous race of half-men, half-horses. By including the Persians among these mythical oddities, the Athenians emphasised their difference and inferiority.

◀ *A Parthenon frieze of Artemis, Apollo and Poseidon.*

THE HARDSHIPS OF HUMANITY

THE HARDSHIPS SUFFERED by humanity were explained in the myths of Prometheus and Pandora. Prometheus (whose name means 'Forethought') was a Titan who befriended mankind but incurred the wrath of Zeus. He tricked the king of the gods out of the best part of the sacrifice, the meat, giving him the bones instead. (From that time, the people offered Zeus the bones of a sacrificed animal, but ate the meat themselves.) As punishment, Zeus refused to let humans have the gift of fire, but Prometheus outwitted him again by stealing a flame and bringing it to earth. Enraged, Zeus ordered Violence and Strength to bind Prometheus to a stake on Mount Caucasus, where an eagle pecked out his liver. As an immortal, Prometheus could not die and his liver was renewed every night for the torture to begin again every morning.

For accepting the gift of fire, Zeus also punished mankind. He commissioned Hephaistus to create a women from clay, and sent her to Prometheus's brother Epimetheus with a jar ('Pandora's box'). Despite Prometheus's warnings, Epimetheus, whose name means 'Afterthought', accepted Pandora. She opened the jar, releasing evil and sickness into the world. Only hope remained, a sign that mankind should not despair.

HEROES AND HERO–CULTS

HEROES WERE USUALLY born of a god and a mortal woman. The hero Perseus was the result of Zeus's love affair with the mortal Danae, while the mighty Herakles was born to Zeus and the mortal Alcmene. They were not divine, but their spirits were thought eternal and they often intervened to help mortals in need. Heroes were not worshipped in Homer's time, but by the fifth century BCE the hero cult had become a widespread form of religious worship. Heroes were worshipped at shrines built on supposed sites of their burial or death. Because heroes were thought to possess exemplary courage and honour, to be associated with them was thought to bring good fortune. Similarly, to neglect a hero risked provoking his anger. Many Greek states claimed a hero as their founder or protector, creating myths to support their lineage, and noble families often claimed to be descended from a hero. There were many local heroes, and heroes often became associated with places, for example Oedipus at Colonus, Ajax at Salamis and Theseus at Athens. Heroes' power brought both good and evil. For example, the hero Oedipus saved his city, but committed terrible crimes.

◀ *Ajax and Cassandra in a scene from the Battle of Troy.*

Myths Retold

THE TROJAN WAR

ARCHAEOLOGICAL EVIDENCE tells us that the city of Troy (called Ilion or Ilium in antiquity) in north-western Asia Minor was destroyed in a war in

▲ *The city of Troy is destroyed by flames during the Trojan War.*

about 1250 BCE. Perhaps this was this war between the Greeks and Trojans which was the subject of Homer's *Iliad* – we just don't know whether or not the myth of the Trojan war had any basis in reality.

The trouble starts when the king and queen of Troy, Priam and Hecuba, expose their baby son Paris, because they are frightened by an omen suggesting that he will destroy the city. (Paris survives and is later welcomed back into the family).

Zeus sets him the task of judging who of the three goddesses, Hera, Athene and Aphrodite is 'the fairest'. Paris chooses Aphrodite, who has promised him the most beautiful woman in the world as his wife. As a result, Paris meets and elopes with Helen, much to the displeasure of her husband, Menelaus. Supporting Menelaus, the Greeks sail to Troy and wage war to recapture Helen.

During the siege, Agamemnon wins Chryseis, daughter of Chryses, the Trojan priest of Apollo, as war booty. Apollo sends a devastating plague upon the Greeks and Agamemnon is forced to return Chryseis. Piqued, the commander steals the Grecian Achilles' war prize, Briseis. Achilles is furious and sulks in his tent, refusing to fight. This allows the Trojans to slaughter many Greeks. Hector, Priam and Hecuba's eldest son, kills Patroclus, who has gone into the fray wearing Achilles' armour to try to intimidate the Trojans.

Achilles is stricken with grief and guilt, and lunges into battle, bent on revenge. He pursues Hector three times around the walls of Troy, kills him in single combat and drags his corpse around the city behind his chariot. Priam begs to be allowed to give his son a proper burial and the angry gods intervene and force Achilles to return the corpse. Achilles dies when Paris' arrow hits him in his only vulnerable spot, his heel. The Greeks win the war with a trick devised by the cunning Odysseus. They build a giant hollow wooden horse, in which the best warriors hide while the fleet sails away as if in defeat. Believing the horse to be an offering to the gods, the Trojans drag it inside the city gates. At night, the Greeks slip out of its belly, burn the city to the ground and enslave the women. Thus did Hecuba's omen that Paris would bring destruction to Troy prove true.

▼ *Greek statue of the sun god, Apollo.*

THESEUS, THE ALL–ATHENIAN HERO

THESEUS WAS THE OFFICIAL hero of Athens. He was not born in Athens and his most famous exploit took place in Crete, where he slew the Minotaur, the man-bull hybrid who lived in a labyrinth and terrorised Athenian youth. However, in the sixth century BCE, the tyrant Pisistratus appropriated Theseus as a panathenian hero. Athenian citizens were encouraged to emulate Theseus and any songs which presented the hero in an unfavourable light were censored. Around 510 BCE an epic celebrating his exploits was composed, called the *Theseis*. It is lost to us now, but might have told how Theseus slew Sinis, the 'pine-bender' who would bend two pine trees together, strap his victim between them and then let the trees go, ripping the man in two. Or perhaps it recounted Theseus' defeat of Procrustes, who victimised travellers by giving them hospitality, but making them 'fit' the bed. Those whose legs were too short, he would stretch on the rack until they fitted, and those whose legs were too long, he chopped down to size. It is unlikely that the real Theseus existed, but Athenians honoured him for unifying Attica (the region of which Athens was the supreme city) into one single state.

HERAKLES, THE HYPER-HERO

HERAKLES, WHO WAS CALLED Hercules by the Romans, was the greatest Greek hero. He was one of the earliest mythological figures to be featured in Greek art (as early as the eighth century BCE) and he was the only hero to be revered throughout Greece. He exemplified the problem that heroes presented Classical Greeks; he was an outstanding individual whose excellence was both a source of admiration and yet also resulted in destruction and dishonour. Among his spectacular achievements are his 12 labours, overseen by king Eurystheus as punishment for killing his family in a fit of

madness visited on him by Hera, jealous of Zeus' liaison with Herakles' mother, Alkmene. Less glorious was his reputation for uncontrollable lust (myth has it that he slept with the fifty daughters of King Thespios in a single night), drinking and gluttony. It was lust that led to Herakles' death. Distressed by Herakles' affection for Iole, his wife Deianeira tried to win back his love with a potion which turned out to be poison. The dying Herakles was placed on a funeral pyre, but as the flames licked around him, his father Zeus snatched him up to heaven, where he was the only hero to be given immortality.

◀ *Herakles and Apollo engage in battle.*

Myths Retold

THE 12 LABOURS OF HERAKLES

1. **The Nemean Lion**
   The lion which terrorised Nemea had a hide so tough that no weapon was able to pierce it. Herakles stunned it with his club before strangling it. He wore its skin for protection.

2. **The Lernaean Hydra**
   In the swamps of Lerna lurked the hydra, a water-snake with nine heads. Whenever Herakles slashed off one serpent head, two more grew in its place. After cutting off a head, Herakles cauterized the stump with a burning torch, thus preventing any heads from growing back.

▲ *Greek amphora showing Herakles capturing Cerberus.*

3. **The Cerynean Hind**
   Herakles had to capture the hind unharmed. It had bronze hooves and gold horns, lived on Mount Cerynea and was sacred to the goddess Artemis. After stalking the hind for a year, Herakles trapped it in a net.

4. **The Eurymathian Boar**
   Herakles managed to chain this boar, who was so fearsome that when Eurystheus saw him he was terrified and hid inside a bronze urn.

5. **The Augean Stables**
   The stables of King Aegeus had never been cleaned and were piled high with dung. Herakles had to clean them out in one day, a task he only accomplished by diverting two nearby rivers through the stables to wash the filth away.

6. **The Stymphalion Birds**
   These man-eating birds had beaks, claws and wings of iron. Herakles frightened them off lake Stymphalos by clashing cymbals and then shot them with his arrows.

7. **The Cretan Bull**

   This monstrous bull ran amok on Crete. Only Herakles was able to overpower it and capture it alive.

8. **The Mares of Diomedes**

   Diomedes fed his wild mares on human flesh. Herakles killed Diomedes and fed his body to the mares who became calm and were easily tamed.

9. **Hippolyte's belt**

   Herakles defeated the warrior women Amazons, in order to steal their queen, Hippolyte's, belt.

10. **The Cattle of Geryon**

    Geryon was a three-bodied monster who guarded his cattle with the help of Orthus, a two-headed dog. Herakles killed them both and drove the cattle home, establishing the Straits of Gibraltar on the way.

11. **The Apples of the Hesperides**

    The apples were tended by the Hesperides nymphs and guarded by a dragon which Herakles had to slay before stealing them.

12. **Cerberus**

    Herakles' final task was to show Eurystheus, Cerberus, the three-headed dog which guarded the gates of the Underworld. He wrestled with the beast, took him to Eurystheus, but returned him to Hades afterwards.

THE ETERNAL SUFFERER

EVERY CULTURE HAS its myths of those who are punished by the gods and sentenced to eternal damnation. Tantalus suffered a particularly nasty fate. He had dishonoured the gods by serving them human flesh (his own son!) instead of meat, and Zeus banished him to the Underworld. He was made to stand in a pool of fresh water which had fruit trees growing overhead. Whenever he tried to eat or drink, the branches and water moved away, condemning him to perpetual hunger and thirst. This myth gives us our word 'tantalise'.

Rome

MANY OF THE GREEK myths were adopted and modified by the Romans, whose empire was the dominant power over and beyond most of the area that we now know as modern Europe for the first four centuries CE. The speed and extent of Rome's expansion was quite extraordinary. When Rome became a republic (governed by elected magistrates) in 509 BCE, it controlled relatively little, but by 241 BCE it had control of most of Italy and by 31 BCE, when Rome became an empire under the leadership of Augustus, it was well on the way to ruling virtually the entire Mediterranean world. Rome's subjects numbered over 50 million, with one million populating the city itself.

THE EXTENT of Rome's dominion is the key to understanding its mythology. The Roman state was simply too large and mutable for only one set of mythological and religious traditions to suffice. As Rome expanded its territories, it incorporated the myths of the conquered peoples into its own. The result is eclectic: Roman mythology is a strange hotch-potch of Greek, Egyptian, Celtic and many other myths.

▲ *Gold coin bearing the portrait of Emperor Julius Caesar.*

▲ God of love, Eros, is punished in front of Aphrodite.

THE BIRTH OF ROMAN MYTHOLOGY

ALL THESE DIFFERENT mythologies, once assimilated, became Roman myths. For example, at the end of the second century BC, the Egyptian goddess Isis was introduced into Italy. A mother goddess associated with fertility, Isis soon became popular and she was sometimes linked with the Roman, Fortuna, spirit of fertility, agriculture and love, becoming Isis-Fortuna. Another Egyptian deity, the ram-horned god Amon, became Ammon in Greek mythology and in Rome became incorporated into the imperial cult. He was a protector of the Roman armies and his image appears on breastplates and medallions.

The Greek pantheon was absorbed into the Roman one, primarily via the Etruscans, an important civilisation on the Italian peninsula between 900 and 500 BCE. Thus, for example, the Roman equivalent of Zeus was Jupiter, of Hera, Juno, of Athene, Minerva, of Artemis, Diana and of Aphrodite, Venus. There were no native myths in which these gods played a part, nor did the Romans have any creation myth. The Roman derivatives proved colourless counterparts to the Greek divinities. The Greek gods were anthropomorphic in more than shape; like humans they fought, swindled, loved and avenged. The Roman deities did not possess human psychology. Instead, they were mostly personifications of various abstract qualities, and their personalities were much less important than their functions.

▲ Dionysus reclines amongst his entourage.

THE GREAT MOTHER

ONE OF THE MOST extraordinary deities introduced to Rome was that of the 'Great Mother' or 'Magna Mater', the Roman name for the Phrygian fertility goddess Cybele. Her cult was brought into Rome in 204 BCE on the advice of an oracle. In one version of the myth by the Christian writer Arnobius (fourth century CE), Cybele was born from a great rock in Phrygia (the one from which Deucalion and Pyrrha took the stones that became human beings). Zeus attacked Cybele and spilled some semen on the rock, which became pregnant. The rock bore a son, Agdestis, a violent and uncontrollable creature. Dionysus drugged him with wine and made vines grow from his genitals. Agdestis tripped over the vines and ripped his genitals. From the blood sprang a pomegranate tree whose fruit made a maiden pregnant. Her child, Attis, became Cybele's favourite and Agdestis protected him. When the king of the capital of Phrygia arranged for Attis to marry his daughter, Agdestis, in anger drove the wedding guests mad and one castrated himself. The distraught Attis castrated himself in kind. This is all very bizarre and the disturbing elements of self-castration and ecstatic ravings were mirrored in the cult practices of the followers of the Magna Mater.

JANUS

JANUS WAS A ROMAN god with no Greek equivalent. He is often depicted on coins as facing in two directions. This is because he was the spirit of doors and archways – at entrances and exits it is sensible to look ahead and behind. He gave his name to the month of January, when we look backwards at the old year and forwards to the new. From the year 153 BCE the Roman year began in January. In the Roman forum stood a gate without a building: a symbol of Janus.

Myths Retold

ROMULUS AND REMUS

ACCORDING TO THIS famous myth, Rome was founded in fratricide. Romulus and Remus were twin brothers born to Rhea Silvia, a woman from the royal family in Alba Longa who was raped by Mars, the god of war. When her uncle, the king Amulius, noticed her pregnancy, he imprisoned Rhea Silvia, and once the babies were born, he exposed them to die by the banks of the river Tiber. The twins were discovered by a she-wolf, who suckled them until a shepherd named Faustulus found and adopted them. When they were young men, Romulus and Remus tried to rob some of Amulius' shepherds and Remus

▼ *A she-wolf suckles the abandoned Romulus and Remus.*

was caught and taken before the king. Meanwhile, Faustulus decided to explain to Remus the circumstances of his birth. When he learned the facts, Romulus rescued Remus, murdered Amulius and made his grandfather, Numitor, king of Alba Longa. Romulus and Remus resolved to found their own city on the site where the she-wolf had nurtured them. However, they argued about the exact location of the site and the dispute ended with Romulus murdering his brother and becoming the sole king of Rome. He gave his name to the city (*Roma* in Latin).

▲ *Surrounded by scenes of torture and evil, Aeneas descends into Hades, or the Underworld.*

INSPIRED WOMEN

WHEN AENEAS DESCENDS to the Underworld in the sixth book of the Aeneid, his guide is the Sybil at Cumae. Myth has it that she was so old because of a punishment inflicted on her Apollo. The god offered her as many years of life as she could scoop up grains of sand. Sibyl accepted, but when she rejected Apollo he kept his word but made her shrivel up like a grasshopper. It is often women who are mouthpieces for prophecy. The oracle at Delphi was spoken through the Pythia and in the Bible the Witch of Endor foretells the future to King Saul.

THE ORIGINS OF ROME

AENEAS, WHO WAS a minor Trojan hero in the Greek epics of Homer, was a significant figure in Roman mythology. Aeneas was revered as the mythical founder of Rome from as early as the third century BCE, but it is in Virgil's monumental epic poem, the *Aeneid*, that this tale of national origin receives its most celebrated treatment. Written in the first century BCE, the *Aeneid* narrates Aeneas' escape from Troy, voyage around the Mediterranean to Italy and fight with Turnus for the hand in marriage of the princess of the Italian kingdom

▼ *The arrival of Aeneas at Pallanteum.*

Latium. In a visit to the Underworld, Aeneas is shown the city he will later found, the future greatness of Rome and the souls of famous Romans of the future who had yet to be born. The poem ends with the defeat of Turnus, but another version of the myth told how Aeneas's son founded Alba Longa. This version made the myth compatible with the myth of Rome's foundation by Romulus, who was descended from the royalty of Alba Longa. Through his *pietas* (devotion to duty), Aeneas was a paradigm of Roman moral values and the Emperor Augustus claimed to be descended from him.

ABANDONED CHILDREN

ROMULUS AND REMUS were abandoned by the banks of the river Tiber where they were expected to die. A she-wolf rescued them and the image of her suckling the twin babies was used by Rome as a symbol of her growing power. Babies being abandoned in the wild, then being saved by an animal or country worker and then returning to take their rightful place in society is a common one in myth. In Greek myth, Oedipus was exposed on the mountainside. In fairytales it is common for babies, or older children like Snow White and Hansel and Gretel, to be abandoned in the woods.

▶ *The she-wolf and a bird nourish and shelter Romulus and Remus.*

 **Myths Retold**

AENEAS AND DIDO

BEFORE AENEAS arrived in Italy, he landed at Carthage on the coast of North Africa. The queen of Carthage, called Dido, had fled from her home city of Tyre in Phoenicia, after her husband Sychaeus, was brutally murdered. Dido had sworn a vow of perpetual fidelity to Sychaeus's ghost, but Aeneas' mother, the goddess Venus, sent Cupid to inspire Dido with passion. Dido fell in love with Aeneas and her thoughts turned to marriage. One day while she and Aeneas were out hunting, they huddled together in a cave while

▼ *Aeneas relates the tales of Troy to Queen Dido.*

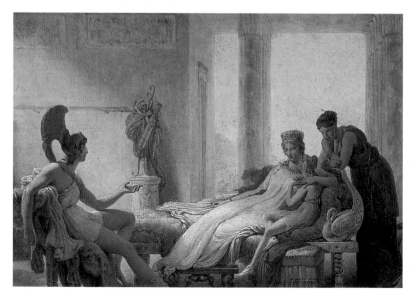

sheltering from a storm and made love there. Their affair blossomed until Mercury, the messenger of the gods, is sent by Jupiter to remind Aeneas that his destiny is to found the Roman race. Aeneas makes secret plans to leave Carthage, but Dido discovers his intentions and confronts him angrily. Aeneas is resolute, and after he departs Dido commits suicide. When Aeneas visits the Underworld later in the epic, he sees the Dido's ghost reunited with the ghost of her husband. This part of the myth is more than a poignant romance. With her infidelity, seductive passion and self-destruction, Dido symbolises Carthage, Rome's greatest enemy, who, under Hannibal (247–183 BCE), almost destroyed Rome.

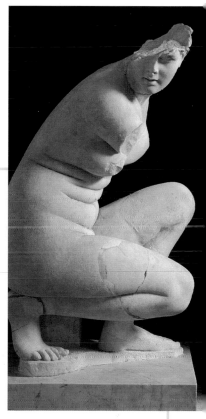

VENUS AND CUPID

VENUS, GODDESS OF sexual desire, plays a major role in the Roman epic poem, the *Aeneid*. She was the mother of Aeneas, and on several occasions intervenes to help her son. Aeneas' father, Anchises, was a mortal man. She is accompanied by Cupid, who is depicted in art as a beautiful winged boy with bows and arrows (much like our St Valentine's Day image). Venus is the Roman equivalent of the Greek Aphrodite and also shares similarities with the Sumerian fertility goddess Inanna and the Akkadian fertility goddess Ishtar.

▶ *The voluptuous goddess of desire, Venus.*

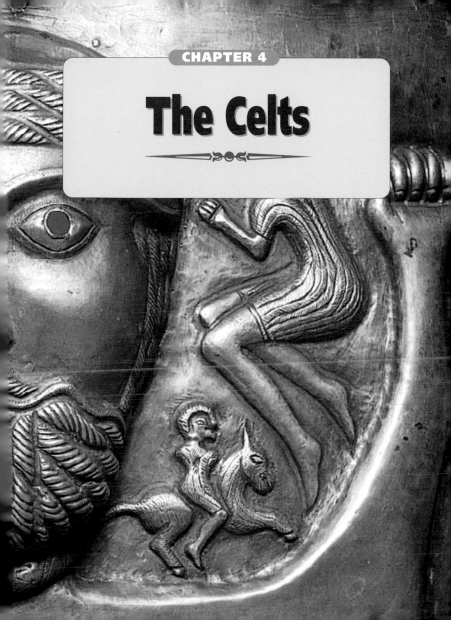

CHAPTER 4

The Celts

The Celts

THE CELTS WERE AMONG the great founding peoples of Europe. Centuries before the Roman Empire, Celtic kingdoms occupied much of the Continent north of the Alps. In the period of maximum expansion, between the fifth and the third centuries BCE, their world stretched from Ireland and parts of Spain in the west to central Turkey in the east.

▲ *Heads held spiritual protective power for the Celts.*

I T USED TO BE thought that the Celts invaded Western Europe some time in the second millennium BCE. The less dramatic but more likely view is that the peoples who had inhabited the area for thousands of years gradually adopted the characteristics we call Celtic.

The Celts were not a united group with a self-conscious ethnic identity. They did not form an empire. Their world was a mosaic of richly diverse chiefdoms and extended families linked by little more than a common language and culture.

Nevertheless, these apparently disorganised peoples dominated Europe for 500 years before they were conquered by the Romans and later driven to the edges of the known world, to Ireland, Wales, Scotland, Cornwall and Brittany.

The pagan Celts left no written records. They passed down their laws, traditions and religious beliefs by word of mouth. Consequently, our knowledge of their culture is based on the testimonies of classical Greek and Roman observers, archeological remains and later Irish and Welsh texts.

At first the ancients did not understand the customs of the Celts and later they needed excuses to conquer and 'civilise' them. Therefore their portrayal of these people as fearsome, undisciplined barbarians who gloried in war and indulged in disgusting rituals is not reliable. Some of their observations, however, have been confirmed by archeology.

▲ *Ornate gold openwork on a Schwazenbrach Celtic decorative bowl.*

From artefacts and Romano-Celtic inscriptions, archeology has also discovered much about Celtic life which is not mentioned by Classical writers. Such discoveries show the Celts to have been an intelligent, complex and wealthy people whose art and technical brilliance was unsurpassed in prehistoric Europe.

The Irish and Welsh texts were written down much later by monks in a post-Roman, Christian setting and they relate entirely to geographical areas which were peripheral to pre-Roman, Celtic Europe. As such, their use is limited in helping us to form a true picture of the mythology of the pagan Celts. Nonetheless, these texts are of enormous interest in themselves and they provide invaluable insights, particularly into those mythological traditions which were to inspire the great Arthurian romances of medieval Europe.

GODS OF THE PAGAN CELTS

FROM THE ROMANS we get a simplistic interpretation of Celtic religion which reduces the abundance and variety of Celtic deities to a convenient system modelled on their own. Hence the Celtic god Lugh is equated with Mercury, Brigit with Minerva and so on.

Fortunately for archeology the Celts were influenced by the Romans when they were absorbed into the Empire. This led to a large-scale representation of their gods in durable materials and to

the production of religious inscriptions. Many Celtic gods discovered in the form of figurines, reliefs and sculpture turned out to be quite alien to the classical system, and the inscriptions have provided us with names for a number of them.

▲ *Head of the female deity, the goddess Brigit.*

The Celts had many gods associated with the most important aspects of life: warfare, hunting, fertility, healing, good harvests and so on. A few, like Lugh, were worshipped by Celts across Europe. In much greater numbers were local, tribal or family deities. Certain gods were associated with particular places such as sacred groves, remote mountains and lakes.

In Gaul, for example, Borvo and Grannos were associated with wells, and in Britain the goddess Sulis gave her name to the healing springs at Aquae Sulis, present-day Bath.

▲ *A stone monolith with Celtic inscriptions.*

 **Myths Retold**

THE COMING OF LUGH

NUADA, THE ONE-HANDED leader of the Tuatha Dé Danann, was holding a great feast at Tara when a young man appeared at the gate. Challenged, the youth identified himself as Lugh, son of Cian of the Tuatha Dé Danann and grandson of their enemy Balor. He had come, he said, to help their incapacitated leader in the imminent battle between the Tuatha Dé Danann and the Fomorians.

No one was allowed into Tara without a skill and Lugh was asked what arts he could offer. He said he was a carpenter, but the gatekeeper was unimpressed. There was already a carpenter in the citadel, he scoffed, by the name of Luchtar. Lugh tried again. This time he said he was a smith. There was already a smith at Tara, came the reply, by the name of Colum Cuaillemech; he was very talented and he had already invented three new techniques.

In successive attempts Lugh told the gatekeeper that he was a champion, a harpist, a warrior, a poet, a historian, a magician and a metal worker. He said he was even prepared to serve as a cup-bearer. But nothing he offered was needed. The Tuatha Dé Danann, he was told, had people who possessed all of these skills.

Eventually Lugh bid the gatekeeper to ask Nuada if there was any one man in his company who possessed all of the skills that he professed. If there was, said Lugh, he would withdraw. So the gatekeeper went to the king and told him that there was a man at the door whose name was Lugh but it should have been Ildanach, the Master of All Arts, because all of the things that different people could do in the Tuatha Dé Danann, he could do himself.

Intrigued, Nuada suggested a test to see just how good Lugh was. He sent the gatekeeper back with a chessboard and told him to pit the young man against their best player. After winning convincingly, Lugh was brought to the king who set him a further test. Ogma, the king's principal champion, hurled a heavy flagstone out of the citadel and Lugh was challenged to return it. Effortlessly, Lugh hurled it back inside where it fell into its original position.

The king was so impressed that he handed over his crown to Lugh who successfully led the Tuatha Dé Danann in their fight against the Fomorians.

FEASTING

RECURRING THEMES IN Celtic mythology are the Otherworld feast and the feast where dramatic events occur. Tales regarding Briccriu and Mac Da Thó revolve around disputes over the champion's portion at feasts; Grainne seduces Diarmaid at a feast; Dierdre is born at one; and the beautiful butterfly, Etain, is born again as a human after landing in a glass of mead at a feast. In the story of Branwen, marriage arrangements and a peace treaty are settled over a feast; Fergus is tragically distracted while feasting; and Bres is satirised by the poet Cairbre for failing to provide lavish hospitality.

THE MYTHOLOGICAL CYCLE

AMONG THE IRISH texts is a collection of prose stories which includes the *Book of Invasions* and the *History of Places*. Both texts were compiled in the twelfth century CE but the more interesting *Book of Invasions* has its origins in earlier attempts by monastic scholars of the sixth and seventh centuries to construct a history of Ireland. In effect it is an Irish creation myth which follows a succession of legendary invasions of the country from the Flood to the coming of the Gaels, or Celts.

The most important invasion is that of the Tuatha Dé Danann, the 'People of the Goddess Danu', the divine race of Ireland. To establish themselves, they had to expel the Fir Bolg and overcome the demonic Fomorians. Their father-god was the Dagda, the 'Good God'. Other deities included a triad of craft-gods called Goibniu, Luchta and Credne and King Nuadu who handed over power to Lugh after he lost an arm in battle. Myths involving Lugh are not confined to the *Book of Invasions*. He turns up elsewhere as the father of the hero Cúchulainn (pronounced 'Koo Hoolin').

The Tuatha Dé Danann are said to have retreated underground when the Gaels conquered Ireland.

◀ *Sheet bronze Celtic divinity with torque.*

EPONA

EPONA WAS AN important goddess of the Continental Celts, commemorated in more surviving sculpture and inscriptions than any other early goddess. Her name means 'Great Mare' and she is usually portrayed on horseback sitting side-saddle and accompanied by a bird, a dog and a foal. Epona was imported to Britain by the Romans and she was the only Celtic deity to be cited in the Roman pantheon. She was popular with the Roman cavalry; she was associated with husbandry and fertility, and shrines were made in stables for her worship and favour. In Britain her cult merged with those of Macha and Rhiannon.

 **Myths Retold**

BRICCRIU'S FEAST

BRICCRIU OF THE Poisoned Tongue built a wonderful hall at Emain Macha to impress his guests and he invited all the men of Ulster and Connacht, traditional rivals, to a great feast. No one wanted to go. They knew Briccriu of old and his love of mischief. But he threatened such retribution if they refused him that they had no choice.

Now, it was the privilege of the most noble warrior present to take the choicest joint of meat at a feast. Briccriu was quick to use this heroic etiquette as an opportunity to cause trouble. He went in turn to the three main contenders, Loegaire Buadach, Conall Cernach and Cúchulainn, and persuaded each of them to claim the 'champion's portion'. To be sure of a fight he also set their wives against each other.

As Briccriu had planned, there was a brawl which was stopped only by the wisdom of Sencha macAilella who suggested that the three heroes should take the issue to Connacht so Queen Medb could decide. After a fearsome ordeal, Medb gave the honour to Cúchulainn but, on their return to Emain Macha, Loegaire and Conall claimed that the queen had been bribed and they refused to accept the verdict.

So the three went to Munster to seek the judgement of the great warrior king, Cú Roí mac Dairi. Following further trials of valour, he

▼ *Cúchulainn sets out on his journey to Emain Macha.*

also chose Cúchulainn and again there was a refusal on the part of the other two to accept defeat.

The matter was unresolved until, one night, when all the men of Ulster were assembled at Emain, an oafish giant entered the hall. In turn he challenged Loegaire, Conall and Cúchulainn to cut off his head on the understanding that he would return the following night to remove theirs. All three agreed and Loegaire took the first turn, decapitating the churl who left carrying his head under his arm. Next evening the giant, with his head restored, returned for his revenge, but the cowardly Loeghaire reneged and refused to submit.

The same thing happened in Conall's case and only Cúchulainn, when it was his turn, was prepared to pay the price. He knelt and waited for the blow. But it did not come. The giant turned out to be Cú Roí mac Dairi himself, come to confirm his previous judgement. He spared Cúchulainn the ordeal and the hero was declared undisputed champion of all Ireland.

GIANTS

GIANTS OCCUR IN CELTIC mythology in several forms. Heroes such as the Irish Finn mac Cool or the Welsh Brân are so great that they are pictured as giants. Some giants are instrumental in the deeds of heroes, such as Wrnach whose sword was one of the items Culhwch had to steal for the hand of Olwen. Others issue challenges, like Cú Roí at Briccriu's Feast. The remainder are either foolish and gentle, or they exist for weaker men to vanquish. There are also giantesses; Bébinn in the Fenian Cycle, for example, and Cymidei Cymeinfoll, in the story of Branwen.

▶ *Surviving stone carvings give an insight into the characters and protagonists of Celtic mythology.*

THE FENIAN CYCLE

THE EARLIEST MANUSCRIPT fragments of the Irish Fenian Cycle date from the eighth century CE although the tales are thought to derive stylistically from the third. The first complete synthesis of its eight major parts did not appear until the twelfth century CE, however. The Cycle comprises a very large body of verse and prose romances from which, it is argued, the themes of the Arthurian sagas are derived.

The supernatural hero of this Cycle is the poet and seer Finn mac Cool, a late development of the earlier god, Lugh. He is the leader of an élite and highly disciplined band of Irish warriors, the Fianna, who are pledged to defend the king and who are chosen for their strength and courage.

▲ *A fifteenth-century manuscript showing the crowning of King Arthur.*

Finn's divine status is confirmed by many features of his life. He is brought up by a druidess and he marries an enchanted woman transformed into a deer. He acquires wisdom from contact with the Salmon of Knowledge, he has the gift of prophecy, he uses magic and he is a superhuman warrior.

These stories are sometimes referred to as the Ossianic Cycle after Finn's principal son, the great poet and warrior Oisin (pronounced 'Usheen'), who features prominently in later tales.

Myths Retold

OISIN IN THE LAND OF FOREVER YOUNG

OISIN, THE SON OF Finn mac Cool, was out hunting one day with his father and their élite band of warriors, the Fianna. They were joined by a beautiful, fairy-like woman on a white horse. Her name was Naim of the Golden Hair and she had come, she said, to take Oisin home with her to Tir na nOg, the Land of Forever Young.

Naim told them that she had loved Oisin since she and her father had ridden through Ireland some years before. She had watched him then, running like a young deer through the meadows, looking every inch a huntsman and a warrior. For seven years and seven days she had returned, invisible, to watch him grow up and, at last, her father had given her permission to declare her love.

She cast a spell over Oisin so that he loved her too, and they rode away on Naim's white steed across lakes, rivers and the misty sea to Tir na nOg. There they married and lived happily for 300 years, a period which seemed like only three weeks to Oisin.

Eventually Oisin became homesick. He longed to see his father and his friends again. Naim did all she could to dissuade him from returning to Ireland. She could not change his

▲ *Oisin loses his magic youth and becomes the old man the Land of Forever Young had disguised.*

mind, however, so she gave him her white horse to make the journey and she warned him not to dismount or he would never return.

When Oisin got back to Ireland he found that everything was different. The countryside had changed, his father and the Fianna were long dead and a new faith was being practised. Deeply saddened, Oisin turned and began his journey

OTHERWORLD VOYAGES

THE 'IMRAM', OR VOYAGE, is a class of Old and Middle Irish narrative in which travellers explore an Otherworld, usually an archipelago of wondrous islands in the western ocean. Typical is the seventh or eighth century Imram Brain, the Voyage of Bran, Son of Febal. Bran's Otherworld goal is the Land of Women where there is no grieving, winter or want. After many adventures he returns home to find that a considerable time has passed in his absence. His family and friends are long dead, and his voyage is remembered as an ancient story. Other notable voyages were made by Ma'le Dúin and St Brendan.

▲ *The Broighter ship, possibly a votive offering to the king of the ocean Manannan mac Lir.*

back to his fairy wife. He had not gone far, however, when a group of peasants struggling to lift a heavy stone into a wagon asked him for help. He agreed willingly but, as he stooped, his reins broke and Oisin fell to the ground. Immediately, the horse vanished and Oisin transformed dramatically into a very old man, blind and near to death.

He was carried to St Patrick who was walking the land and preaching of the new god. The saint received him into the new faith. He also managed to take down some of Oisin's stories of the old days when the Fianna ruled the land. But soon, the warrior-poet, and the world he had known, passed away for ever.

THE ULSTER CYCLE

THIS IS THE NAME given to a collection of Irish epic prose stories of which the most important is a group called the *Táin* (pronounced 'toyn') or the *Cattle Raid of Cooley*. The oldest manuscript, which was compiled in the twelfth century CE, is called the *Book of the Dun Cow*. The story is much older in origin, however, and can be traced to the eighth century and possibly earlier.

The *Táin* is not a tale of mundane cattle rustling; it is about supernatural beasts around whom a battle myth is woven. The fighting over the Brown Bull, the Donn and the White Bull, Finnbennach, symbolises the prolonged and fruitless struggle between Ulster and Connacht, the two most northerly of the five ancient provinces of Ireland. Traditional rivalry between the provinces is suggested by the fact that the bulls have already pursued their ferocious conflicts in various guises.

Compiled in a Christian setting, the story must have undergone some reinterpretation. Nevertheless, a considerable mythological content remains: the superhuman warrior, Cúchulainn champions the Ulster cause; Connacht is ruled by the queen-goddess Medb (pronounced 'Maeve') and the destiny of the two kingdoms is in the hands of the death and destruction goddess, the Morrigan.

 **Myths Retold**

THE BROWN BULL OF ULSTER

QUEEN MEDB of Connacht and her consort, Ailill, lay chatting in bed one night, boasting of their possessions. They were evenly matched except for Finnbennach, the great, white-horned bull owned by Ailill.

Medb searched her lands in vain for a comparable beast until she heard of the Donn, the magnificent Brown Bull of Ulster which was owned by Daire mac Fiachniu. Daire might have been willing to lend Medb the Donn for a year if he had been made a generous offer, but he overheard the queen's drunken envoys bragging that they would take the animal with or without his consent. So he refused to co-operate and he sent the bull into hiding.

On hearing the news Medb was livid and she bullied Ailill into invading Ulster to steal the Brown Bull. They amassed a huge force including a well-disciplined contingent from Leinster. Jealous of their performance, the evil Medb contemplated sending them home, or even killing them. However, wise counsel prevailed and she was talked into dispersing them throughout the rest of her army to spread their good influence.

A bitter struggle ensued between the forces of Connacht and King Conchobar of Ulster, often pitting relations and old friends against each other. For much of the time the great warrior Cúchulainn fought the Connacht army single-handed because he was the only Ulster hero unaffected by a curse of weakness which descended periodically on the men of the land. Medb failed to defeat him with bribes and tricks and he killed large numbers of her men, many sent against him in single combat and others attacking a hundred at a time. Eventually the men of Ulster regained their strength and, rallying in support of Cúchulainn, they routed Medb's army.

In the meantime, Medb's scouts had found the Donn and they had driven it back to Connacht along with 50 heifers which followed it from Daire's herd. When the Brown Bull

▶ *Queen Medb of Connacht on her throne.*

came into contact with Ailill's white-horned animal, there was instant hatred between them. The great beasts lowered their horns and fought a great battle, rampaging over the whole of Ireland. At last the Brown Bull was seen galloping back victorious to Ulster, scattering Finn-bennach's entrails across the plain. But the Donn was exhausted and mortally wounded, and it died soon after.

Thus, in the space of a month, thousands died over a greedy whim and neither side won the great bull.

CERNUNNOS

CERNUNNOS WAS A principal god among the
pagan Celts. His name means 'The Horned One' and
he was a lord of nature, animals, agriculture, prosperity
and the Underworld. He is portrayed with a man's body
and the antlers of a stag; he adopts a characteristic
Buddha posture and he wears or holds the sacred torc
in one hand and a ram-headed serpent in the other.
Cernunnos is possibly the closest the Celts got to a
universal father god. There are traces of him in the
literary traditions of Ireland and Wales and he is the
model in later Christian iconography for the Devil.

▲ *Cernunnos,*
'The Horned One'.

EARLY WELSH MYTHS

THE MASTERWORK of medieval Welsh literature is the *Mabinogion* made up
of the Four Branches, or tales, of the Mabinogi and 12 other stories.

The earliest surviving manuscripts of the *Mabinogion* are the *White Book of
Rhydderch* and the *Red Book of Hergest* which date from the fourteenth century.
The stories must be much older than this, however, because they contain so many
ancient, Celtic elements such as god-like heroes, enchanted animals, the love of
feasting and the Otherworld. By the time they came to be written down they
were overlaid with elements of chivalry, knights on quests and ladies in distress,
which are all products of later, Continental influence.

The Four Branches, three of which concern the hero Pryderi, are the stories
of Pwll, Branwen, Manawydan and Math. The remaining stories fall into two
groups: 'Four Independent Native Tales' and 'Three Romances'. The story of
Taliesin is included in later compilations.

Among the 'Native Tales', the collection boasts the earliest surviving
Arthurian tale in Welsh, *Culhwch and Olwen*, which shows forms of eleventh
century style, vocabulary and custom. In this story, Arthur appears as something
between a crude Celtic chieftain and a courtly king.

BRANWEN, DAUGHTER OF LLYR

BRANWEN WAS THE SISTER of Brân the Blessed of Wales. To ensure peace between Wales and Ireland she was betrothed to Matholwch the Irish king. Her brother Efnisien objected to the match, however, and he insulted Matholwch when he travelled to Harlech for the wedding by mutilating his horses so badly that they had to be destroyed.

Brân appeased his guests with apologies and gifts, the most precious being a magic cauldron of Irish origin which could restore dead warriors to life, lacking only the power of speech.

Branwen was taken to Ireland as Matholwch's queen and they lived happily together for a while. But the king's resentment smouldered, fuelled by his counsellors, and he began to take it out on his wife. He relegated her to the kitchens, where she was subject to daily bullying by the servants, and he took measures to

▲ *Ornamental fittings, such as these for a shield, were decorated with symbols representing divinities.*

ensure that Brân would not find out. However, Branwen trained a starling to carry a message to her brother who responded by invading Ireland.

Brân was a giant and he waded across the Irish sea, leading his fleet and carrying his harpists and lute players on his back. The Irish retreated beyond the river Shannon and destroyed the crossing. But Brân was so huge that he was able to form a bridge for his army to cross over.

To pacify Brân, Matholwch told him that he was giving up the crown in favour of the son Branwen had given him. But, at the investiture, Efnisien felt slighted and threw the boy into the fire. Fighting resumed and, using the magic cauldron, the Irish were gaining the upper hand. However, Efnisien destroyed the cauldron and himself in the process, and the Welsh won with only seven men left.

Brân himself was mortally wounded by a magic dart and he decreed that his head should be cut off and born to the White Mount in London where it was to be buried facing east to deter invaders. On the way the party rested at Harlech for seven years. They visited the Otherworld of Gwales and they spent eight years in Pembroke. All the while the head remained alive and did not decay; indeed, it was a most congenial companion.

Eventually the head was buried in accordance with Brân's instructions. As for Branwen, she died of a broken heart in Wales lamenting that, because of her, two great countries were in ruins.

ARTHURIAN ROMANCES

THE ORIGINS OF THESE legends are obscure. *Culhwch and Olwen* is the earliest, fully fledged Arthurian tale in a Celtic language and the tenth century Welsh poem, 'The Spoils of Annwn', is a prototype for the Grail quest. Arthurian tales became popular in Irish literature because of similarities with Finn mac Cool and the Fianna. But the Irish Arthur is a rapacious invader.

It was Geoffrey of Monmouth who began the popular myth of King Arthur. His twelfth century *History of the Kings of Britain* inspired the Norman poet, Wace, whose version provided a more courtly setting and introduced the Round Table. Later in the twelfth century the story was expanded by the French poet, Chrétien de Troyes, who introduced novel elements from

Continental sources. He added the idea of courtly love and provided the earliest version of the Grail legend.

There followed an English version by the poet Layamon, mixing-in some Celtic folk traditions, and in the thirteenth century there was a German contribution. The fourteenth century saw the writing of the greatest single Arthurian legend in Middle English, *Sir Gawain and the Green Knight*, and in the fifteenth century Sir Thomas Malory gave the saga its final shape in *Le Morte D'Arthur*.

▼ *Knights surrounding the Round Table, in the centre of which sits the Holy Grail.*

FABULOUS CAULDRONS

MAGIC CAULDRONS FEATURE repeatedly in both Irish and Welsh mythology. Some, like the Dagda's, never empty, except for cowards; some, like Brân's, revive the dead while others contain greals or brews of wisdom. Ultimately the miraculous cauldron becomes the Holy Grail which promises immortality to those who have earned it.

Surviving cauldrons from the pagan Celtic period are made of bronze, copper or silver and they are richly decorated. The best example is the Gundestrop Cauldron from the first century BCE displaying what is thought to be the embossed figure of the god Cernunnos holding a torc and a serpent.

▼ *Detail from the Gundestrop Cauldron, showing a magnificent bearded deity.*

 **Myths Retold**

CULHWCH AND OLWEN

CULHWCH GOT HIS name from the pig run in which he was born. As a young man he angered his stepmother who swore that he would never know the touch of a woman until he won the hand of Olwen, the beautiful daughter of the giant, Ysbaddaden.

Culhwch went to the court of Arthur, his cousin, to ask for help. There, a group of extraordinary characters was assembled to accompany him in his search for Ysbaddaden's castle. In their travels they encountered the giant's herdsman whose wife turned out to be Culhwch's aunt. When she heard of his quest, she was reluctant to help, having lost twenty-three of her twenty-four sons to their master. Nevertheless, she arranged a meeting between Culhwch and Olwen.

Olwen was more beautiful than Culhwch could have imagined and he swore his undying love for her. Olwen was equally smitten, but she would not leave her father without his consent because it was destined that he would die

▼ *The boar is the most widely depicted animal in Celtic art; these figures were probably votive offerings.*

on her wedding day. Culhwch would have to go to Ysbaddaden, she said, and ask him what he would accept in exchange for her hand.

Culhwch and his companions fought their way into the castle where Ysbaddaden kept them waiting for three days for his reply. Eventually he relented and gave Culhwch a daunting list of tasks to perform. There were thirty-nine in all, many of which revolved around the hunting of Twrch Trwyth, the son of prince Taredd, who had been magically transformed into a wild boar. Ysbaddaden was particularly keen to acquire a comb and shears from between the ears of the boar; none of his own were strong enough to give him a decent shave.

Arthur himself led the expedition which finally tracked down Twrch Trwyth and his seven young pigs to Tsgeir Oervel in Ireland. After a long and bitter battle, Arthur and his men chased them across the sea to Wales. There they continued to create havoc before the boar was driven into the river Severn. As he struggled against the current two of Arthur's men, snatched the comb and shears from between his ears.

Culhwch returned to Ysbaddaden's castle with these and all the other objects he had been challenged to collect. He claimed Olwen as his bride, and the giant was shaved of his beard. Then Goreu, the last remaining son of the herdsman, cut off Ysbaddaden's head and displayed it on a stake.

SHAPESHIFTERS

THE ABILITY TO CHANGE SHAPE, or to transform into another object or creature, is common in Celtic mythology. The Morrigan, the frightful Irish goddess of war, appears as a crow feeding off the bodies of fallen warriors. Arawn, king of the Welsh Otherworld exchanges forms with Pwll, and Sadb, the enchanted mother of Oisin, takes on the form of a doe. Merlin, of course, can also change his shape as well as that of others. He facilitates the union between Arthur's father, Uther, and Igraine, the wife of Gorlois (Duke of Cornwall), by casting a spell to make Uther appear temporarily as Gorlois.

THE SACRED HEAD

CELTIC MYTHOLOGY is full of stories in which giants and enemies are beheaded or heroes are challenged to decapitation contests. We know, too, that the Celts were head-hunters; they kept them as trophies or sacrificial offerings, believing them to contain the essence of the person to whom they belonged and to be a source of wisdom. While human figures are rare in Celtic art, the head or face alone is not, although in two dimensional art forms the face may be difficult to make out among the decorative details. The wearing of jewellery decorated with faces may have followed from the belief that it possessed protective powers.

▼ *This double head is believed to be a symbol of defeated enemies.*

CHAPTER 5

Central and Eastern Europe

Central and Eastern Europe

WITH THE NOTABLE EXCEPTION of the Romanians, Hungarians and Albanians, the peoples of Central and Eastern Europe are predominantly of the Slav family which established an ethnic identity some 1,500 years ago. About that time, in the fifth century, the Slavs began to migrate through eastern Europe: up to the Baltic Sea in the north; down to the Adriatic in the south; and Bohemia in the centre eastwards, travelling half way round the world to the Pacific Ocean.

THOSE WHO SETTLED in the north – the Poles, Belorussians and Russians – found themselves in a mainly flat and marshy terrain, interspersed with broad rivers and covered in snow for up to six months in the year.

Those who inhabited the central parts – the Czechs, Slovaks and Ukrainians – encountered a largely treeless steppe of feather grass.

The families that trekked south through the Balkans, the Yugoslavs (meaning 'southern Slavs' – the Serbs, Croats, Slovenes and Macedonians) and the Bulgarians – found a milder climate beside the warm Adriatic, Aegean and Black seas, and surrounded by snow-topped mountains.

▲ *Fundamental to Central and Eastern mythology is the fish-faced creator god.*

The hardy tribes that went due east – the Rus or Russians – cleared a way by axe and fire through dense forest watered by bog and lake and full of large numbers of nourishing wild animals – wolf and bear, sable and mink.

Each of these terrains left a deep imprint on the civilisation and mythology of the Slavs. The forest taught caution and kindled fantasy. The steppe's endless expanse gave the feeling of vast horizons and distant dreams. Yet it was even more menacing than the forest, for it offered no hiding place from enemies. As for the river and sea, the Slavs placed their homes on their banks, and for most of the year the waters fed them. At the same time, the waters were full of demons, gods and mysteries.

Here, then, are the main offspring of Mother Nature that formed the Slav culture and lent Slav myth its special character.

WATERS OF THE WORLD

RIVERS, LAKES AND SEAS were vital to the ancient Slavs; the motion of water naturally suggested that it was alive. Each stretch of water therefore had its spirit – old, ugly, greenbearded – who when drunk made the waters overflow; when pleased, guided fish into the nets; when cross, raised storms, sank ships and drowned sailors. In the depths of the waters lived the rusalka or water nymph – a lovely naked girl who so charmed passers-by with her laughter and song that some would drown themselves for her sake.

▲ *The Slavic divinity Vodianoï was believed to favour stretches of water near mills.*

FORCES OF NATURE

UNLIKE THE SUMERIANS, Egyptians and Ancient Greeks, the Slavs left no written record of their myths. Only after their Christianisation in the late tenth century did literacy and literature appear. Although the names of pagan gods have been preserved, we nonetheless know little of their cults and stories.

Like other peoples, the primitive Slav believed that some mysterious and fantastic power controlled the sun, sky, stars, rivers and seas. The best-known collector of folklore, Alexander Afanasiev (1826–71), had a romantic theory about myths. In the story, 'Fair Vassilisa and Bába Yága', for example, the

witch (Bába Yága) symbolises the dark storm cloud that wants to destroy the sun (the young girl, Vassilisa); but the sun frees itself from the power of the storm and other dark clouds (the stepmother and her daughters). In the dragon stories, it is the storm cloud (the dragon) fighting the sun (the hero) who destroys and disperses it with lightning (his sword). When Fenist the Falcon is woken by a maiden's kiss (a change of gender role from the West European *Sleeping Beauty*), it is really Nature woken by spring, the earth kissed by the sun.

◀ *Bába Yága the witch — an illustration from the tale of the beautiful Vassilisa.*

 **Myths Retold**

SNOWMAIDEN

▲ *Palekh papier-mâché plaque, showing the Snowmaiden watching the villagers dancing and playing.*

SNOWMAIDEN (Snegurochka) is the daughter of Fair Spring and old Red-Nose Frost. Until she was 16, she grew up in her father's icy realm – lest Yarilo the sun god see her and melt her away.

Early one spring, when Fair Spring and Frost met, they argued about their daughter's future. While her mother wanted her to be free, her father was afraid the sun would kill her. Finally, they decided to put her into the care of an old childless couple.

So it was, one morning, as the old man and woman are walking in the snowy forest, the man set to making a 'snowgirl'. To his surprise, the snowgirl's lips grow red, her eyes open and she steps out of the snow – a real, live girl.

Snowmaiden grows up not by the day but by the hour. Soon spring sunshine warms the land and patches of green grass appear. Yet the young girl hides from the sun, seeks a chill shadow and stretches out her pale arms to the rain.

One day, as summer is approaching, some village girls invite Snowmaiden out to play. Reluctantly, she joins them, picking flowers, singing songs and dancing with the village lads.

Snowmaiden hangs back until a shepherd boy plays his flute for her, and then takes her by the hand and whirls her around in a dance.

From that day on, Lel the shepherd calls on Snowmaiden. But although he loves her dearly, he feels no response in her cold heart. Finally, he leaves her for another village girl. In her grief, Snowmaiden runs to a lake in the middle of the forest and begs her mother to give her a human heart.

'To love for a moment is dearer to me than a frozen heart,' she says.

Her mother takes pity on her, places a crown of lilies on her head and warns her to guard her love from Yarilo's fiery gaze.

Rushing through the trees, Snowmaiden finds Lel and declares her love for him. As she speaks, the radiant sun rises higher in the cloudless sky, dispelling the mists of dawn and melting the remaining snow. A ray of sunshine falls on her and, with a cry of pain, she begs Lel to play her one last tune.

As he plays, her body sinks into the ground; all that remains is a crown of lilies.

Yet as one life passes, another is born. Sunshine awakens the frozen earth with a kiss and gives birth to plants and flowers. As for Lel, he waits for the winter snows to bring him back his beloved Snowmaiden.

PALEKH FOLK ART

THE ANCIENT RUSSIAN folk art, palekh, originated in the village of Palekh, some 480 km (300 miles) north-east of Moscow. Palekh lacquered miniatures are paintings mainly on papier-mache jewellery boxes and brooches. They most frequently depict folk themes (such as the Firebird, Sadko, Bába Yága) or religious images – the icons, best seen in Palekh's beautiful Krestodvizhensky Cathedral.

For the paint, finely-ground pigments are rubbed into an emulsion made of egg yolk; the separated yolk is returned to the shell, water and vinegar are added, and the emulsion is stirred with a special nine-hole whisk.

◄ *The magnificent Krestodvizhensky Cathedral, depicted here by the palekh artists, itself contains many other such artworks.*

THE CHURCH

MYTHS WERE THE SLAV story of Nature. The heroes are the gods of sun, sky, light, thunder and water, while their foes are the gods of darkness, winter, cold, storms, mountains and caves.

When Christianity came to the Slavs (the western Slavs – Poles, Czechs and Slovaks – took religion from Catholic Rome; the eastern and southern Slavs from Orthodox Greek Byzantium) in the tenth century, it outlawed the pagan gods, although some of their features appeared in the legendary feats of the saints. But the old cults continued: either they were adopted by the Church as its own rites, or they became magic. Thus, Perun (god of thunder and lightning) became Ilya the Prophet; Volos (guardian of herds and flocks) became St Vlasia; Kupalnitsa (goddess of rivers and lakes) became St Agrippina.

The spring rites now coincided with Easter (the main celebration of the Orthodox Church), the winter Calendae was replaced by Christmas, and the festival of Yarilo (god of the sun and all earthly life) became St John's Day. Like religion elsewhere, the Orthodox and Catholic churches did all they could to stamp out primitive belief, preventing the literate from reading 'human fables' and cutting out the tongues of the wandering storytellers.

▲ *The spectacular St Andrews Church in Kiev.*

THE OTHERWORLD

THE 'OTHERWORLD' is sometimes portrayed as an island, Booyán, far out to sea (where the sun goes down and rises), a place of eternal sunshine and happiness. This is where the souls of the dead and those not yet born dwell – as well as the seeds, plants and birds that appear in springtime. To reach this mystic isle, the hero has to travel beyond the realm of three times ten, often on foot, wearing out three pairs of iron shoes and three stone staffs, eating through three stone loaves and climbing a mountain of iron or glass.

Myths Retold

SADKO THE MINSTREL

SADKO LIVES IN Novgorod and plays his Maplewood lute at banquets for rich merchants. But times grow hard and no one wants to pay for his music. One day, as he is playing his lute by the river, the waters begin to foam and the mighty head of the sea god rises from the waters.

'Sadko,' he says, 'I want you to play for me in my palace. I'll reward you well.'

No sooner has Sadko agreed than he finds himself upon the ocean bed in a palace of white stone; there is the sea god in a great hall sitting on a coral throne. As soon as Sadko strikes up a tune, the sea god begins to dance. Overhead the waters froth and foam, and waves as big as hills roll across the swell, dragging ships down to the depths.

After a while, Sadko grows so tired he can barely play another note. All at once, he feels a hand upon his shoulder and, glancing round, he sees a white-bearded man.

'You are weary, Sadko,' the man says. 'Snap your strings to stop the dance. The sea god will then offer you a bride. But don't be hasty in your choice. Let the first three hundred girls pass by, choose the last and marry her. But heed my warning: don't touch her or you will stay forever beneath the sea.'

So Sadko chooses the last maiden, Chernava, the fairest of them all. He marries her and that night he lies down without touching his new bride. In the middle of the night, however, he turns over and touches her with his foot. So cold is she that he wakes up with a start.

▲ *Water, its gods and mythical inhabitants form the basis of many Central and Eastern European myths.*

Imagine his surprise to find himself lying on the steep bank of the Chernava River that runs past Novgorod, his left foot dangling in the icy waters. For the rest of his life he is lame in that foot. And there are those who say that when a storm rages upon the sea or lake, it is really Sadko the minstrel playing his lute and the sea god dancing a jig upon the ocean bed.

GODS AND BELIEFS

IN THE ABSENCE of written myths, stories such as that of Márya Morévna gives us clues to the Slav gods and beliefs. In this tale Ivan's three bird brothers-in-law are really the Rain, Wind and Thunder. The three princesses they wed are the Sky, Moon and Stars. Márya Morévna (meaning 'Daughter of the Sea') is the Sun which at dawn and dusk 'bathes' in the sea. Old Bones is the storm cloud chained by winter frosts. He gains strength when he drinks his fill of melting spring waters, tears himself free and carries off Márya Morévna, so clouding over the Sun. Winds bring rain clouds that pour the water of life upon the earth. Prince Ivan is Perun, the pagan god of thunder, who smashes the storm cloud and saves the Sun, leading her out of darkness.

Bába Yága is the best-known figure of Slav myth. She commands Night and Day, and appears as the guardian of the 'Other World'. In some tales, she is helpful to the hero/heroine, suggesting that her origins go back to the once-powerful goddess of life, death and rebirth, and sentry of the Other World.

SPIRITS OF THE HOME

EVERYWHERE THE ANCIENT Slavs turned, they found spirits, good and bad. Each had to be treated with care. At home the domovoi was the spirit of the dead ancestor who watched over the house. He had to have his favourite food left out for him at night. When angered, he would smash the crockery and make the animals sick. If ever the family moved house, they had to coax the domovoi along with them, usually in a bast sandal or in the ashes of the hearth fire.

 **Myths Retold**

MÁRYA MORÉVNA

WHILE OUT RIDING one day, Prince Ivan comes upon the slain army of Old Bones the Immortal; it has been defeated by the warrior queen, Márya Morévna. Ivan finds the lovely queen, falls in love with her and they marry, before she goes off to war again, warning him not to enter a certain room in her palace.

As soon as she is gone, however, he opens the forbidden chamber and finds an old man chained inside an iron pot over a blazing fire. Taking pity on him, Prince Ivan gives him a drink of water. At once Old Bones's strength returns, he bursts his bonds and carries off Ivan to his own realm.

When Márya Morévna finds out, she rides off to rescue her husband, but is caught and cut to pieces. At this point, Ivan's brothers-in-law – a falcon, raven and eagle – come to the rescue and sprinkle the water of life over the pieces of the corpse. The body grows whole and she comes back to life.

This time, to rescue Ivan, Márya Morévna sets off to obtain the only horse that can outpace Old Bones's steed. It belongs to Bába Yága who lives in a

revolving hut on hen's legs, surrounded by a fence of human skulls. The witch lives at the ends of the earth, and to get there Márya has to cross a burning river.

Eventually, she wins the steed from Bába Yága who flies after her. But Márya escapes over a magic bridge across the burning river and rescues Prince Ivan. Then she strikes Old Bones dead and scatters his ashes to the winds.

◀ *Illustration of Bilibine's tale showing Prince Ivan fleeing with his beautiful wife, Queen Márya Morévna.*

CHAPTER 6

Northern Europe

Northern Europe

NORTHERN MYTHS TELL OF conflict between gods and giants, between chaos and order. The evidence for the myths is fragmentary, but this mythology's influence on the English-speaking world is far-reaching, and its position as an important heritage of the English-speaking people undeniable. Indeed, in English the days of the week are still named after Northern Gods: Tuesday – Tyr's day; Wednesday – Woden/Odin's day; Thursday – Thor's day; Friday – Frigg's day.

WHEN THE ROMAN Empire declined, Germanic tribes pushed forward from east of the Rhine over lands formerly defended by the Romans. The Germanic peoples were those who spoke Germanic languages, as opposed to Celtic, Slav or Latin-based tongues. From the fourth to the sixth century CE Europe was the scene of continual movement. Some Germanic dialects disappeared and the rest developed eventually into what are now German, Dutch, Flemish, English, Danish, Swedish, Norwegian and Icelandic. To these regions the Germanic people brought not only their language, but also their myths,

▲ *Church carvings such as this were a means of ensuring that tales stayed part of a culture's heritage through time.*

religion and beliefs. In mainland Europe and England, relatively early conversion to Christianity means that little evidence for these beliefs remains, so we have to turn to Sweden, Denmark, Norway and particularly Iceland, where Christianity was embraced much later (only finally taking over in the eleventh century) to construct a picture of Germanic myth.

The only contemporary written evidence we have is from outside observers such as the Roman historian, Tacitus, as the Germanic people did not write. Their runic alphabet, which had mystical significance, was designed for carving inscriptions on wood or stone – not for lengthy treatises. The most important written sources for the mythology date from around the thirteenth century, when the authors were already Christian, and come from Iceland, where

▲ *The illustrations and texts of ancient manuscripts record myths and legends for prosperity.*

interest in the old gods lasted the longest. In around 1220, Snorri Sturluson, a brilliant Icelandic scholar who was also a major landowner, an important political figure and a Christian, wrote a book about the heathen gods and myths so that they would not be lost forever to poets of the future. It is from Snorri's book, the *Edda*, that we have our fullest picture of Northern mythology. Also written down in thirteenth-century Iceland, though presumably dating from earlier, was another major source: a collection of mythological poems known as the *Poetic Edda*. Additionally, we have fragmentary evidence from Icelandic sagas, and evidence from archaeology, such as the finds from the magnificent ship burials excavated at Oseberg in Norway and Sutton Hoo in eastern England.

CREATION

IN THE BEGINNING there was Ginnungagap – a gaping void. Fiery Muspell lay to the south of this and freezing Niflheim to the north. Eleven rivers flowed from the heart of Niflheim, whose poisonous flow hardened into ice. Vapour rising from the poison froze into rime, and layer upon layer the rime increased until it spread right across Ginnungagap.

▲ *Odin, skilled magician and god of war.*

The part of Ginnungagap facing Niflheim was filled with ice and rime, but the southern part was warmed by hot wind coming from Muspell. When the ice met the heat this fusion brought about the first signs of life.

The melting drops of ice formed into a huge giant, Ymir. Three gods: Odin, Vili and Ve, killed Ymir and created the world from his body. They carried him into the middle of Ginnungagap and formed the earth from his flesh and rocks from his bones. His blood they made into lakes and the sea. They formed the sky from Ymir's skull and set it up over the earth, placing one of four dwarves: Nordri, Sudri, Austri and Vestri, at each corner. Ymir's hair the gods used to create plants and trees, and they scattered his brains into the sky to form clouds

COSMOLOGY

THE WORLD WAS thought to consist of three levels, one above the other like a series of plates. The gods lived in Asgard, on the top level. Also on this level was Vanaheim, dwelling place of the Vanir (another group of gods), and Alfheim, domain of the elves. On the level below was Midgard, where men lived; Jotunheim, land of the giants; Svartalfheim, the abode of the black elves and Nidavellir, home of the dwarves. Asgard and Midgard were connected by a flaming bridge called Bifrost, otherwise known as the rainbow. On the level below was cold Niflheim.

The central column of the World Tree, the great ash Yggdrasill, passed through each level. Yggdrasill's branches extended over the whole earth and its three roots burrowed into the three levels of the universe. The well of Urd (fate), where the gods held council each day, lay under the root that reached into Asgard. Beneath the second root, which delved into Jotunheim, was the well of Mimir, where Odin pledged one of his eyes in return for a wisdom-giving drink. Under the root which extended into Niflheim was the spring of Hvergelmir, the source of the eleven rivers of the creation process.

THOR

ARMED WITH HIS HAMMER, Thor, god of thunder, protected the world. His most famous attribute was his mighty strength, excelling that of all others. He was enormous, with red hair, a red beard, red eyebrows and fierce red flashing eyes. Thor's main occupation was destroying the giants who constantly threatened the worlds of the gods and men. Thor actively sought these beings out, with the express intention of their annihilation, and seldom hesitated to raise his hammer aloft when he encountered one. Should any of the other gods be threatened he could also be called upon, and would instantly appear.

▶ *Tapestry detail showing one-eyed Odin carrying an axe, Thor carrying his symbolic hammer and the fertility god, Frey.*

THE AESIR

CHIEF OF THE GROUP of gods known as the Aesir was Odin, a skilled magician and god of war, death, kings, poetry and magic. Odin was a frightening character, not always to be trusted, who was more concerned with magical power than with his subjects. His queen was the beautiful and gracious Frigg, who shared with him the ability to foresee the future.

Thor, protector of Asgard, was Odin's son and god of thunder. He was always called upon if the gods were in trouble with giants, and would instantly appear, wielding his invincible hammer, to save the day. This role as protector also extended to men: Thor could be relied upon and the population put their trust in him.

Balder, another son of Odin, is the most well known of the other Aesir, mainly on account of the myth of his death. Balder was the wisest, kindest, most beautiful and most beloved amongst the gods – but was killed through the treachery of Loki, the trickster. Tyr, also a god of war, was the bravest of the gods. Bragi, a god of poetry, and Ull, god of archery and hunting, were also of the Aesir.

▶ *Tyr, god of the sky, with a chained animal, probably Fenrir, whom Tyr fettered at the cost of his hand.*

 **Myths Retold**

THOR FISHES FOR THE WORLD SERPENT

THOR'S PARTICULAR adversary was
the monstrous Jormangand, the World
serpent, who lay coiled around the world
at the bottom of the sea. On one occasion,
Thor assumed the appearance of a young
boy and lodged for a night with a giant
called Hymir. When Hymir prepared to go
fishing the next day, Thor asked to
accompany him. Hymir sneered that he
would be useless as he was so young and
small. Infuriated, Thor retorted that he was
not sure who would be the first to beg to
row back, and was just about to crash his
hammer down on Hymir's head, when he
remembered his secret plan to test his
strength elsewhere. Instead he asked Hymir
what they would use for bait. 'Get your
own bait,' said Hymir. Thor tore the head
off the biggest ox in Hymir's herd.

▲ *Thor with his symbolic hammer,
catches Jormangand, the World Serpent.*

Thor took the oars first, and it struck
Hymir that Thor rowed particularly hard. When they reached the usual
fishing ground, Thor said he wanted to row further out. A little later, Hymir
warned they were now so far out it would be dangerous to proceed on
account of the World Serpent. Thor said he would row on, and did so, which
made Hymir very anxious.

When Thor finally laid down the oars he fastened the ox head onto the
end of a line and threw it overboard. Deep under the sea the serpent closed its

mouth around the bait. Inside was a huge hook which stuck into the roof of its mouth, and the serpent jerked violently. Holding the other end of the line, Thor summoned all his strength against the serpent. He pushed down so hard that both his feet went through the bottom of the boat, bracing him against the sea-bed. He pulled up the serpent, but Hymir panicked and went very pale, and just at the moment that Thor lifted his hammer to strike the serpent its deathblow Hymir cut Thor's line. The serpent sank back into the sea and Thor threw his hammer after it. Thor was furious at Hymir's ruining of his plan, and punched him so hard that he fell overboard. That was the end of Hymir, and Thor waded ashore.

▲ *A Rune stone, believed to have held magical or protective power.*

RUNES

THE EARLY NORTHERN European runic alphabet was designed for cutting on to wood, stone or metal and consisted of straight lines, easier to carve than curves. Runes were not used for long documents. They have been found extensively on memorial stones, on wooden tallies used in trade and on weapons. Runes were also thought to have magical significance, and spells could be cast by carving them or protection afforded by wearing them. Odin, powerful god of magic, was thought to have introduced the Runes to the world by performing an excruciating self-sacrifice by hanging for nine nights on the World Tree.

THE VANIR

FERTILITY DEITIES known as the Vanir lived alongside the Aesir. Njord, god of the sea and its bounty, was invoked for riches, success in fishing and sea travel. He lived at Noatun (ship enclosure/harbour) and was the father of the twins Freyr and Freyja.

The principal fertility god, Freyr, was a radiant and bountiful god of sunshine and increase. He ruled harvests by controlling the sun and the rain. Marriages were also occasions to invoke Freyr, as he was responsible for human increase too. Freyr was called upon for prosperity and thought to be a bringer of peace. Weapons were banned in his temples and the shedding of blood in his sacred places was taboo.

Freyja, principal goddess of the Vanir was more than just a fertility goddess: she was also goddess of love, an expert in magic and a receiver of the slain.

THOR'S HAMMER AS PROTECTOR

Amulets in the shape of Thor's hammers, made of silver or other metals, have been found in Scandinavian graves, demonstrating the faith placed in Thor's protection. Most date mainly from the later tenth century and were found in Denmark, southern Norway and south-eastern Sweden. Some are very tiny, perhaps 2 cm (1 in) long, and many have loops attached, showing they could be worn. As a protective symbol, they were perhaps the pagan version of the miniature cross worn by Christians – moulds have been found in which hammers and crosses could be manufactured side by side to suit the requirements of customers.

◀ *Thor's hammer, used to protect the gods from their foes.*

LOKI – FRIEND AND FOE OF THE GODS

ONE OF THE MOST extraordinary characters in Northern mythology is Loki. Not strictly a god (he was descended from giants), he lived among the Aesir: joining their escapades and often helping them out. However, while he was the gods' friend and companion, and blood brother of Odin, Loki was also their adversary and at Ragnarok – the end of the world – Loki would fight against the gods on the side of the giants.

▲ *Detail of a forge stone incised with the face of Loki with his lips sewn together.*

Loki was handsome and witty, but malicious and sly. He was also extremely cunning, and always full of tricks and schemes. A shape-shifter, he was able to take on the shapes of animals or birds when wreaking his mischief. Snorri Sturluson refers to Loki as the slanderer of the gods and the origin of all lies and falsehood.

There is no evidence that Loki was worshipped, but he was integral to the mythological canon. His presence causes many of the events in the mythology. Loki's mysterious nature is revealed by the fact that although he constantly caused trouble for the gods, it was often his quick thinking and cunning that got them out of trouble again, and his influence could be beneficial to them as well as malign.

LOKI AND IDUNN

THE GODDESS IDUNN guarded the golden apples of eternal youth which the gods had to eat to keep from growing old. Mischievous Loki caused both Idunn and her apples to be stolen away by a giant, yet it was also Loki's cunning that reversed this calamity and brought Idunn back again.

Loki was captured by a giant called Thjazi, who refused to free him unless he promised to bring Idunn out of Asgard with her apples. Loki at once vowed to do this and the giant let him go. Loki went to Idunn and told her he had seen some apples in the forest that she might think were very precious. He suggested that she come to see and bring her apples with her to compare. As soon as the two were outside the walls of Asgard, Thjazi arrived in the shape of an eagle and snatched up Idunn with the apples, taking her back to his home.

▲ *Both Loki and Thjazi transform themselves into birds in this myth in order to overcome their adversary.*

The disappearance of Idunn and the apples affected the gods greatly and they began to grow old and grey. They met together to discuss the last sighting of Idunn, and realised the last time she had been seen she was going out of Asgard with Loki. Loki was seized and threatened with torture and death. Terrified, he promised to go and look for Idunn if Freyja would lend him her falcon shape.

Transformed into a falcon, Loki flew to Giantland and came to Thjazi's castle. Thjazi was away and Loki found Idunn alone. He quickly turned Idunn into a nut and flew home to Asgard with her in his claws.

When Thjazi returned and discovered that Idunn had been taken he transformed himself once more into an eagle and gave chase. The Aesir saw the falcon flying with the nut and the eagle following and built a fire in Asgard. The falcon, Loki, flew in over the wall and dropped straight down – the eagle could not stop and flew over the fire and caught alight. So the Aesir killed Thjazi, and Loki had both caused the disappearance of Idunn and her apples and brought them back.

▲ *Thor and his hammer Mjölner, and his spear Gungner.*

LAW AND ORDER

THE THEME OF ORDER pervades Northern mythology, where the gods constantly strive to maintain or restore order in the face of dark and unpredictable forces, mainly in the shape of giants. Thor's strength and his hammer are the main weapons in this fight, and Thor's overriding concerns were justice, law and order. Therefore, among men, Thor was closely associated with the law, and the populace relied on and placed their trust in him. The annual Icelandic assembly, at which the laws were recited, disputes were settled and legal cases heard, always opened on a Thursday, the day sacred to Thor.

VALHALLA

NOBLES AND heroes who died in battle were believed to go to Odin's magnificent hall, Valhalla (hall of the slain), where they became part of the Einherjar, Odin's personal army. They dwelt there gloriously, feasting and sporting, until the end of the world, when they would be called upon to fight for Odin in the last great battle.

Valhalla was an enormous building with many doors. Its rafters were fashioned from spear shafts and its tiles from shields. Every day the Einherjar would put on war-gear and fight one another for their entertainment. At the end of the fighting all those who had fallen miraculously rose, and in the evening they all sat together again: eating, drinking and carousing.

▲ *Detail of a carved funerary stone. The soldiers in the top panel carry their swords pointing down, signifying death.*

The warriors ate the meat of a boar named Saehrimnir, which was cooked each day in the pot Eldhrimnir by the cook Andhrimnir. Saehrimnir's flesh would always be sufficient to feed the Einherjar, regardless of their number, and each morning it was whole again, ready to be cooked for the next day. The Einherjar's drink was an endless supply of mead produced by a goat named Heidrun who, each day, filled a vat big enough for all to drink their fill.

RAGNAROK

DESTINY COULD NOT be avoided. This concept culminated in Ragnarok (destiny of the gods), the inevitable destruction of the world. Ragnarok will be presaged by three years of fierce battles, followed by three years of terrible winter with no summer. Then a huge earthquake will break all bonds. The wolf Fenrir will become free, and so will Loki. Jormangand, the World Serpent, will come to shore, making the ocean surge onto the land. The ship Naglfar, made from dead men's nails, will be carried along on the flood, filled with giants, with Loki at the helm.

Fenrir will advance with mouth gaping. Beside him will be Jormangand, spitting poison. They will advance to Vigrid, the plain where the last battle will take place, as will the gods with the Einherjar, led by Odin who will make for Fenrir. Thor will vanquish the serpent, but will succumb to its poison. Fenrir will swallow Odin.

▲ *The Andreas Stone with a relief depicting Odin being eaten by the Fenrir, from the story of the Doomsday of the Gods.*

Flames, smoke and steam will shoot up to the firmament. The sky will turn black and the stars will disappear. The earth will sink into the engulfing sea.

However, Ragnarok will not be the end of everything. Eventually the world will re-emerge, green and fertile, and a new age will be ushered in. Crops will grow unsown. The children of the old gods will sit on the grass where Asgard had previously been, and discuss former times. The

▲ *Brooch in the form of the World Serpent, who will come to shore at the final destruction of the world.*

human world will be repopulated by two people, Lif and Lifthrasir, who will have hidden in the ash Yggdrasill. Thus the end will contain a new beginning, and the cycle will begin again.

ODIN

ODIN, KING OF THE GODS, was powerful and terrifying – certainly not a benevolent father figure. He was the special god of kings, nobles and poets, and a god of war, magic and wisdom. Odin's mastery of magic was legendary. He could change his shape at will, and his magical abilities made him a formidable opponent. He had only one eye, having pledged the other at the well of Mimir in return for a knowledge-giving drink. Odin was invoked for victory in battle, but the promotion of strife was in his interests, and he was often accused of awarding triumph unjustly.

 **Myths Retold**

BALDER'S DEATH

BALDER DREAMED of mortal danger to his life, which was of great concern to the Aesir. His mother Frigg hit on a plan to safeguard him. She extracted oaths from everything not to harm Balder – from fire, water, animals, birds, snakes, plants, stones, trees, earth, metals, diseases and poison.

The Aesir then found it greatly amusing for Balder to stand up and the other gods to throw things at him, for nothing would harm him. When Loki saw this, he changed himself into a woman and went to visit Frigg. He told Frigg the Aesir were all shooting at Balder, but he was not being hurt. Frigg said: 'Neither weapons nor wood will harm Balder, I have received oaths from them all.'

'Has every single thing had sworn an oath not to hurt Balder?' Loki asked. Frigg replied that one plant, mistletoe, had seemed too young to swear an oath.

Loki went away and found the mistletoe and pulled it up. He approached the blind god, Hod, who was standing alone, and asked why he was not shooting at Balder.

'Because I cannot see where he is,' replied Hod, 'and besides, I have no weapon.'

'I will help you to honour Balder,' said Loki, 'I will show you where he is and you can shoot at him with this stick.'

Hod took the mistletoe shaft and shot as Loki directed. The stick pierced Balder through and he fell down dead. When they saw Balder fall, all the Aesir were speechless with shock. All they could do was weep. Frigg eventually spoke out. She asked

▲ *Odin rides his horse, Sleip-ner, who is also used to carry dead warriors in Valhalla.*

SHIP BURIALS

THE ANGLO-SAXON EPIC poem *Beowulf*
describes a spectacular ship funeral given for
the Danish king, where the dead king was laid
in a ship with much valuable cargo and a golden
standard above him. The ship was launched and
bore him away. In Norse mythology the god
Balder is given an elaborate ship funeral, on a
ship sent blazing into the ocean. These
mythological funerals reflected real burials: a

▲ *Carved dragon-head
post from the burial ship
discovered at Oseberg.*

magnificent burial in a ship of a ninth-century woman, surrounded by
much treasure, was discovered at Oseberg in Norway, and ship burials
have been found in other parts of Northern Europe.

who amongst the gods would ride down to Hel, the Underworld, to find Balder,
and offer a ransom to Hel's guardian, also called Hel, to let Balder come back to
Asgard. Hermod, Balder's brother, volunteered. Odin's horse Sleipnir was
summoned, and Hermod galloped away.

Hermod rode until he came to the gates of Hel, where he saw Balder in the
seat of honour. Hermod begged Hel to let Balder come home to Asgard,
describing the great weeping amongst the Aesir. Hel said the strength of feeling
for Balder must be tested before she would release him. 'If all things in the world
will weep for Balder, then I will let him go, but if any object refuses to weep then
I will keep him.'

The Aesir then sent messengers all over the world to ask that Balder be wept
out of Hel. Everyone and everything did this – people and animals, the earth,
stones, trees and every metal.

On their way back, the messengers came across a giantess called Thokk. They
asked her to weep Balder out of Hel, but she refused, saying, 'Thokk will weep
dry tears for Balder. Let Hel keep what she has.' So Balder was not released. It was
widely thought that Thokk was Loki in disguise.

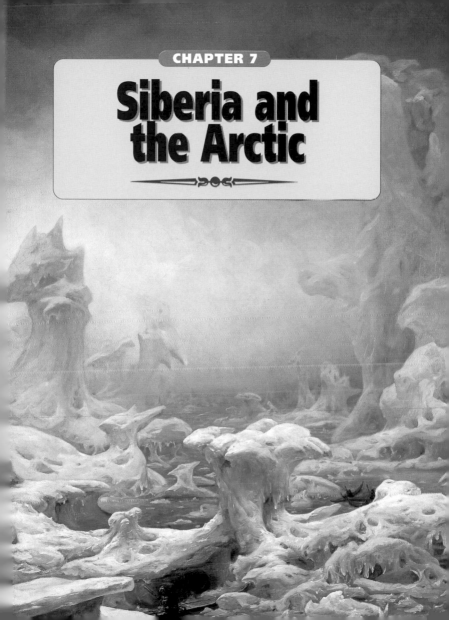

CHAPTER 7

Siberia and the Arctic

Siberia and the Arctic

THE ARCTIC REGIONS OF Siberia, Alaska, Canada, Greenland and northern Scandinavia are homelands for diverse groups of indigenous peoples. In Siberia, these peoples include the Chukchi, Even, Evenk, Nenets, Nivkhi, and Khant; in Alaska they are known as Inupiaq and Yup'ik Eskimos, Alutiiq and Athabaskans; in Canada and Greenland they are the Inuit; while in Scandinavia the indigenous population is the Saami. The Saami also inhabit the Kola Peninsula in north-west Russia, while Yup'ik Eskimos also live along the far eastern coasts of Siberia. The circumpolar peoples are hunters, fishers and reindeer herders. They have similar origins in Central Asia – the Inuit, for example, are nomadic migrants who arrived in Alaska from Siberia during the last Ice Age, and moved gradually across the vast tundra plains of northern Canada, eventually reaching the mountainous and ice-filled coasts of Greenland some 4,500 years ago.

DESPITE DIFFERENCES in lifestyle, language and social and economic organisation, the indigenous peoples of the Arctic have one thing in common – they have a unique and special relationship to the Arctic environment, which is essential for social identity and cultural survival. The peoples of the Arctic are not only sustained by the environment in an economic sense, the Arctic nourishes them spiritually and provides a fundamental basis for their distinctive cultures and ways of life.

This relationship that Arctic peoples have to the environment is reflected

▲ *Indigenous peoples have learned to survive the Arctic conditions of semi-permanent ice and darkness.*

in the richness of their mythology, and underscored by an elaborate system of beliefs and moral codes. Spiritual forces are inherent in humans, animals and all natural phenomena. Because of this, the Arctic is perceived as an environment fraught with danger and uncertainty. Part of this danger is due to the fact that hunting peoples, such as the Inuit, rely on hunting animals that have souls that must be propitiated by the hunter after being killed. Similarly, reindeer herders such as the Evenk must make sure that reindeer are slaughtered correctly and their meat, bones and hide utilised in ways that will not offend the animal's guardian spirit. Offences by an individual against animals and spirits in the natural world can cause pain to the souls of recently killed animals and entice vindictive and malevolent spirits, putting an entire community at risk. This finely tuned balance between humans and the environment can be restored through the intervention of the shaman, who visits the spirit world and acts as a curer of illness, affliction and misfortune.

RESPECT FOR THE SOULS OF ANIMALS

THE MYTHS AND ORAL histories of Arctic peoples mainly emphasise the spiritual relationship between humans and animals. Animals are the principal supply of food, and elaborate rituals are associated with the hunting of animals

and their subsequent treatment. Among the Nenets, Chukchi and Evenk of Siberia, reindeer, bears, wolves and foxes are dominant animal characters in myths and stories, whereas for the Inuit myths revolve around seals, whales, walrus and fish, such as Arctic char. Animals are spiritual beings endowed with souls. As such, they are potentially dangerous to humans if mistreated. Myths relate how the everyday and ambivalent preoccupations of Arctic hunting peoples are their hopes for good hunting and abundance of game, but also their fears of starvation and bad luck. Specific measures must be taken to ensure a successful hunt, and myths describe how the animal must be propitiated and respected in order to ward off the vengeance of its soul. A fundamental belief across the Arctic is that animals have a guardian, or master, who releases

▲ *The Arctic fox is hunted for food and for its pelt, yet they also command respect from the Arctic peoples.*

the animals in their care only if people treat them with courtesy and respect. The myth of the Sea Woman (called Sedna or Nuliayuk) reflects this belief in the unity of all life, but also symbolises the tensions between the human and animal worlds, of which Sedna is mediator.

▶ *This Polar bear, made from marine ivory, originates from the Inuit civilisation.*

Myths Retold

THE SEDNA MYTH

SEDNA WAS A GIRL who refused to get married. As punishment, her father married her to a dog and they went to live on a nearby island. Sedna was lonely in her exile and longed to be reunited with her people. One day, when her dog-husband was away from home, a stranger appeared in a boat and called to her to join him. Sedna seized upon this opportunity to leave the island and stepped into the stranger's boat.

After a long journey, they reached his village and Sedna took him as her new husband. Sedna soon discovered that her husband was not a man after all, but was a petrel who could assume the appearance of a human. Sedna was now afraid and wished she could escape from her new husband. Sedna's father in the meantime had been searching for his daughter. Eventually he succeeded in finding her, hidden behind some rocks, and waited for the petrel to go fishing. When the petrel was gone, Sedna's father took her away from her husband's village. The petrel returned in time to see the boat disappearing around a headland. Chasing after it, he caused a heavy storm, which rocked the boat. To save himself, Sedna's father had no choice but to throw her overboard into the sea.

Clinging on to the side of the boat, Sedna pleaded with her father to save her. The storm grew wilder and, one by one, Sedna's father cut off the joints of her fingers. As they hit the water, Sedna's fingers were transformed into seals, whales and narwhals. Before Sedna slipped beneath the waves, her father poked out one of her eyes. Sedna descended to the lower world at the bottom of the sea, where she became mistress and keeper of the sea mammals which had once been her fingers. Sedna's father reached his village and lay in his tent, while the tide rose and swept him away. He now lives in Sedna's house and her dog guards the entrance.

Sedna is usually generous to humans, and releases the sea mammals in her care. But there are also times when she retains the animals because hunters have caused pain to the animal's soul. When the animals are scarce, a shaman must journey to Sedna's abode and plead with her to release them. Sometimes the sea mammals are tangled in Sedna's hair, which has been made dirty by humans violating taboos. When this happens, the shaman must visit Sedna and comb her hair, and so release the animals.

MYTHS ABOUT THE SUPREME BEING

FOR THE PEOPLES of the Arctic, everything in the world, animate or inanimate, has a life force and shares the same spiritual nature. Some groups, such as the Chukchi, believe in a Supreme Being, which they call the Creator, or Life-giving Being. But the nature of the Supreme Being is uncertain and difficult to conceptualise. For the Chukchi the Supreme Being is indistinguishable from the master of the reindeer herds, and is also known as Reindeer Being. The Evenk believe the Supreme Being consists of two aspects, *Amaka*, which looks after the fortunes of people, and *Ekseri,* which rules over all animal guardians and the great Siberian forests. *Amaka* is also the Evenki word for bear, which is visualised as the form of both the Supreme Being and the master of the animals.

▲ *An Inuit woman drinks from a melt-water stream.*

The Supreme Being is the personification of the life force which flows through and animates the human and animal worlds. The Inuit call this vital principle *inua*. But they also talk of *sila*, ruler of the elements and the universe. *Sila* is all of the individual powers and forces of nature, the fundamental principle which pervades the natural world. *Sila* is also manifest in each and every individual person – the vital force which connects and integrates a person with their immediate environment.

THE MASTER OF THE ANIMALS

THE ARCTIC PEOPLES believed that a great spirit protected the animals and supervised their correct ritual treatment by humans. This master, guardian, or owner of the animals, also prevented or facilitated the hunting of animals. In Siberian reindeer-herding societies, such as the Chukchi and Nenets, the master is protector of the herds. The Naskapi of Labrador visualised the caribou guardian as a white bearded man, who could also take the form of a bear. For the Inuit, whose spiritual culture is closely linked to water, the Sea Woman is owner of the sea mammals. A widespread myth of the North Pacific coasts of Siberia and Alaska relates how the master of the water is a killer whale.

▲ *Reindeer provide transport as well as food and clothing.*

ORIGIN MYTHS

A WIDE VARIETY OF MYTHS tell of how the world came into being. A common theme is that before the beginning of time, there exists only darkness until a trickster figure creates the world. The Inupiaq Eskimos have oral histories which describe how Raven Man was first created by the figure of a primal shaman. Raven Man harpoons a whale whose body becomes land, then Raven reveals the daylight and creates the first people. Other myths describe the origin of the sun and the moon, which are related to myths about the balance between daylight and darkness, time and space and the year's hunting activities. Many origin myths serve to remind people that, in the distant past, animals and humans were not as clearly distinguished in the same way as they are today. Yup'ik and Inupiaq Eskimo myths relate how all animate beings have a dual existence, so that an animal can become a human at will, or vice versa. The myth of Raven Man tells how, set adrift on an ice floe, Raven comes across a village of people and takes a wife from among them. Raven and his wife have children who, travelling to their father's land, become ravens themselves, retaining the power to change back into human form. Eventually, their descendants forget how to change into people and remain ravens.

THE SHAMAN

THE SHAMAN IS A UNIVERSAL FIGURE across the Arctic, acting as intermediary in the transactions between humans, the souls of animals and the master of the animals. Myths relate how the shaman must first undergo a long, solitary and arduous initiation, wrestling with spirits and aquiring his powers, before returning to his home community. As the shaman goes into a trance, his soul leaves his body and journeys to the spirit-world. Once there, the shaman bargains with the master or guardian of animals for the animals to be sent to the hunter to be converted into food, and for the return of any human souls that may have been captured by malevolent spirits.

▼ *This Shaman in ritual clothing invites the spirit of the fire to give a blessing.*

Myths Retold

THE ORIGIN OF THE SUN AND THE MOON

LONG AGO, BEFORE the world had taken its present form, a man lived in a coastal village. He had no wife, but he did have a younger sister with whom he was in love. At night, when she put out the seal-oil lamp in her iglu, she found that a man would come in and make love to her. In the darkness, she could not see who the man was, but she was determined to find out. One night, before she put out the light, she dipped her fingers into the soot at the bottom of the lamp. When the man came in and made love to her that evening, she smeared his forehead with the soot.

▲ *Traditional Eskimo villages would have consisted of igloo houses created from the frozen landscape.*

The following day, she went looking for the man and found her brother sitting in the men's house with lamp soot on his forehead. The girl was both ashamed and angry. In a fit of rage she cut off one of her breasts and placed it on a dish, which she then offered to her brother, saying 'Since you desire me so much, eat it!'. Her brother refused and chased her as she ran off, still carrying the dish. As she was running, the girl picked a clump of moss and lit it. Her brother did the same. The girl ran faster and faster until she ascended skywards and became the sun. Her brother followed her but the flame on his moss went out, leaving only the burning embers, and he became the moon. To this day, the sun is chased by the moon. Occasionally they embrace, causing an eclipse. The sun loses height in the middle of winter, but gains in strength and beauty throughout the spring and summer, which only increases the moon's desire for her. The moon is without food and gradually wanes from hunger until it is lost from sight, but then the sun reaches out and feeds it from the breast which the girl had placed on the dish. Once the moon is nourished it continues to chase the sun, who allows it to starve again before allowing it to feed once more.

REINCARNATION OF THE HUMAN SOUL

MYTHS AND STORIES surrounding personal names and human reincarnation are universal themes throughout the Arctic. The person consists of three souls; the personal soul, the breath or free soul and the name soul. In Greenland, the

▲ Aurora borealis, *believed to be the souls of those awaiting rebirth.*

SIBERIAN YUP'IK CEREMONIAL MASKS

MASKS EXPRESS THE UNITY between humans and animals, and bring the mythical world of the past into the present. The Siberian Yup'ik Eskimos of the coasts of south-west Alaska, the Bering Straits and eastern Siberia carved elaborate masks from driftwood for ceremonial purposes. These masks depicted animal spirits and mythical figures. Masks were worn at community feasts, ritual trade festivals and dances to celebrate the memory of the ancestors. According to Yup'ik myth, a person can be incarnated into the animal or its spirit by using its own form. A person wearing a mask can gain influence over the animal's spirit, and shamans commonly wore masks in rituals to ensure success in hunting and fishing.

Inuit believed that after death the personal soul travelled to either the Underworld, a place with an abundance of game animals and where the souls of dead kin and friends would be reunited, or to an upper world of eternal starvation and cold. The breath or free soul can leave the body at will, often when the person is asleep. If it strays too far, it may have to be retrieved by a shaman. Throughout Siberia, Alaska, Canada and Greenland, people believe that a person's name is also a soul. At death the name soul leaves a person's body and is said to remain 'homeless' until it is recalled to reside in the body of a newborn child. While the deceased are waiting to be reborn, their souls form the *aurora borealis*, the northern lights. Myths and stories tell of the soul's wanderings after death, and relate how, through the name soul, the deceased become the guardian spirits of their descendants.

▲ *Walrus being fished by Greenlanders.*

THE SACRED LANDSCAPE

RESPECT FOR NATURE and animals is a fundamental theme in the traditional worldview of Arctic peoples, and is reflected in both mythology and practice. Many features in the landscape are sacred places, where animals reveal themselves to hunters in dreams, or where people encounter animal spirits while travelling. In Siberia, reindeer antlers are placed at sacred sites and adorned with gifts; in Greenland pieces of the veterbrae or hide of a hunted polar bear are left to flutter in the wind to ensure the release of its spirit; while in northern Scandinavia, the Saami place sacred stones (seiteh) on mountain tops and near lakes and rivers.

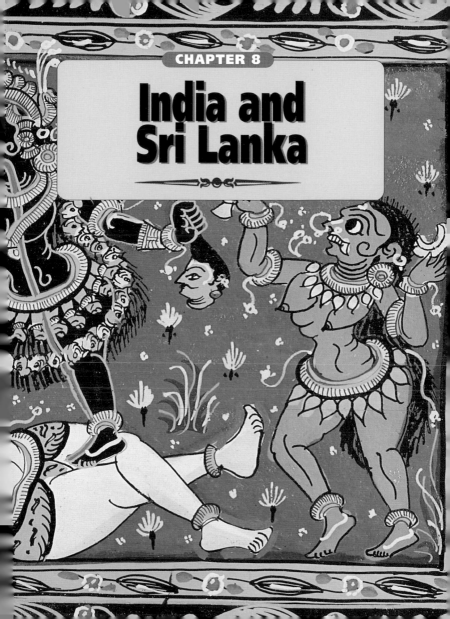

CHAPTER 8

India and Sri Lanka

India

THE WORLD OF INDIAN myth is more than a selection of stories: it provides a complete alternative reality and belief system which forms the basis of the Hindu religion and, to some extent, Buddhism.

▲ *Theatre and dance, such as this Dance of Krishna, are the media through which Indian myths and beliefs are retold.*

INDIA'S TRUE NAME is Bharat, after King Bharat whose life is a key to understanding Indian myth. In old age he retired to the forest to prepare for death. He wanted to be released from the cycle of re-birth. But he adopted an orphaned deer which he grew to love so dearly that when he died, instead of being liberated from the cycle of re-birth he entered the body of a deer to live in that same forest. He was, however, blessed with the memory of his former royal birth, and in time was re-born as a human. This time, to avoid further ties of affection, he pretended to be dumb, and shunned all human contact. Thus he gained enlightenment and at the end of that life was not re-born.

Bharat's story illustrates an underlying theme of Indian myth: the search for a higher reality, in which the soul may journey through many births to find a way out of this world. In this sense the mythology of India is not myth

◄ The Indian oral tradition was maintained by spiritual teachers, or brahmins.

but truth, a body of wisdom as relevant today as it ever was.

The oral tradition of India is called the *sruti*, meaning 'that which is heard'. It was passed down through chains of spiritual teachers, called brahmins, who were the keepers of the wisdom. We are told that 5,000 years ago, at the dawn of the present age of Kali Yuga, the wisdom was recorded in Sanskrit to preserve it for future generations. In the process it was expanded into a vast corpus of spiritual learning, collectively called the Vedic literature.

EARLY BEGINNINGS: THE *RIG VEDA*

THE EARLIEST MYTHS were gathered in the *Rig Veda*, believed to be the world's oldest surviving text, written at least 3,000 years ago. It is a collection of hymns to accompany the rituals offered to the cosmic deities. Among its stories we find the cosmic initiation ritual which took place at the beginning of this universe, when the primeval male was sacrificed by the deities of space and time. This event symbolised the union of gods and men in acting out the play of life, in which all sacrifice their time and energies in service to the Supreme Being. The Supreme Being is himself the substance of the universe, offered in sacrifice to himself. This theme of self-sacrifice recurs throughout Indian mythology as duty and honour. The Sanskrit word approximating 'duty' is *dharma*. Roughly translated, it means 'the essential purpose of life'. It gave rise to a set of principles governing behaviour, such as obedience to one's father. These principles at their best embodied a spirit of service which expressed love. The spirit of love was later to flower in the bhakti, or spiritual devotion, of the *Bhagavad Gita*.

THE PANTHEON OF GODS

THE UNIVERSE is pervaded by the great spirits called in Sanskrit, *devas*. They each have responsibility for an aspect of nature, which in their personal form they embody, such as Agni, the god of fire. Another example is the goddess Ganga, spirit of the River Ganges. She is daughter of the Himalayas. She was taken up to heaven as the celestial Milky Way and brought back to earth by the penances of King Bhagiratha to be caught in Shiva's hair. Her devotees believe that she washes away sins. This mystical story co-exists with the physical existence of the river in a union of myth and reality which typifies the world of Indian myth, where the line between the visionary and the material substance is subtle and shifting.

The gods have their devotees and their festivals. The high gods, such as Indra, the king of heaven, or Kartikeya, the god of war, are celebrated throughout India. At the local level village gods are worshipped, such as Sitala, the goddess of smallpox, who gives protection from the disease. All the gods and goddesses, however, are intermediaries of the three great deities, Vishnu, Shiva and Devi, and ultimately of the one Supreme Spirit.

 **Myths Retold**

THE VEDIC CREATION STORY

LONG AGO VEDIC sages described Vishnu as the One whose existence spans the cosmos. When this universe first came into being it was but one of countless seeds springing from the body of Vishnu, seeds which floated in the Ocean of Creation like clusters of bubbles. Each seed became a golden egg into which Vishnu entered as the Purusha, the Cosmic Man. Appearing inside its dark hollow, he transformed primeval matter into earth, water, fire, air and ethereal space. As his universal body developed, corresponding elements of the physical and mental world came into being.

The Vedic hymns recount the sacrifice of Purusha, the Cosmic Man, at the dawn of the universe. The gods prepared a sacrifice in which the principal offering was the gigantic form of the Purusha himself. From the different

▼ *Vishnu rests between the destruction of the world and the creation of the new universe.*

parts of his body were produced the elements of the universe. His mouth became Speech, presided over by the fire god Agni; his nostrils became Breathing and the sense of Smell, controlled by the wind god Vayu; his eyes became the sense of Sight, controlled by the sun god Surya; Movement appeared along with his legs, rivers along with his veins and Mind along with his heart. Brahma and Shiva were his Intellect and Ego. The four

▲ *The creator god Vishnu, seen here riding on Garuda with the goddess Lakshmi.*

divisions of human society, priests, rulers, merchants and workers came from his mouth, his arms, his thighs and his feet.

Elsewhere are more specific accounts of the development of the universe undertaken by Brahma, the creator-god born from the navel of Vishnu. Brahma made the planets and stars and all the thousands of demi-gods, each of whom was given charge of a particular part of the cosmic order. Indra was given the rain, Vayu the wind, Surya the sun, Chandra the moon and Varuna the oceans and rivers. Goddess Bhumi was given the earth.

Brahma and the gods produced the myriad life-forms of the universe, among them human beings. The gods were given the power to grant great blessings to their worshippers. They are the powers behind the elements of the natural world such as wind, rain and the earth itself. The goddess of the Earth, Bhumi, is considered by Hindus as one of the seven mothers. However, powerful though the demigods are, behind them lies Vishnu, and it is really he who creates and controls all. Without him they can do nothing.

VISHNU

THE TWO GREAT deities to emerge from the early myths are Vishnu and Shiva, the gods of Maintenance and Destruction respectively. Both have their ardent devotees who honour them as the Supreme Deity, and their separate traditions of learning and worship.

Vishnu is the background to existence, who enters the universe as Narayana, the One Who Lies on the Waters of Life. He sleeps at the base of the universe, attended by the Goddess Lakshmi. Whenever there is disturbance in the balance of the universe, he enters the human world to restore the true religious teachings and protect righteousness. He is characterised as full of mercy and patience and his symbols are the lotus flower and the conchshell by which he blesses the good, and the club and discus with which he subdues the bad.

His role as keeper of the balance is well-illustrated in the story of Kurma, the tortoise incarnation, where he sets out to help both the demons and the gods, but finally takes the side of the gods. His role as teacher is exemplified by Krishna who taught the Bhagavad Gita. In the form of the fish incarnation, Matsya, he re-established the Vedic teachings, which were lost in the great flood, by instructing King Satyavrata.

▼ *Vishnu rests with his ever-present attendants, on the serpent, Ananta.*

 **Myths Retold**

MATSYA, THE FISH

ONCE A KING NAMED Satyavrata found a tiny fish in the river and took it in a bowl to his palace. Next morning the fish had grown so he transferred it into a pond, but it very quickly outgrew that too, so he put it into a lake. Soon it had grown so large that it had to be put in the ocean.

The king asked the fish asked why it had taken this form. The fish replied that he was Vishnu, come to save all the creatures of the earth from a devastating flood. The king should gather samples of all species of plants and animals to be saved.

Soon huge clouds appeared and poured water on land and sea, and the ocean overflowed onto the land. Then Satyavrata and all his companions saw a large boat floating towards them across the waves. Satyavrata led them aboard, and Matsya, by now a golden fish of inconceivable size, towed the boat with its precious cargo of all species of life across the waters of devastation. For countless years darkness covered the worlds and they travelled across the stormy wastes. During their journey Matsya instructed King Satyavrata in spiritual knowledge.

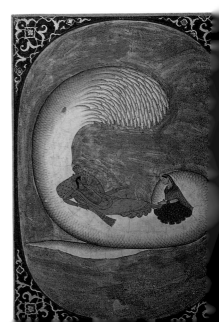

It is said that whoever hears this story is delivered from the ocean of sinful life.

▶ *Vishnu and Lakshmi repose on the Serpent of a Thousand Heads.*

THE WORLD AS SYMBOL

INDIAN MYTH HAS made every aspect of nature into a symbol of divinity, celebrated in dance, poetry, music, sculpture, painting and architecture. One of the oldest symbols is the ritual fire sacrifice, in which the fire symbolises Agni, the fire god, or Vishnu the preserver, and becomes the mouth of god to accept the offerings of grains and fruits placed in it. Another daily ritual is meditation on the sun at sunrise, noon and sunset, in which the brahmin prays: 'O Sun, who illuminates the three levels of the universe, upper middle and lower, similarly illuminate and inspire my inner consciousness.'

AVATARS OF VISHNU

THE 10 INCARNATIONS of Vishnu are called *avatar*, meaning 'one who descends'. They take progressively more developed forms, from aquatic to mammal to human. Their stories have had a profound influence on Hindu culture. They are:

1. Matsya the fish
2. Kurma
3. Varaha the boar, who rescued planet earth from the bottom of the universe
4. Narasimha the man-lion, who protected the boy Prahlad
5. Vamana the dwarf, who defeated the demon Bali
6. Parasurama the warrior, who defeated the warlike kings and established peace
7. Rama the good king
8. Krishna the cowherd and his brother Balarama
9. Buddha the teacher, who taught non-violence and compassion
10. Kalki the slayer, who will come at the end of this age riding a white horse to kill the demons and inaugurate a new cycle of the universe

Thus, from outside Vishnu reassures the good that he will always ensure that evil never triumphs. Meanwhile he is also revered as Antaryami, the One Within, the eternal friend who lives in the heart of each being and gives inner wisdom and guidance.

 **Myths Retold**

KURMA, THE TORTOISE

ONCE, THE GODS AND the demons both wanted the Nectar of Immortality. On the advice of Vishnu they made a pact to co-operate together. Vishnu told them to throw all kinds of vegetables, grass, creepers and herbs into the Ocean of Milk and churn it. To churn the ocean they would have to use the golden mountain, Mandara, as a churning rod and Vasuki, the giant serpent, as a rope. Taking the mountain and wrapping the serpent around it, the demons held his head and the gods held his tail.

They tried to churn, but the mountain sank into the ocean floor, so Vishnu appeared as a gigantic tortoise, Kurma, to support the mountain on his back. Using Kurma as the pivot, they began to churn. The first thing the churning produced was a deadly poison, which was drunk by Shiva. They continued to churn and eventually the ocean produced the Nectar of Immortality. Both groups wanted it, and a quarrel developed. Vishnu came to the aid of the gods and helped them win the nectar for themselves. The demons, seeing they had lost the nectar, attacked the gods, but after a terrible battle the demons were defeated.

SHIVA

SHIVA MANIFESTS the dark side of the divinity, the power of death and destruction. He is easily moved to anger, and can be a frightening figure surrounded by ghostto the wayward elements in the universe, called the *asuras* (the 'ungodly'), and those who are at odds

◀ *Stones such as this are believed to have been phallic symbols representing the mighty Shiva.*

with the world. He carries a small drum to accompany his dance of destruction, and his carrier is the bull Nandi. On his head is a crescent moon and a symbol of the descending waters of the Ganges, which he caught in his hair to save the mountains from being crushed by her weight. His mountain home is Mount Kailash, and his followers are numerous in the Himalayas, but he is also found in cremation-grounds where he smears his body with ashes and sits in trance

▲ *Bronze statue of the volatile deity, Shiva.*

CYCLE OF LIFE

PERHAPS THE GREATEST theme which underlies all Indian myth is the everlasting play between the world of illusion and the world of reality: on the one hand the perpetual cycle of birth and death, of creation and destruction, of the duality of good and bad, set against on the other hand the divine existence of the immortal soul and the Supreme Deity. This tension is replayed in the drama of re-incarnation, and the periodic descent of the avatars ('incarnations') of Vishnu from the eternal to the temporary worlds, and the tireless search of the ascetics and devotees for mukti ('liberation') from the world of birth and death.

of meditation. Among his followers are the ascetics who wander India smeared in ashes, semi-naked, smoking *ganja*.

Shiva's and Vishnu's followers, the Shaivites and the Vaishnavas, are often at odds with each other, and the myth of Daksha's sacrifice, told here, accounts for the origins of this enmity. But they each acknowledge Vishnu and Shiva to be aspects of the same Supreme Divinity.

▲ *Traditional art depicting the followers of Krishna.*

KRISHNA, THE COWHERD

INDIANS HAVE PERSONIFIED all aspects of nature and spirituality in the form of their numerous deities. For some these deities are symbolic only, whereas for others they have a life and reality beyond the temporary world. The best-loved deity is Krishna the cowherd, eighth incarnation of Vishnu. He lives as a child in the forest surrounded by his childhood friends, and by the cows and peacocks. There he dances with his young lover, the divine Radha, rejoicing in the bounty and simplicity of rural life. Together they share perfect spiritual love. Followers of Krishna offer him their unconditional devotion as the one Supreme God.

▲ *Krishna dances to the music of the young women to call the rain.*

 **Myths Retold**

SHIVA'S ANGER AT DAKSHA

THE GODS ONCE ASSEMBLED for a thousand-year sacrifice. When Daksha, leader of the brahmins, arrived everyone stood to receive him except Shiva, who was deep in meditation. Although Shiva was married to his daughter, Daksha was offended.

'Shiva is not worthy to be part of this sacrifice,' he cursed. Then he stormed out of the arena.

This led to a confrontation between the followers of Shiva and the followers of Daksha, from which originated the age-old antagonism between the worshippers of Vishnu and the worshippers of Shiva.

Daksha organised another sacrifice and Shiva was not invited. But Shiva's wife, the goddess Sati, went to the ceremony. She found that no oblation had been offered to Shiva, and she was insulted by Daksha, her father, who refused to acknowledge her presence. It was as if she and her husband did not exist.

▲ *Shiva and the female aspect of this deity, Parvati.*

'Daksha is envious of Shiva,' she declared. 'I no longer want to be his daughter, or to keep this body which was born of him.'

So saying, she sat on the ground and focused her fiery anger between her eyes. Flames burst forth and consumed her body. A great cry went up from the followers of Shiva. When Shiva heard of this terrible event he laughed in demented rage and began his dance of cosmic destruction. Plucking a hair from his head he dashed it to the ground. From it a great demon sprang up, high as the sky and bright as three suns.

'What would you have me do, O master?' the demon cried.

'Kill Daksha,' shrieked Shiva.

Darkness fell over the arena of sacrifice as the great demon appeared. He caught Daksha and in a moment cut off his head, throwing it onto the sacrificial fire. The brahmins fled for protection to Brahma, the father of all beings, but he told them they must beg forgiveness from Shiva himself.

Mount Kailash is the heavenly home of Shiva, surrounded by forests of flowering trees, filled with the cries of peacocks and the sound of waterfalls. In its midst, beneath a huge banyan tree where the air is cool and silent, sat Shiva, grave and peaceful in the company of sages. The brahmins fell before him in contrition. Shiva gladly forgave them and agreed to bring Daksha back to life. Since Daksha's head had been burnt to ashes he gave him a goat's head instead.

This story illustrates how Shiva is easily angered and easily satisfied. It is said that one who hears it with faith is released from sin.

COSMIC DESTRUCTION

WHILST BRAHMA is the creator and Vishnu the preserver, Shiva's anger is the destructive force which annihilates the cosmos. Death is the inevitable consequence of life, and holds no fear in Indian myth, for in this world of duality neither life nor death have meaning without each other. Death is the precursor of life, which all must come to terms with, as described in the Bhagavad Gita:

'One who is born must die, and one who dies must be reborn. Do not mourn the inevitable.'

At the end of the universe the sun and moon shine no more and all becomes dark. Shiva begins his *pralaya*, dance of destruction, accompanied by

his drum called *damaru*, to draw the curtain on the universal act. With his hair scattered he subdues the lords of all planets with his trident. He generates the fire of eternal time, which blazes throughout the universe. This fire blazes for a hundred celestial years, destroying all creatures. From Shiva's scattered hair torrential rains fall for a further hundred celestial years, inundating all directions. The universe fills with water and is swept by howling winds. Then follows the long silent night which precedes the next cycle of creation.

▲ *A young woman gives offerings in worship of Shiva.*

THE INTERPLAY OF MALE AND FEMALE

THE BALANCE OF MALE and female is at the heart of Indian myths. All deities have their female aspects, such as Vishnu and Lakshmi, Krishna and Radha, Rama and Sita and Shiva and Parvati. The female aspect of the deity embodies mercy and the spirit of devotion to that deity, while the male aspect represents the outward flow of power and protection. The union of male and female as the creative source of the energy of life is symbolised in the image of the Shiva surrounded by the Yoni of the mortals, yet who have direct access to the eternal realm, beyond this temporary world, inhabited by the Supreme Being, in his forms as Vishnu or Shiva.

▲ *Bronze statue of Shiva and Parvati.*

◄ *The decoration on this jewel casket depicts Rama and Sita.*

Sri Lanka

SRI LANKA IS A small island located just north of the equator, off the southernmost tip of India. Its location – on the sea-routes between Europe, Africa and Asia – has ensured contact with many great civilisations and it had a highly developed culture as early as the fifth century BCE.

T HE EARLIEST INHABITANTS were probably related to the Dravidian hill tribes of southern India. The first Sinhalese speakers arrived in around the fifth century BCE. Tamils, probably immigrants from Dravididan India, arrived on the island between the early centuries CE and *c.* CE 1200. There are also Moors of Arab origin and Burghers, descendants of Portuguese or Dutch settlers.

Buddhism was established between 270 and 232 BCE. Monks from Buddhist monasteries in northern India travelled and taught along the eastern coast of India before crossing to establish monastic communities on the island. Buddhism quickly became the dominant religion, and remains so today.

▲ *The teachings of Buddha had a strong influence on Sri Lankan mythology.*

Foreign contact with Africa and the Middle East was common in coastal areas. The Portuguese, Dutch and British were involved in trade on the island from the sixteenth century. In the nineteenth century the British, who had annexed the island in 1815, introduced Tamil workers from southern India to work the plantations, further emphasising the division of the population into the majority Buddhist Sinhalese and the smaller Hindu Tamil community.

Types of Sri Lankan Myth

SRI LANKA POSSESSES a rich store of myths which fall into various categories: myths concerning spirits, origin myths, Hindu myths concerning the gods and heroes, and Buddhist myths, including the Jataka stories.

There is evidence that even before the arrival of the Aryan peoples there had been a preoccupation with nature spirits, fertility deities and the solar bodies. The gods of the sun, moon and stars were known and worshipped. Gods such as Sumana, prince of *devas*, may have originated as solar deities. There were both local and national deities who acted in a protective capacity, and there were *devata* who were similar to the Southeast Asian nature spirits. Fertility spirits such as the goddess Pattini were also popular.

▲ *The detail on this casket depicts two spirits in a ritual dance.*

Hindu myths are well known. Vishnu, Shiva, Brahma and the other major gods and goddesses all feature in innumerable tales, and stories explaining the status of the various castes are also told. The great epics the *Ramayana* and the *Mahabharatha* are popular and are frequently enacted in dance and drama.

Buddhist myths, especially the life of the Buddha are extremely popular. The *taka* stories, which relate the previous lives of the Buddha, provide Buddhists with moral guidance.

 **Myths Retold**

THE VIJAYA LINE

THE BUDDHIST CHRONICLE the *Mahavamsa* records the arrival of the first Sinhalese colonists. In the fifth century BCE. Prince Vijaya and seven hundred followers landed on the island and defeated a band of demons, or *yaksas*, whom they chased into the interior. Vijaya, descended from a lion (*inha*), later married a *yaksa* princess who bore him two children which he sent away. He then sent to India for another princess, and wives for all his

SRI LANKAN GODS

ANCIENT GODS SUCH AS PATTINI, goddess of fertility, and Sumana, once a solar deity, still hold a place in Sri Lankan mythology everywhere. Nature spirits and household spirits are still widely respected. Vishnu, Shiva, Brahma, Ganesha and the goddess are all worshipped by the Tamil community, whereas the Buddha is revered by the Sinhalese. In addition Sri Lankan mythology is full of creatures which populate Indian and Southeast Asian mythology: demons or *yaksas*, *nagas* or serpent deities, *garudas* or part bird-part human beings, *devas* or angels, and *brahmas* or lesser gods.

◀ *Shiva is brought to the floor and attacked by the she-ogre, Kali.*

followers. His nephew continued the Vijaya line. This probably reflects actual events when the early Dravidian inhabitants were pushed further inland by the Indo-Aryan settlers.

Ravana, the villain of the Ramayana, is referred to as lord of the demons, or *ksas*, and rides in a sky chariot. In the ancient past he was probably associated with the sun. According to one account the Buddha is believed to have preached to Ravana at the summit of Sumanakutu, the sacred mountain, suggesting the ascendance of Buddhism over the earlier sky deities. The sun god Sumana, mentioned in the *Mahavamsa* may have been a later Buddhist substitute for Ravana.

IMAGES OF THE BUDDHA

HINDU AND BUDDHIST myths are depicted in painting, sculpture and architecture. It is believed that the Buddha stepped across the sea to visit Sri Lanka, and carvings of his footprint are sacred. They are marked with the 107 symbols of the universe to symbolise the Buddha's ascendence over all phenomena. The Buddha image is popular, usually seated in the gesture of 'Calling the Earth to Witness' or protected by the *naga* (see Southeast Asia), and Jataka stories are often depicted in mural painting and silver work. The most sacred Buddhist *stupas* are believed to contain relics of the Buddha's body, brought to Sri Lanka after his death.

▶ *The lotus position and the position of Buddha's hands indicate that he is teaching.*

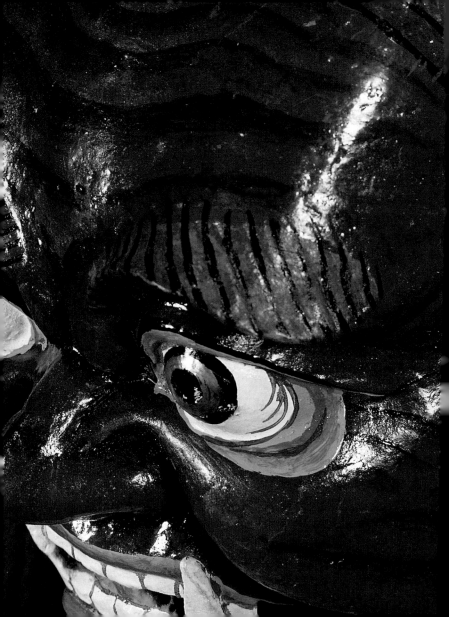

CHAPTER 9

Tibet and
Mongolia

Tibet and Mongolia

AT A CROSSROADS between India and China, the original religion of Tibet is typically animistic and based on dualism. The religious aspiration of its inhabitants is to live in harmony with the unseen forces operating all around them: benevolent spirits are to be thanked for their kindness with regular offerings, and caution must be exercised at all times so as not to offend the malevolent.

BEFORE THE DAWN of history, Tibet is said to have been held together by a succession of non-human rulers. Eventually the first human ruler of Tibet 'descended from the sky' onto a mountain in Kong-po and was proclaimed king by a grateful people. At the end of his reign he ascended

THE FIVE AGGREGATES

THE INNUMERABLE transcendent gods of tantric Buddhism imported from their homeland in India, cluster around the five families of buddhas headed by Vairocana, Akshobhya, Ratnasambhava, Amitabha and Amoghasiddhi. Typically arranged in the circular formation of a *mandala*, with one in the centre.and the others surrounding him in the four cardinal directions of the compass, each buddha has his own distinctive colour, posture and attribute. Evoked during the

once more to the heavens from whence he had come by means of a *dmu* cord, leaving no earthly remains. When the seventh of his royal line finally cut the magical cord connecting his family to the sky, he was buried in the Yar-lung valley and thus began the cult of the royal tombs.

THE FIRST HUMAN RULER

AFTER 27 GENERATIONS of kings from the time of Tibet's first human ruler, Lha-tho tho-ri came to the throne and, in the water-bird year of 433, at the age of 60 years, he became the first king to learn of Buddhism. Legend has it that the sky one day filled with rainbows, and onto the roof of his palace fell Buddhist texts and images. Unable to comprehend even a single syllable of the sacred writings, it was predicted to the king that their meaning would be

course of profound meditation, these five buddhas are thought to arise naturally from the basic constituents of the human personality, known as the five aggregates, and they sit in union with their female consorts who embody the five elements of earth, water, fire, air and space.

◀ *A Tibetan wooden plaque decorated with a figure of Vairocana.*

▲ *Traditional Tibetan art depicts ancient rulers and divinities.*

revealed to his family after five generations. Worshipping the miraculous objects as sacred, Lha-tho tho-ri lived to the age of 120 although his body appeared no older than 16.

In fulfilment of the prophecy, after five generations, King Srong-btsan sgam-po (CE *c.* 617–650) commissioned the production of an alphabet for the language of Tibet, thus introducing the art of writing. Among his five wives, also, were counted two Buddhist princesses from the neighbouring countries of China and Nepal. It is said that these two queens, as part of their dowries, brought with them precious statues of the Buddha and Buddhist saints. At their insistence, Srong-btsan sgam-po began to tame the wild terrain of Tibet which was thought to be in the form of a malignant ogress, and prepare the country for the advent of their foreign religion.

 **Myths Retold**

THE BIRTH OF PADMASAMBHAVA

THE INDIAN MYSTIC Padmasambhava is popularly believed to have emanated miraculously as an eight-year old youth within the heart of a lotus blossom in the Dhanakosha lake in Oddiyana, Swat valley in modern Pakistan.

Raised by the king of Oddiyana as his own son, Padmasambhava enjoyed all the luxuries of palace life until the time came for his great renunciation. Having murdered a minister of the king, he was banished from the kingdom and condemned to live the life of a penitent ascetic in the fearful channel grounds beyond the borders of human habitation. There he is said to have conversed with supernatural beings and attained great spiritual power. He is believed to have been ordained as a Buddhist monk by Ananda, the Buddha's cousin, and to have lived for over a thousand years as a follower of the Buddhist path. Arriving in Tibet as a result of the king's invitation, Padmasambhava travelled throughout the land and subdued the hostile forces that arrayed them-

▲ *Padmasambhava sits with a vajra in his right hand, a skull and bowl in his left.*

selves against the new religion, so that he remains worshipped as the founder of Buddhism in Tibet.

DURING THE SECOND half of the eighth century, King Khri Srong-lde'u-btsan, full of admiration for the sophisticated cultures of his Buddhist neighbours, sent messengers to India in search of the most learned men of his day whom, he hoped, would found a new temple and teach his people the ways of righteousness. In particular, the king was advised to invite the tantrika (practitioner of occult religion, thus *tantra* means 'occult religion', i.e. esoteric Buddhism) known as Padmasambhava, 'the Lotus-born Guru', and thus a new wave of mythology inherited from the Buddhist magicians of India swept the land.

THE CREATION

THE EARLIEST MYTHS of the shamanic culture that was once prevalent over the whole of Central Asia and the north of the continent concern the origins of the world and all that it contains. According to these tales, the world is created and sustained by an enormous number of gods and demons that reside unseen in countless locations of power. Their assistance is called upon before the commencement of any undertaking and they are to be controlled and exorcised by the shaman priest whenever they cause trouble, stagnation or sickness. While the allotted realm of

◀ *Shamanic mask representing the queen of the demons.*

man covers the face of the earth, the gods and demons dwell in the heavens above and in the subterranean labyrinths beneath the surface.

Only a shaman in trance has the power to travel the three realms and understand the intricate workings of the universe. Only he may divine the causes of illness and misfortune, or retrieve lost souls abducted by spirits. It is he who recommends the performance of a particular sacrifice, typically the weaving of a 'thread cross' (*mdos*) and the presentation of a ransom to the offended or malicious spirit. It is he who points out the sacred features of the landscape and keeps the myths alive.

STATUES OF THE BUDDHA

DEMONSTRATING HER skill in the ancient Chinese art of geomancy, Queen Kong-jo, the Chinese bride of Srong-btsan sgam-po, pointed to those locations in the land where specially designed temples could be built to press down upon the earth-demoness' shoulders and hips, elbows and knees, hands and feet, and heart. The large, jewel-encrusted golden image of the 12-year-old Buddha that she brought with her from China is nowadays to be found in the Ra-sa 'phrul-snang temple, built upon a lake in Lhasa formed of the ogress' heart blood. This statue remains the most revered image in the whole of Tibet.

▶ *A wooden figure sitting in a traditional Buddhist position.*

 **Myths Retold**

GURU PADMASAMBHAVA

HAVING INVITED Padmasambhava to assist him in Tibet, the king and the guru were of different opinions concerning who should salute whom. Guru Padmasambhava therefore made a gesture of salutation to the king's staff, causing it to break into a hundred pieces, so that the king immediately raised his hands in salutation. Muttering a spell and throwing some mustard seed, Padmasambhava then caused fire to blaze up all around them.

At that time Pe-dkar, the leader of the *rgyal po* demons, could not bear to see a human with miraculous powers to rival his own and therefore dispatched his retinue of one thousand *the'u rang* demons to destroy the guru. When they arrived, however, they had no opportunity to kill him due to the burning fire and they returned to their master in defeat. Even by the time Pe-dkar himself arrived, the fire had not died down so he began to wonder how it could have been caused. Inquisitive about the spells the guru had recited, he crept forward to listen. Knowing this, the guru pierced him in the hearing ear with his magic *kila* and made his ear deaf. Piercing him in the seeing eye, he made his eye blind. Piercing him in the leg, he crippled his leg. Pe-dkar was thus subjugated and bound under oath to protect the doctrine of Buddhism evermore.

▶ *A bodhisattva – one who has renounced nirvana to help people on earth.*

168 ≈

FORCES OF NATURE

THE CHAOTIC FORCES of nature, variously feared and honoured by the original shamanic tradition of Tibet, became systematically categorised and ordered under the influence of Buddhism and made to fit harmoniously into the Indian cosmological model. The wild spirits of the land are all said to have been 'converted' and tamed as protectors of the Buddhist faith. Stripped of their former malignancy, they would now harm only those whose own wrongdoings were the cause of their misfortune. According to the doctrine of *karma*, the moral citizen has nothing to fear from the unseen world of spirits, and the patterns of nature became respected as the unfolding of natural *dharma* or universal law. Indeed, as the special protectors of the doctrine, these forces could be summoned by the Buddhist meditator and set to work at his request. Old shamanic rites of healing, ransom and exorcism were readily adopted by the Buddhist clergy and heavily overlaid with Buddhist liturgy and symbols.

DARKNESS AND LIGHT

THE CONCERNS of Tibetan mythology are categorised as either worldly or transcendental. Mundane myths concern the origin of the world and the history of all that has taken place here since time began. Within this ongoing story are count- less episodes of struggles between the forces of darkness and light engaged in by gods, demons and men from the realms above, below, and upon the surface of the earth. In the realm of the enlight- ened ones, however, beyond the understanding of ordinary mortals, are the countless buddhas of the five families whose existence is symbolically expressed in sacred texts of tantra and in artistic representations of circular *mandala*.

▲ *Red Yama, the Lord of Death, shown here turning the Wheel of Life.*

Mongolia

THE SHAMANIC ART of travelling in a trance to unseen worlds, in order to resolve the dilemmas of life (once common across the whole of Central Asia), is said to have been introduced to Mongolia in ancient times by a

15-year-old youth called Tarvaa. This lad, having fallen ill and fainted one day, was mistaken for dead. In disgust at the haste in which his relatives removed his body from the house, Tarvaa's soul flew off to the spirit realm where he was accosted by the judge of the dead and asked why he had come so early.

▲ *Skulls are used in masks such as this as they are believed to hold the personality of a being.*

PLEASED BY THE boy's courage in travelling to that realm where no living man had travelled before, the lord of the dead offered the boy any gift of his choosing to take back with him to life. Shunning the proffered offerings of wealth, pleasure, fame, longevity and the rest, Tarvaa chose to return with a knowledge of all the wondrous things that he had encountered in the spirit realm, and the gift of eloquence. By the time he returned to his body, crows had already pecked out the eyeballs but, although blind, Tarvaa could forsee the future and he lived long and well with his tales of magic and wisdom brought back from the far shore of death.

GESAR KHAN

GESAR KHAN WAS A ruthless and powerful warrior king who crushed violent
injustice wherever he encountered it. Having
descended from heaven to earth, commissioned to destroy certain demons whose
maledictions threatened to destroy the stability of human
existence, Gesar often became forgetful of his quest in the
aftermath of individual victories and required the prompt-
ing of his guardian angel (now identified as a Buddhist
dakini, a female spirit of wisdom) to set his feet back on
the path. The tales of his exploits, passed down
through oral tradition, are full of the dramatic
effects of mortal weaknesses, and the episodes
arouse great emotion in the listener as they
twist and turn in an unpredictable manner
as a result of treachery, deceit,
cowardice, greed and envy.

▶ Dakini, *a female spirit of wisdom.*

SHAMANS

SHAMANS THAT HAVE followed in the wake of Tarvaa speak of being
summoned by the spirits of their ancestors who force themselves upon the
young person and cause his or her personality to crumble. As the neophyte
shaman experiences the dismemberment of his physical body on the worldly
plane, his spirit takes refuge in a nest upon one of the branches of the World
Tree. There it stays until it has been nurtured back to health, and the spirits
that attend it have taught it how to see the world from the high vantage point
of the tree.

Whilst resting in their nests in the branches of the world tree, fledgling
shamans learn the way of sacrifice to ensure harmony and order within the

▲ *Modern societies still pay homage to ancient shamanic rituals.*

web of life. They return to men with a knowledge of the gods of wind and lightning, the gods of the corners and the horizon, of entrance and borders, of steam and thunder and countless other gods, and such knowledge gives them great power. Able to summon with their drums whomsoever they please, it is said that the god of death himself, in a fit of rage, reduced the originally double-headed shamanic drum to its current single-headed style in order to protect his sovereignty, for early shamans could call back the souls even of those long deceased.

THE SACRED COW

AMONG THE KHALKHA tribe of outer Mongolia there is a belief that their origin is due to the love of a shamanic nature spirit and a cow. The first Khalkha, having been born from a cow and raised on her creamy milk, bequeathed to the tribe a natural inclination towards cattle rearing and the nomadic life. In order that their coming into being should not be forgotten, married women of this tribe wear their hair parted in the middle and combed outwards, stiffened with mutton fat, in the form of a long pair of horns. Their dresses, also, are notable for the high projections that they wear on their shoulders, reminiscent of the prominent shoulder blades of cattle.

 **Myths Retold**

THE WASP AND THE SWALLOW

AT A TIME WHEN the world was yet still young, the king of all flying creatures ordered the wasp and the swallow to go and taste the flesh of all living creatures. The two subjects were to report back to him in the evening and declare which meat was sweetest, most fit for the diet of a king. It being a beautiful day, the swallow lost himself in transports of joy singing and soaring in the blue, blue sky. The wasp, on the other hand, did as he was bid and spent the day biting whoever he met and tasting their hot blood. When the two met up at the end of the day, prior to their reporting back to the king, the swallow asked the wasp for his verdict. 'Without

HAYAGRIVA

RENOWNED AS 'THE five animal people', Mongolians are pastoral nomads with sheep, goats, cattle, camels and horses under their care, and animals as familiars and helpers are important in their native shamanic cosmology. With the introduction of Buddhism, however, the animal fables of the distant past have largely given way to such tales as those of the horse-necked tantric deity Hayagriva who resides as the fierce aspect in the heart of the bodhisattva Avalokiteshvara. The horse dance is thought to pound down upon the heads of demons and conquer the world.

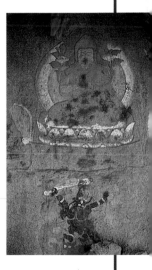

▲ *Depiction of Avalokiteshvara.*

doubt,' said the wasp, 'The sweetest food to eat is humans.' Fearing that this could cause great trouble for the future, the swallow pulled out the tongue of the wasp with his beak so that when the king asked him again that night, all the poor creature could do was buzz incoherently. 'We have decided, your majesty,' said the swallow, 'That the meat most suitable for a king is the flesh of serpents.' To this day, then, the eagle and the hawk who are the descendents of that royal line, love to dine on snakes.

▲ *Stones dating from the time of Chinggis Khan, possibly tombs or places of worship.*

MYTHOLOGICAL GROUPS

MONGOLIA WAS twice converted to the Buddhism of Tibet. In the thirteenth century, Khubilai Khan, grandson of the great Chinggis Khan, together with members of his court, adopted the religion, when Khubilai became ruler of an empire stretching from China to the gates of Europe. Three hundred years later, virtually the entire population of Mongolia became converted as Altan Khan also professed his faith in the religion. It was Altan Khan who gave the Mongolian title 'Dalai Lama' to his priest, the title by which he subsequently become known throughout the world in all his successive incarnations.

THE GER

TRADITIONALLY A NOMADIC culture, Mongolians have very little permanent architecture but prefer instead to dwell in domed tents called *ger*. These circular constructions of latticed wood and felt are symbolic of the universe, with the roof representing the sky and the smoke hole the sun. The central hearth brings all the elements together in harmony: a metal grate on the foundation of earth contains wood and fire which heats water for cooking. Thus the fireplace is sacred and no stranger will ever take a light from it, nor will any member of the family ever throw in rubbish for disposal.

▲ Gers *on the Mongolian plains.*

Since the introduction of Buddhism to Mongolia during this period, the ancient shamanic myths have become devalued and lost. The Mongolian Buddhist figure of the 'white old man', for example, represents all that remains of the once proud shamanic deity that ruled as father over the 99 regions of heaven. It is said that he was converted during a meeting with the Buddha, and now he acts as an assistant to the clergy and as a supporter of the Buddhist path.

CHAPTER 10

China

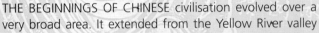

China

THE BEGINNINGS OF CHINESE civilisation evolved over a very broad area. It extended from the Yellow River valley in the north to the central region of the Huai River and south-east to the lower Yangtze basin. At first its culture took the form of numerous ethnic communities whose traits were equally developed by the Neolithic era of 5000 BCE. One of these ethnic groups emerged in about 1700 BCE as the dominant power in the Yellow River region. It progressed to become the first Chinese state, the Shang Dynasty, with its nucleus of power in Anyang city, modern Henan province.

▶ *Chinese Buddhist saint from the Qing Dynasty.*

THE SUCCESS OF THE Shang was due to its superior system of military organisation, urban settlements, its institutions of kinship and priesthood, methods of transport and communication, and its distinctively robust artistic expression. Two cultural traits played a crucial role in the rise of the Shang state and early Chinese civilisation. Technological expertise in metallurgy meant supremacy in war and material culture. The invention of a usable writing system consisting of graphs or characters by around 1200 BCE led to improved methods of social organisation through bureaucratic and administrative control, commerce, calendrical regulation of agriculture, foreign affairs, kinship structures, alliances, and religious practices. The main function of the Shang script was divination. The thousands of inscriptions found at Anyang consist of oracle bones. In these early writings no Shang myths are recorded. Only late in the succeeding Zhou Dynasty were the myths of ancient China written down. The Zhou people were from north-west China, modern Gansu province. They belonged to a different ethnic group from the Shang, but they had absorbed Shang cultural influences. Zhou society was organised into strictly defined social classes and functions, with a dual emphasis on warfare and agricultural productivity. By

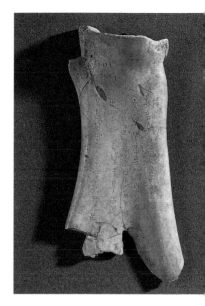

▲ *Ancient inscribed oracle bone, used for divination.*

around 1123 BCE the Zhou conquered the Shang and began to unite the communities of ancient China into a loose federation of kingdoms to form the Zhou dynasty. This political system flourished for several centuries, but it disintegrated in the Warring Kingdoms era of 403–221 BCE. The decline of the Zhou coincided with the emergence of great thinkers and writers such as Confucius, Mencius, and Zhuang Zi, who began to record the beginnings of their civilisation and to set down in writing their sacred history in the form of myths. Very few recognisably Shang or Zhou myths survive. Most recorded myth is undatable and derives from an archaic oral tradition.

THE COMPLEXITY OF THE COLLECTION OF CHINESE MYTHS

THE MYTHS OF ANCIENT China emerge from the oral tradition to be preserved in classical texts in the Age of the Philosophers and with the advent of early literature. China had no Hesiod, Homer, or Ovid to retell the mythic oral tales. Instead, Chinese writers introduced fragmentary passages of mythic narrative into their works to illustrate their argument and to give authority to their statements. Chinese myth exists as an amorphous, diffuse collection of anonymous archaic expression preserved in the contexts of philosophical, literary, or historical writings. They are brief, disjointed, and enigmatic. Incorporated into miscellaneous classical texts, these mythic fragments vary in their narration. Often authors adapted the myth according to their point of view. The result is that Chinese myth exists in numerous versions, mostly consistent but with significant variation in the details. Whereas the reshaping of archaic oral Greek and Roman myths into artistic narrative literature meant the loss of the authentic oral voice, the Chinese method of recording mythic fragments in a wealth of untidy, variable narrative forms demonstrates a rare aspect of primitive authenticity.

CALENDRICAL AND CULTURAL DEITIES

CLASSICAL TEXTS RELATE MYTHIC episodes of numerous famous or shadowy deities. Two play a role in creation myth (Woman Gua and Pan Gu) and four play a role in the flood myth (Woman Gua, Gong Gong, Gun, and Yu). While the celestial and calendrical deities are female (Xi He, the sun goddess, and Chang Xi, the moon goddess), the cultural deities are male (The Farmer God and Fu Xi). Deities of destruction have different functions. Chi You is the god of war, Gong Gong the marplot and Queen Mother of the West the sender of plagues and punishment.

▶ *Spectacular statue of the sky god.*

Myths Retold

THE ORIGIN OF THE WORLD
FROM THE BODY OF PAN GU

CHINA HAS A RICH TRADITION of creation myth. There is the world picture of a primeval earth covered by a sky cupola fastened together by cords, mountains or pillars. There is the creation of the universe from vapour. A third myth relates that the world was created from matter like a chicken's egg that separated into sky and earth. Another, more obscure myth tells how the goddess Woman Gua created all things through her seventy transformations. The most colourful creation narrative derives from a minority ethnic group in south-western China, recorded in the third century CE, and probably

transmitted from Central Asia. It relates how the world and humans were formed from the dying body of the first-born, semi-divine human, the giant Pan Gu. His breath became wind and clouds, his voice thunder, his eyes the sun and moon, and his limbs mountains. His bodily fluids turned into rain and rivers, his flesh into soil. His head hair became stars, his body hair vegetation. Teeth, bones and marrow became minerals. His bodily bugs turned into humans. This myth is a series of metamorphoses. It is referred to as the myth of the cosmological human body.

THE VARIETY OF TEXTS THAT PRESERVED THE MYTHS

THE EARLIEST CLASSICAL text which preserved mythic narrative is a Zhou dynasty anthology of poetry of 600 BCE. It contains the rare myths of the divine origin of the Shang and the Zhou, each through an ancestral goddess. The later texts of Confucian philosophy refer only briefly to mythical figures, but the Confucian text, Mencius (350 BCE), records two versions of the myth of world catastrophe by flood. The anonymous *Ancient History* adopted by the Confucian school relates myths of the origin of government, the concept of the sage-king and the transfer of political power. The texts of Daoist philosophy, especially *Zhuang Zi* (340 BCE), recounts the myth of Chaos, the god Hundun and the metamorphoses myth. The two major sources of myth are the 'Questions of Heaven' chapter of *Songs of Chu* (400 BCE), and the *Classic of Mountains and Seas* (third century BCE–second century CE). The first text records the sacred narrative of the people of Chu in central China from creation to the era of human history. The second text contains numerous narratives of over one hundred mythical figures. Both texts preserve major and minor myths in their great diversity. Miscellaneous ancient and medieval writings, and later encyclopedias also preserve fragments of myth.

▲ Top: *Confucius (in yellow) was one of the first philosophers to record his beliefs and thoughts;* bottom: *A page of a sutra, discourse of a Buddha.*

Myths Retold

THE CREATION OF HUMANKIND
BY THE GODDESS WOMAN GUA

THE PAN GU CREATION myth relates one of three versions of the myth of the creation of humankind. A second relates that out of primeval vapour two gods formed and divided into the cosmic powers Yin and Yang. They produced all living things and humans were created from primeval vapour. A third myth is female-gendered. It contains dramatic and colourful detail.

The narrative begins after the creation of the world. The creator goddess Woman Gua kneaded yellow clay like a potter and made images of humans which came to life. She wanted to create more but could not. So she made a furrow in mud with her builder's cord and lifted it out so that the falling mud became humans. The myth goes on to explain the origin of social hierarchy. The yellow clay humans became the class of plutocratic nobility, while the inferior mud produced the mass of the poor underclass. The colour motif of yellow resonates through Chinese culture. The Yellow Emperor god was the supreme deity of philosophical and religious Daoism; yellow symbolised the divine earth; and it was the emblematic colour of some dynasties. Woman Gua's emblems are her knotted cord and compass.

▲ *The Yin and Yang symbol represents opposing forces that interact to produce harmony.*

FIGURES AND ARCHETYPES IN CHINESE MYTHOLOGY

MANY FIGURES DEPICTED in mythical episodes represent cultural archetypes. Woman Gua and Pan Gu in creation myth, Yi the Archer in the world catastrophe of fire, and Yu in the flood myth symbolise order out of chaos, and they are archetypal saviour figures. The mothers of the suns and the moons, Xi He and Chang Xi, and the culture-bearing deities are archetypal nurturing figures. The female Drought Fury and Responding Dragon denote divine vengeance. Gun is the archetypal failed hero, who also represents the trickster-figure. The grain god Hou Ji, Shun and Yu are stereotypical successful heroes. Shun is the archetypal moral leader.

WAYS OF READING CHINESE MYTH

THE NATURIST APPROACH identifies solar and lunar myths of the goddesses Xi He and Chang Xi. Modern gender theory underscores their myths and those of the creatrix and saviour goddess Woman Gua. The anthropological approach uncovers important charter myth in the transfer of power from the sage-kings Yao and Shun. The ethnographic approach reveals the creation myth of Pan Gu from the south-western subculture of ancient China. The aetiological approach underscores myths of origin, from the creation myths of Woman Gua and Pan Gu to the discovery myths of the culture-bearing deities, such as the Farmer God and Fu Xi. Aetiological myth is evident in the female-gendered foundation myths of the Shang, through a bird's egg, and the Zhou, through a god's footprint, beside the animalian myth of the Yao people through the divine dog Pan Hu. The motif or mythic theme approach helps the reader to discern myths of world catastrophe by fire and flood through the figures of Yi the Archer, Woman Gua, Gong Gong and Yu. The stereotypical features of the hero figure identify the child hero and grain god Hou Ji, the failed hero Gun and the successful heroes Shun and Yu.

Myths Retold

THE WORLD CATASTROPHE OF THE FLOOD

THE FLOOD MYTH is told in four main versions. The myth of the worker god Gong Gong relates how he stirred the world's waters so they crashed against the sky barrier, threatening a return to chaos. The myth of the dual catastrophe of flood and fire is recounted through the figure of the goddess Woman Gua who controlled the disaster. Another account tells how the hero Gun risked all by stealing divine cosmic soil to stem the flood, but he failed and was executed. His son Yu was born from his belly; Gun then metamorphosed into a bear. The version of the flood myth which became standard relates how the hero Yu controlled the flood through his superhuman physical prowess, intelligent flood plans and his moral virtue. Supernatural creatures, the aquatic dragon and turtle, aided his labours. Yu worked so long and hard that his body became disfigured. After controlling the flood, he divided the world into nine regions and he became the founder of the mythical Xia dynasty, the first in the Golden Age. In Chinese Flood myth, the themes of the flood as divine punishment, the drama of human escape and the recommence-ment of humankind by divinely favoured survivors do not occur.

▲ *Chinese plate decorated with a green and red dragon motif. Dragons are often central to Chinese mythology.*

WORLD PARALLELS AND INDIGENOUS TRAITS

THE MAIN THEMES of Chinese myth reveal significant parallels with world mythologies. Chinese creation myth differs by the absence of a creator or the concept of divine will, and by the absence of an authorised version, such as Genesis. The myths of creation and of catastrophe by flood each have four distinct versions. World catastrophe by fire has only one mythic version, whose central concern is with the solar calendar, but there are several drought myths. In myths of cultural benefits the two themes of deities voluntarily bestowing gifts on humankind and of first teaching humans how to use them find close parallels in world mythology. Several divine gifts from Fu Xi, such as divination through the Eight Trigrams (the Yi jing), are uniquely Chinese. The archaic Shang and Zhou foundation myths are vividly detailed. The absence of a foundation myth of a named city derives from the custom of multiple capital cities in ancient China rather than one sacred citadel, such as Rome. The myth of the hero reveals stereotypical parallels, such as divine birth and trials of the child hero Hou Ji. But Chinese heroic myth differs in its early emphasis on the moral virtue of the warrior hero, such as Yu.

MAJOR CHINESE THEMES

MAJOR MYTHIC THEMES are narrated in several versions, such as the four creation myths and the four flood myths. Divine warfare and the marplot themes are significant. The re-establishment of natural order after world catastrophes is followed by the theme of a Golden Age of sage-kings. The theme of the warrior and moral hero is represented in numerous episodes. The rarely expressed theme of love occurs in the myth of stellar lovers. Less emphasised themes include agricultural and pastoral, migration and exile, animalian and vegetal, gendered conflict, and the cultural other.

▶ *As in other mythologies, the Chinese believe in the occurrence of a catastrophic flood.*

Myths Retold

THE DISCOVERY OF MEDICINE BY THE FARMER GOD

THE MYTH OF THE Farmer God relates how he taught humans the discovery and uses of medicine. He took pity on humans who were suffering illnesses from eating toxic plants and drinking contaminated water. In an effort to help these humans, the god tasted all the plants and taught humans the difference between those that were poisonous and those that were edible. His method was to thrash plants with his rust-coloured whip and then judge their value by their taste and smell. He organised plants into four categories – bland, toxic, cool and hot. This taxonomy forms the basis of traditional Chinese medicine. The Farmer God also taught humans how to distinguish between types of soil and terrain. He created a wooden plough and taught humans how to till the soil and sow the five grains. His function as agricultural deity overlaps with that of the grain god Hou Ji. The Farmer God's emblem is a forked plough. He became the divine patron of medicine.

THEMES IN ART

THE EARLIEST artistic expression of myth occurs on funereal stone carvings and murals. Favourite themes are the acts of the deities, flood and fire myths, the tree of life, the paradise of Queen Mother of the West and the trials of the hero, such as the filial Shun. The most popular poetic theme is the tragic myth of two stellar lovers. In novels, recurring figures are military heroes of antiquity and intelligent animals, such as Monkey. Temple architecture colourfully represents deified figures like Confucius. The life-giving symbol of the dragon appears on textiles and ceramics.

▲ *Vase with a dragon motif, dating to the early Ming Dynasty.*

CHAPTER 11

Japan and Korea

Japan

THE FOUR MAIN ISLANDS that make up the Japanese archipelago have been inhabited for at least 50,000 years. Land bridges linking present-day Japan to mainland Sakhalin in the north and Korea in the south existed until about 12,000 years ago and these overland routes would have enabled early migrants to settle in Japan. Traces of the various waves of people who arrived in Japan can be distinguished archeologically into the Old Stone Age (50,000–12,000 BCE), the Jomon culture (11,000–300 BCE) and the Yayoi culture (300 BCE–CE 300). Jomon culture sites are located throughout Japan, especially in the north of the main island, Honshu. The settlements of the later Yayoi people, however, were centred on Kyushu, Shikoku and the Kii Peninsula south of Osaka and Nara. The proximity of Korea suggests a close racial connection with these people.

THE YAYOI PEOPLE are thought to be the main cultural and racial ancestors of the present-day Japanese population, with the exception of the small group of Ainu, numbering around 20,000, who live on the northern island of Hokkaido. These Ainu are possibly the remnants of the Jomon people.

◀ *Japanese god encounters an apparition of the fox goddess.*

THE RISE OF THE ICON

THE NUMEROUS *kami* or gods of Japanese mythology and the Shinto religion based on them, were not represented in any art form prior to the introduction of Buddhism, with its complex range of scriptures, paintings and sculptures. Instead the gods were thought to be invisible spirits or the spiritual power that inhabited objects, whether living or inanimate. Shinto shrines usually have no statues in them but only symbolic objects. The introduction of Buddhism resulted in the identification of the mythological gods with various Buddhist deities and this facilitated the depiction of the gods and goddesses in visual forms.

▶ *Shinto shrine in Kyoto.*

THE CREATION

THE *NIHON-SHOKI* and the *Kojiki* generally agree in their accounts of the creation. Some scholars discern a degree of Chinese influence in these accounts. It is possible that this is not because of later influences after the introduction of Chinese culture to Japan, but perhaps because these myths came from people who migrated from northern China and Korea. According to these myths, the universe originally existed only as an unformed, oily lump. Eventually, a the god Amanominakanushi-no-kami arose from this mass. He was followed by another four gods, forming a group of five primordial gods. Then a further seven generations of gods and god-desses came into being. All these divine beings inhabited the High Plains of Heaven (*Takama-gahara*) because there was no solid land. The youngest of these gods were Izanagi and Izanami, who began to create land. Standing on the Floating Bridge of Heaven, they stirred the depths with a sacred spear. When they lifted the spear out, drops fell down and formed the first land, an island called Onogoro.

THE ROLE OF IZANAGI AND IZANAMI

IZANAGI AND IZANAMI descended from the heavens to the newly formed land and built a palace for themselves there. As they were the first couple, they invented the ritual of marriage and then procreated. Their first-born, Hiruko (Leech Child), was deformed so they placed the child in a reed boat and set it adrift in the sea. Divination showed that this child was deformed because the goddess Izanami had spoken first during the marriage ritual. After performing the marriage ritual again correctly, Izanami gave birth abundantly. Her first group of offspring were the islands that make up the Japanese archipelago. Next, she gave birth to a series of gods and goddesses linked with natural phenomena such as the wind and the mountains. Finally, she gave birth to the god of fire (Kagutsuchi) who burnt her so badly as he was being born that she died. More gods arose from her dead body and also from the tears of Izanagi. After she had entered the Underworld realm of the dead, Izanagi tried to visit Izanami and have her return with him to the land of the living. However, he failed in his attempts as Izanami was already a corpse.

▲ *Raijin, Japanese god of thunder.*

The events surrounding this first death also reflect the early Japanese concern with taboos and pollution. Some scholars believe that the repeated relocation of the capital during the Yamato and the Nara periods following the death of the ruler is linked with this myth with its decisive separation of the living and the dead.

Myths Retold

IZANAGI AND IZANAMI

AFTER IZANAMI'S DEATH she entered into Yomi, the dark Underworld realm of the dead. Overcome with inconsolable grief, Izanagi decided to visit Izanami to entreat her to return with him, but Izanami told him that she would need to talk to the gods of the Underworld about this, warning him not to look at her. Overcome by a desire to see her once again, Izanagi broke off a tooth from his hair-comb and lit it as a torch. He was horrified to see that Izanami was now a maggot-infested rotting corpse and tried to flee from her. Angered by his act, Izanami sent a horde of demon hags and warriors to pursue him. When he reached the entrance back into the realm of the living, Izanagi found three peaches which he threw at the frightening horde chasing him and managed to turn them back. At this point, Izanami herself, transformed into a demon, gave chase. Before she could reach him, Izanagi barred her way with a great boulder with which he sealed the entrance to the Underworld. Here they confronted each other a final time and dissolved their marriage vows.

UNIVERSAL THEMES

THOUGH GENERALLY less complex than those found elsewhere, Japanese myths share some features in common with those of other cultures. The emergence of certain deities, land and food from the living and dead bodies of the gods have echoes in the dismemberment concept of creation found in India and elsewhere. The first death of Izanami and Izanagi's visit to the Underworld is similar to the Greek myth of Orpheus and Eurydice, as well as that of Persephone and that of Yama and his sister in Indian mythology.

EARLY RULERS

INITIALLY, THE YAYOI people were organised on the basis of loosely related clans with their independent territories. Strong ties with Korea on the mainland were maintained by these people and their descendants even as late as the seventh century CE. The earliest accounts of Japan survive in Chinese annals from the first century CE, which mention the names of the various clan 'kings' or chiefs. However, by the third century CE, a process of conquest and consolidation of these small separate territories led to

▲ *Ancient Yayoi terracotta vase.*

the emergence of the large single state of Yamato which included southern Honshu and Shikoku. The lineage of the present-day emperor of Japan can be traced in an unbroken line back to the early legendary rulers of Yamato.

Most surviving Japanese mythology concerns the divine ancestors of these early rulers as recorded in the *Nihon-shoki* and the *Kojiki*, written during the eighth century CE. It may be assumed that this mythology was primarily linked to the Yayoi people and may have formed part of their culture even prior to their arrival in Japan.

DESCENDANTS OF THE YAMATO STATE

THE SOURCES OF surviving Japanese myths are very limited and derive almost entirely from two sources: the Kojiki and the slightly later Nihon-shoki. The mythological sections of these records were written with the explicit intention of establishing the divine descent of the Japanese imperial family. It is likely therefore what we have now were the clan myths of the particular group which eventually became overlords of the early Yamato state, to the exclusion of rival claimants. For this reason there are few recurrent figures or themes in the mythology, with the exception perhaps of the small group of myths connected with Susa-no-o and his sister Amaterasu.

 **Myths Retold**

AMATERASU

FOLLOWING IZANAGI'S return alone to the land of the living, a number of important gods and goddesses emerged from his body and clothing. The most important of these were the sun goddess Amaterasu, the moon god Tsuki-yomi and the storm god Susa-no-o. Izanagi set Amaterasu up as the ruler of the High Plains of Heaven (*Takama-gahara*), Tsuki-yomi as the ruler of the night and Susa-no-o as the ruler of the seas. However, Susa-no-o was jealous of the status of his sister Amaterasu, rebelled against his father's wishes and hence was banished by Izanagi.

Suspecting that he was plotting to overthrow her, Amaterasu armed herself and confronted her brother. He challenged her to a contest which would prove who was really the mightiest – whoever could give birth to male gods would win. Though Amaterasu won, Susa-no-o refused to accept defeat and embarked on a series of foul outrages against Amaterasu which so terrified her that she sealed herself inside a cave. The world and the heavens were cast into darkness and misery. In vain the gods tried to lure her out.

▼ *The goddess Amaterasu emerges from the earth.*

Then the beautiful goddess of the dawn, Ama-no-uzume, a prototype of early Japanese female shamans, stood on an upturned rice barrel and began a sacred erotic dance. The other gods were greatly excited by this. Hearing the excitement of the gods and their praises for Ama-no-uzume, Amaterasu peeped out and asked what was happening. She was told that the gods were rejoicing at the sight of a goddess more beautiful than herself. As she peeped out, one of the gods held up a sacred mirror and Amaterasu saw her own reflection in it. At this moment, one of the other gods seized her by the hand and pulled her out of the cave. Finally, the entrance to the cave was blocked. Amaterasu then resumed her place in the heavens and Susa-no-o was punished by the other gods and banished to the land of mortals. Amaterasu is viewed both as the chief protector of Japan and as the ancestor of the emperors.

She is worshipped to this day at the most important shrine in Japan at Ise.

SACRED OBJECTS OF THE GODS

THE THREE MOST important religious symbols associated with the Japanese gods are still enshrined in Shinto shrines. These are: a necklace of *magatama*, curious comma-shaped stones, like those given to Amaterasu by Izanagi as a symbol of sovereignty; a metal mirror representing the one used by the gods to lure Amaterasu from her cave; and a sword symbolising the Kusanagi found by Susa-no-o and later owned by Jimmu, the first Japanese emperor. Shinto shrines are usually marked with avenues of trees or rocks with a sacred gateway or *torii* through which the gods enter into the shrine itself.

◀ *The sacred gateway, or torii, leading to a Shinto shrine.*

 **Myths Retold**

SUSA-NO-O

SUSA-NO-O WAS A TROUBLE-MAKER even before he quarrelled with his sister Amaterasu, and he caused a number of earlier conflicts with other gods. According to the *Nihonshoki,* he made advances towards Ogetsu, the goddess of food. He demanded that she give him some food to eat but he flew into a rage when she drew this from her nose, mouth and rectum. He killed Ogetsu, but after her death the various orifices of her body gave rise to the staple crops eaten by the Japanese: rice, millet, wheat, red azuki beans and soya beans. After his exile to the Land of Reed Plain, he encountered an old couple with their beautiful daughter Kusanada-hime (Rice-Field Princess). They were being terrorised by an eight-headed and eight-tailed monster which had eaten all their other daughters. Susa-no-o agreed to kill this

▲ *The trouble-maker Susa-no-o.*

monster if he could marry the daughter. Leaving tubs of rice wine for the monster to drink, Susa-no-o succeeded in killing it. In one of its tails he found the legendary sacred sword, the Kusanagi (Grass-Cutter). He then married Kusanada-hime and took up residence in a palace at Izumo.

Korea

THE ORIGINS OF THE Korean people can be traced to around 1000 BCE when Bronze Age warriors belonging to the Tungusic racial group invaded Manchuria and the Korean Peninsula, mixing with its original inhabitants. The Tungus are one of the three major ethnic groups in northern and central Asia, today occupying most of Manchuria and south-eastern Siberia. Thus, the Korean people have a distinctive racial and cultural origin from the Chinese people, although they have also absorbed considerable elements of Chinese élite culture and use substantial amounts of Chinese vocabulary in their language.

▲ *Ch'amsong-dan altar, said to have been erected by Tan'gun, mythical founder of the Korean nation.*

THEIR MYTHOLOGY, however, is a reflection of a non–Chinese culture. The structure of the tales, the characters and the motifs which appear in them are on the whole remnants of an earlier period. Korean myths are of two types: foundation myths about the people and state, and creation myths about the origin of the world. Because the foundation myths are so ancient, most of them are known only from ancient Korean or Chinese records and not from narration by contemporary storytellers. The only exception to this statement are the creation myths which are sung by shamans as part of their ritual repetoire.

STRUCTURAL TYPES OF KOREAN FOUNDATION MYTHS: THE TAN'GUN TYPE

THE NATION OR STATE foundation myths of Korea may be divided into three principle types based upon the formal structure of the mythic narrative

– the Tan'gun Type, the Chumong Type and the Three Clan Ancestors Type. In addition there are clan foundation myths, describing the origin of individual clans, particularly the three royal houses of the Kingdom of Silla (traditional dates 35–936 BCE).

The Myth of Tan'gun, Lord of the Sandalwood Tree, is the quintessential foundation myth of Korea describing how:

▲ *Bronze decoration in the form of a tiger.*

1. The son of the Ruler of Heaven was selected to go to rule mankind

2. Heaven's son descended to earthand established culture there

3. A tiger and a bear vied to become men

4. The transformed bear-woman pleaded to have a child

5. The child Tan'gun established the first Korean kingdom

Assuming the pre-existence of humanity, the tale serves three functions, to describe how civilisation was brought to this world, how the first Korean royal house was established and how the first Korean kingdom was created. Among the motifs used in the myth are the world tree and a cosmic mountain which form the link between earth and Heaven.

Myths Retold

THE MYTH OF TAN'GUN

THE RULER OF HEAVEN had a concubine's son called Hwanung who wanted to descend from Heaven and rule the world of men, so his father gave him the three heavenly regalia, and commanded him to rule over mankind. With the Earl of Wind, Master of Cloud and Master of Rain, Hwanung descended upon the summit of the Great White Mountain by the Sacred Sandlewood Tree. Hwanung called the spot the Sacred City and he was known as the Heavenly King.

At that time, there was a bear and a tiger living in a cave who constantly pleaded with Hwanung to transform them into men. Hwanung gave them some Sacred Mugwort and twenty pieces of garlic, telling them to eat the plants and avoid daylight for one hundred days. The bear and tiger ate the plants and fasted for three times seven days. The bear received a woman's body, but the tiger who was not able to fast, did not. As there was no one with whom the Bear Woman could marry, she went every day to the Sacred Sandalwood Tree to pray for a child. Hwanung changed form and married her. She had a son, who was called Prince Tan'gun, Lord of the Sandalwood Tree. Tan'gun made P'yongyang his capital and called the nation Choson.

THE MOUNTAIN GOD

PAINTINGS OF THE Mountain God are found in shrines on mountain passes, and in shrines within virtually every Buddhist temple. Called *sanshingak*, these shrines are dedicated to the Mountain God as the ruler of all the mountains of Korea. In the pictures hung behind the altar, San-shin is often depicted as a grandfatherly figure with a long white beard, seated on a tiger and resting beneath a pine tree. He is identified with Tan'gun who upon his death is said to have been transformed into the Mountain God.

STRUCTURAL TYPES OF KOREAN FOUNDATION MYTHS: THE CHUMONG TYPE

THE MYTH OF CHUMONG relates the story of the founder of the Kingdom of Koguryo, a militarily powerful state ruling most of Manchuria and half the Korean peninsula from the fourth to the seventh centuries CE. The mythic narrative as recorded in the *Samguk yusa* is composed of four distinct scenes which describe how:

1. A king discovered the daughter of a river spirit who had been raped
2. The river spirit's daughter gave birth to a giant egg out of which the hero emerged
3. The hero fled because of the jealousy of his half-brothers
4. The hero established his kingdom

The four-fold pattern of the narrative scenes in the myth is the basic pattern of the foundation myths of the Tungusic peoples of north-east Asia, whether the people had state-level societies such as the Manchus or lived in tribal communities. This myth is only concerned with the establishment of the state and not with the origin of the people's culture. It also differs from heroic tales told in Europe and the Mediterranean area which use the motif of the flight of a hero from his place of birth. In those myths the hero eventually returns home. In the Chumong myth the hero never returns.

◄ *Typical image of the mountain god, seated upon a tiger under a tree.*

THE MYTH OF CHUMONG

TRAVELLING NEAR the Great White Mountain, King Kumwa met the daughter of the Earl of the River, who told him she had been raped by the son of the Ruler of Heaven, near the Bear Spirit Mountain on the Yalu River. Angered, her parents had banished her. The king secluded Yuhwa in a room. Sunlight caressed her body, she became pregnant and gave birth to a large egg. The king gave the egg to the dogs, pigs, cows and horses, but they would not harm it. Not being able to smash the egg, Kumwa gave the egg back to its mother. A

◄ *San-shin accompanied by his messenger tiger.*

heroic baby broke open the egg and came out. When the boy was seven he could make his own bows and arrows, and hit the target one hundred times in succession. He was called Chumong, 'Good Shot'. As his half-brothers were jealous of him, his mother told him to flee. He took some good horses and with three friends fled until they came to a river. Chumong cried out that he was the descendant of the Ruler of Heaven and the Earl of the River. Instantly, terrapin and fish rose up, and formed a bridge. Chumong crossed over, built a capital city, called his nation Koguryo and gave himself the surname Ko.

▶ *Tombstone of a Korean saint, with the base formed by a granite terrapin.*

SPIRITS OF NATURE

SAN-SHIN, THE MOUNTAIN god, is ruler of all the mountains and owner of all the creatures and objects on the mountains. He is thought by many to be Tan'gun, the father of the nation. The tiger is his messenger. The spirits Earl of the River, Earl of Wind, Master of Cloud and Master of Rain are master spirits, rulers of aspects of nature. The terms are similar to spirit names from the Zhou Dynasty (eleventh to third centuries BCE) of China.

CHAPTER 12

Southeast Asia

Southeast Asia

SOUTHEAST ASIA IS a complex region both geographically and ethnically, and this complexity is reflected in the rich cultural diversity of its people. Much remains to be discovered about its ancient past and extensive mythology.

▲ *Ornate head of a Buddha.*

BORDERING THE Pacific Ocean, Southeast Asia is made up of the mainland and the island arc. The mainland comprises Burma, Thailand, Cambodia, Laos, Vietnam and Malaysia. The Indonesian archipelago, which contains 13,677 islands, lies across one of the earth's most active and dangerous volcanic regions. The Philippine Islands also form part of the region. The majority of the population is of Mongoloid extraction.

Between 5000 and 1000 BCE there was a continuous drift of peoples possibly from southern China, into Southeast Asia and the islands of Indonesia and the Philippines. Some practiced shifting agriculture in remote upland regions whilst the majority settled in river valleys and along coastal strips.

Apart from the huge influx of peoples from Southern China, the greatest influence on Southeast Asia was India. Indian traders frequented the coastal towns and there was also interaction between the courts of India and Southeast Asia. From about the beginning of the Christian era the Buddhist and Hindu religions were introduced to the larger, more cosmopolitan groups in the region; Buddhism remains the principal faith in Burma, Thailand, Laos and Cambodia, and is also practiced in Vietnam. In the fourteenth century Islam, brought by Arab traders, began to be adopted in the islands of Sumatra and Java and the Malay Peninsula, and in this southern region it remains the principal faith.

Southeast Asians have long been skilled navigators and sailors, trading for centuries with China. Arabia and India. From the early sixteenth century European powers also competed for trade in Southeast Asia, which was on the sea route between China and India, and was itself a vital source of spices. Europeans also traded here, becoming increasingly powerful politically. During this period Christianity was introduced, especially into remote regions. The Philippines, which also experienced a strong American influence, is largely Christian today.

During the nineteenth century Chinese and Indian migrants moved to the cities, attracted by economic opportunities. The population of Singapore is today largely Chinese. Many Chinese Southeast Asians practise Confucianism and Buddhism, as do large numbers of Vietnamese, whilst Hindu temples serve the smaller Indian communities.

▲ *Cloth worn in Indonesian ritual ceremonies; the two figures are symbols of male achievement.*

NATURE SPIRITS

THE MAJORITY OF Southeast Asians still live by the land, as can be seen by the many myths connected with nature spirits. These may inhabit unusual trees, rocks and other natural phenomena, and offerings are often made to

them by passers-by. Sometimes stories recount the unnatural death of a person whose spirit has sought refuge in such a place. These spirits can be malevolent if not respected.

The importance of the sea has given rise to many myths about great ocean journeys, princesses on far islands, magical fish and fearsome monsters. Many boats are decorated with painted eyes which protect the sailors from sea monsters known to lurk in the deep. These monsters or Makara also adorn temple gateways, where they are thought to ward off evil.

The ritual of human sacrifice is a common legacy of Southeast Asia, and heads were regularly taken in some areas well into the twentieth century. The life force, which is seated in the head, was thought to increase the store of fertility within the head-hunter's community.

▲ *A male figure rising from a tree – it is the wood that is considered sacred in Indonesia, not the figure.*

CHARACTERS, PROTAGONISTS AND ARCHETYPES

THE BALANCE BETWEEN the forces of good and evil, light and dark, male and female are played out in dance-dramas typified by Bali's Barong dance, in which the lion-like Barong and the witch-like Rangda enact the eternal battle. The heroic prince, courageous, modest and pure, appears in many dramas. The Buddha, himself of royal blood, is known throughout Southeast Asia as a symbol of detachment and enlightenment. In Javanese and Balinese shadow theatre there is found a grotesque clown-like figure, a member of the court. A figure of fun, he nevertheless speaks word of true wisdom and is ranked with the gods. He may have developed out of an ancient deity in the region.

◄ *Balinese performance of the mythical lion Barong fighting the witch Rangda.*

Myths Retold

ANIMAL MYTHS

THE DRAGON-SNAKE or *naga* is a fabulous creature known throughout the region. It appears in many Indian myths where it is associated with both Vishnu and Shiva. The Angkor dynasty in Cambodia and the Mons of Burma traced their descent to the union of a brahmin prince and a *naga* princess. Also frequently seen, from Burma to New Guinea, is the familiar image of the serpent fighting the bird, presumably symbolising the balance of the elements of sky and earth.

In New Guinea the Bird of Paradise is thought to have received its feathers from the spirits of Heaven, or indeed to have escaped from Heaven, for it is so beautiful and rarely touches the earth. In Indonesia the souls of the dead may take the form of birds, which fly above the lands of their descendents.

▲ *Turtles, snakes and other Underworld creatures support this temple's pagoda roof.*

CENTRAL THEMES

CREATION MYTHS occur throughout the region, and myth also accompanies the ritual of death and the passage to the world of the dead. Myths concerning heroic figures are popular, and often relate to the glorious past of the community or to a founding ancestor. These tales may tell of great ocean crossings in the dawn of time, or of unions between men and gods or semi-divine creatures.

◄ *This cloth painting shows the churning of the ocean by gods and demons at the dawn of creation.*

The turtle is a popular figure, often appearing in Hindu myth, sometimes supporting the world on its shell, or acting as a wise councillor and guide on the journey of life.

Werewolves and weretigers are feared in deeply forested areas, and there are also tales of women walking in the forest becoming possessed by spirits, whom they are forced to marry.

THE ORIGINS OF MYTH

SOCIETIES OFTEN TRACE their descent to a semi-divine common ancestor who may have been human or animal, and ancestors are often deified. Stories relate the founding of ethnic groups by such mythical figures. In the south, tales are told of the arrival of the original man by canoe.

Hindu myths, particularly stories from the *Ramayana* and the *Mahabharatha,* are well-known throughout Southeast Asia and appear in the dance-dramas and puppet theatre of most countries. Buddhist stories are very popular in the north, and in the Muslim south Islamic legends of semi-historical kings and warriors are enacted alongside Hindu myths in dance-drama.

▲ *Illustration from the* Ramayana *showing a nymph seducing the king of the demons.*

Twentieth century political upheavals produced a legacy of stories concerning the struggle for independence. Some nationalist leaders such as Ho Chi Minh have aquired a legendary status; in some countries the exploits of these men and their comrades are enacted in drama and shadow theatre, and may well prove to be the basis for myths of the future.

▲ *Mask representing benevolent rice spirits in dances held to promote crop fertility.*

 **Myths Retold**

SPIRITS AND SAINTS

IN BURMA THE SPIRITS are called *nats*. A pantheon lists the spirits of thirty-seven *nats* who died unnatural deaths, often after a tragic love affair. The brother and sister Nga Tin De and Shwemyethna are probably the most well known of the *nats*. Nga Tin De, the strong and handsome blacksmith, was killed in a jealous rage by the king. On hearing the news, his sister, who was married to the king, burned herself to death rather than continue to live with his murderer.

Very popular in the north of the region, is the story of how the Buddha-to-be, on the point of Enlightenment, is challenged by *Mara*, the Evil One. The Holy One points to the earth, calling upon it to bear witness to his countless good deeds in this and previous lives. The earth quakes in response, causing *Mara* to flee

GODS AND SPIRITS OF SOUTHEAST ASIA

AMONG NATURE SPIRITS the rice goddess is particularly honoured, and the god or spirit of the mountain or volcano is also feared, especially in the islands. The god of the sea, too, is respected. Every house has its guardian spirit to whom offerings are made daily, regardless of the nominal faith of the household. In the Hindu phase many temples were dedicated to Shiva and Vishnu. In Hindu Bali these gods and many others remain, their characteristics merged with those of ancient indigenous deities. In northern Southeast Asia the Buddha is revered, and Hindu deities such as Indra, Sri Devi and Brahma, who feature in Buddhist mythology, are still known.

The arrival of Islam in the south is remembered in myth: An Islamic saint laid a curse on the Hindu Raja of West Java, prophecying – accurately – that he would be the last Hindu ruler, and that a new religion would soon sweep the land.

CHAPTER 13

Oceania

Oceania

OCEANIA IS USUALLY DIVIDED into three regions, the larger islands north of Australia, or Melanesia, long settled by dark-skinned agricultural people, scattered groups of small islands contiguous to Asia, or Micronesia, settled by seafaring folk of Asian origin and the far-flung islands of Polynesia forming a triangle enclosing Hawaii in the north, New Zealand in the south and Easter Island in the east. Unlike the Melanesians and Micronesians who spoke hundreds of languages and had as many mythologies, the Polynesians all spoke languages belonging to one language group though their mythologies reflected different influences.

▲ *Huge monolithic figure sculptures on Easter Island.*

THE PRIMAL MYTHOLOGIES of Oceania mostly reflected their shamanic origins, the attempts by skilled practitioners and mediums to manipulate and control the spirit world and even visit it. Throughout the region legends and folk tales told of celebrated tricksters, shape-changers and spiritual voyagers. There were, however, great differences. In much of

▲ *Oceanic fertility god.*

Melanesia and some of the other island groups the more negative facets of the shamanic experience had developed into magic and sorcery. Elsewhere in the region strong religious cults developed or were introduced, some harking back directly to Asia or even the Americas, with their own distinctive shamanic underlay. The Polynesians were the great navigators and explorers and had settled in Samoa and Tonga by 1000 BCE. Over 25 centuries they spread to other island groups in the triangle. Although many of the myths of exploration reflected real voyages they were also understood to represent spirit journeys. Insofar as demi-gods such as Rupe and Maui were originally real people they were more likely to have been famous shamans than explorers. Apart from the folk tales or fables, the older myths in the region usually concerned nature, especially the stars, and the origin of places and obvious things such as fire or animal species. These stories were often told in narrative cycles added to from time to time by the storytellers on ritual occasions.

One of the migrations from Southeast Asia into Polynesia, possibly via the island of Futuna, introduced an Indo-European cosmology of numerous heavens and Underworlds, a world tree, waters of life and a mirror-image world called Pulotu. The Pulotu people dominated in western Polynesia and Fiji, while the Papatea people, those who supported a pantheon emanating from the parent gods Papa and Atea, held sway in eastern Polynesia including New Zealand, where Rangi replaced Atea.

TRANSMISSION OF KNOWLEDGE

MYTHS HELPED THE people of the islands to relate to their environment and were the basis of their religion. In most societies there were men or women who had the task of transmitting such knowledge either within a family or as custodians of knowledge for a high chief. In one of the Cook Islands, for instance, the system of ultimogeniture applied to high priestly titles, that is an old priest passed on his mythological and related knowledge to his youngest son who inherited his title. Craftspeople passed on their specialised knowledge which was often inseparable from the mythology. In the highly stratified societies specialised and esoteric knowledge was taught at schools of learning. The Maori schools in New Zealand were taught by priestly 'experts' known as *tohunga*, those in Hawaii by their equivalent the *kahuna*. In the Society Islands the youth were trained by the principal chief and senior members of the 'Arioi society' or players. The myths were often presented to the people in the form of dance or drama with elaborate costumes, Greek-style choruses, falsetto voice parts and clowning.

CARVING

WOODCARVING WAS THE great mythic art of Oceania, though mythological motifs were also rendered in stone, ivory and greenstone. Sennit-binding, barkcloth, feather and shell decoration and dog hair were also used in representing the gods, often portrayed as kites, adzes and ceremonial artefacts. Mythological symbols were also used in tattooing. Carved objects ranged from large and elaborate god figures to decorative war clubs, pedigree sticks and bowls for domestic use. Canoe prow carving was widespread through Oceania while elaborate house lintel carving was restricted to New Zealand.

▲ *Carved figure and hook used for hanging skulls on.*

Myths Retold

THE ORIGIN OF KAVA

THE MAN FEVANGA attended the Tu'i Tonga and
invited his master to visit him and his wife Fefafa on
Eueiki Island. The visit took place during a famine and
there was nothing to eat except one big *kape* plant with
its edible peppery root. The chief Lo'au rested his canoe
so that it sheltered the *kape* plant. Fevanga then persuaded
Lo'au to move and dug up the root which he put into the
earth oven together with his leprous daughter Kavaonau.
When the food was presented to Lo'au he would not eat
the girl but had her head and body buried separately. After
five nights a big kava plant grew from the head and sugar
cane from the body. Lo'au ordered Fevanga to bring the
kava and sugar cane to him and said, 'chewing kava, a leper
from Faimata, the child of Fevanga and Fefafa! Bring some
coconut fibre to strain it, a bowl to contain it, someone as
master of ceremonies, some young leaves of the banana as a
receiver and someone for the bowl to be turned to,' thus
celebrating the occasion when an only child had been
cooked for the reception of the ranking chiefs.

MYTHS OF EXPLANATION

MANY OF THE MYTHS throughout the region were
simply fables to explain geographical features and natural
phenomena such as fire. Invariably particular gods such as
Tangaloa in Samoa and Tonga were attributed with having

◀ *Cook Island statue of the creator god, Tanganoa.*

thrown down rocks which became islands. Kura in the Tuamotus, Motikitik in Yap and Maui in Tonga and New Zealand were credited with having fished up islands from the sea with magic fishhooks. All the islands, however, from Guam and New Guinea in the west to remote Easter Island had entertaining myths that explained the markings on certain creatures or why certain characters became particular birds, animals or stars. One popular myth in central Polynesia was that of the rat and the octopus which explained the markings on the octopus. Myths relating to one flood, one famine or the exploits of one hero usually reflected cumulative experiences scattered over time incorporated by the storytellers into shamanic song cycles. Numerous myths told of battles between birds and fish, fish and ants or between different species of birds. These myths may have been referring to real battles between totemic groups; more likely they referred to struggles, not necessarily physical, between rival groups of shamans.

THE PANTHEON

GODS AND SPIRITS were legion throughout the region particularly in Melanesia and the Marquesas where tribal groupings were separated by mountains and valleys. High gods were more prevalent in eastern Polynesia and Tonga than in Samoa and Micronesia where spirits predominated. Each Polynesian group developed its own pantheon often grouped around its three most important gods as in Tonga, Tahiti and Hawaii. Samoa had two main cults while the Marquesas and New Zealand had family pantheons which seemed to reflect multi-tribal diversity. Most gods had human or anthropomorphic forms though they could also be worshipped as inanimate objects.

▼ *Statue formed around a central 'eye of the fire', itself encircled by a snake biting its own tail; the ends are the heads of mythical fish.*

Myths Retold

THE ORIGIN OF MAKING FIRE

THE TRICKSTER GOD was always responsible for stealing fire and bringing it to earth. Olifat, the son of a woman of the Carolines and the sky father, accidentally saw his father through a hole in the coconut he was drinking and determined to visit him. He ascended to the heavens on the smoke from a burning pile of coconut shells. After various adventures in which he was killed by his relatives and restored by his father, he was given a place in the heavens. He sent a bird back to earth with fire in its beak which was placed in certain trees thus enabling men to obtain fire by rubbing sticks together.

Unlike the Micronesian tricksters the Maui heroes of Polynesia brought fire from underground. In the Maori versions Maui changed to a bird to visit the Netherworld where he fetched fire from the goddess Mahuika whose fingertips and toes glowed with fire. Mahuika gave him the end of a big toe as a firestick which he extinguished in a stream and returned until she had

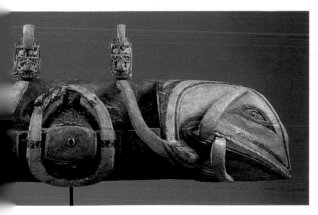

removed all her fingers and toes, but one. This she threw after him in anger with a curse that it would consume forests, but he called on the rain gods to save him. Enough seeds of fire were left in certain trees for firemaking.

SHAMANS OR SPIRIT-ANCHORS

THROUGHOUT THE Oceanic world ancestral and other gods were believed to communicate through mediums – persons of both sexes and of varying social status – who became possessed, shook violently and spoke in the voice of the spirit or god. These mediums were supposed to travel in the spirit world, heal diseases, change shape, levitate and fly to distant places in the flick of an eye. In Polynesia the mediums were known as 'spirit anchors'. A Samoan myth of a pigeon with nine heads

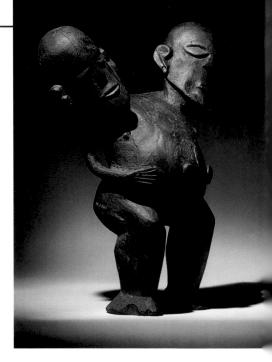

▲ *Double-headed wooden figure, possibly used for sorcery.*

refers to a shaman (symbolised by a winged creature) who had access to the nine heavens of Samoan mythology. In another myth Maui had eight heads suggesting that the most popular trickster was not fully adept. Tafaki, on the other hand, was a master shaman who had 'climbed' to the uppermost heaven in Maori legends. He acquired many characteristics of the Christian god which suggests that the storytellers were influenced by the ideas of early Spanish or whaling residents. Just as the shamans were shape-changers the gods also appeared in their favourite animal forms – particularly the shark and the octopus. The Tongan spirit Fehuluni regularly changed sex to entrap both men and women.

 **Myths Retold**

THE OCTOPUS AND THE RAT

THREE LAND ANIMALS once joined a party of birds to travel in a canoe. When a kingfisher picked a hole in the bottom of the canoe it filled and sank. The birds all flew off. The flying fish emulated them but fell into the water and found that it could swim. The hermit crab fell on to the reef below and found that it could come and go on the reef as it pleased him. The rat, however, floundered about expecting to drown until a passing octopus answered his cries of distress and agreed to take him to the shore. The rat refused to hang on to the tentacles so climbed onto the head of the octopus where he urinated and defecated on it. Indeed, he was so ratty that he would not jump off but insisted on his obliging carrier taking him to dry sand so that he would not get his feet wet. The rat then rudely asked the octopus to feel his head. On discovering the rat droppings the octopus was incensed: that is why it has tubercles on its head and why it always attacks the imitation rat used as a lure by fishermen.

THE SEARCH
FOR IMMORTALITY

A CARVED LINTEL from a Maori meeting house exhibited in the Wanganui Museum in New Zealand, replicated in many villages, shows Maui attempting to pass through the body of his ancestor Hinenuitepo, the personification of death. Maui, accompanied by a flock of birds, came upon the goddess asleep. Warning the birds to be silent Maui wriggled his way into her body. Hardly had he got his head inside when the birds could not control their mirth and the fantail's twitter woke the goddess who brought her giant thighs together in a thunderous clap and snapped Maui in two, ending his quest for immortality.

ASTRONOMICAL MYTHS

MANY OF THE EARLIEST myths were universal in type because they drew on the antiquity of star lore. As the Maori scholar Hare Hongi pointed out, many of the Greek and Oriental solar and star myths could only be interpreted properly when compared with their Maori variants which retained essential detail. Maui in particular was the demi-god who ordered, arranged and controlled the solar system. While the classic myth of his snaring the sun survived, his own cult was superseded by the cults of Rongo, Tane and Tangaroa. All events and seasons were determined by the movements of the heavenly bodies, and the gods associated with certain stars and planets became the tutelary gods of certain crops. The rising of the Pleiades signalled the coming of the wet season and was often an occasion of great excitement. In one Maori myth the Pleiades were seven white pigeons being snared by Tautoru the fowler or Orion.

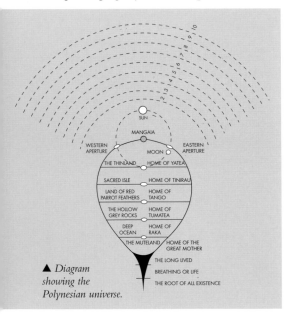

▲ *Diagram showing the Polynesian universe.*

Hina, the name of numerous goddesses and manifestations, was identified with phases of the moon, appearing in myths as the goddess respectively of death, childbirth, the tides, the west wind, fire, water and women's crafts, her styles being similar to those of the Virgin Mary.

 **Myths Retold**

MAUI SNARES THE SUN

WHEN MAUI WAS young the sun travelled so swiftly across the sky that his mother and other earth people did not have enough time to complete their work in the gardens. Maui determined to slow the sun down so, armed with strong ropes and a club, he travelled to the east to wait for the sun to appear. When the sun put his head into the snare Maui got his brothers to pull on the rope ends until the sun was completely at his mercy. According to the Hawaiians Maui lassoed six of the sun's legs or rays and lashed them to a tree. Maui then gave the sun a sound beating with the club which was said to be the jawbone of his grandmother. The sun was only released when it agreed to travel more slowly and allow the earth people more time to tend their gardens. This myth was retold to suit the conditions of many islands and formed part of the song cycles of Maui in Tonga and Samoa, Hawaii, New Zealand, the Tuamotus and the Marquesas.

HIKULE'O

HIKULE'O, AN ANCESTRAL DEITY from Samoa, was the great god of the Tu'i Tonga, or sacred king, of the Tongan Islands to whom first fruits were offered. The god dwelt in the mirror-image world of Pulotu. He had a reptilian tail like the god Dengei in Fiji which encircled the world tree and was tied down by his brothers to prevent him from wrecking the earth. He sometimes appeared as a white shark. When the Tu'i Tonga line passed through two females Hikule'o took on a female manifestation and is now regarded as a goddess on Tongatapu.

SOCIAL MYTHS – CREATION STORIES

THROUGHOUT OCEANIA myths were used to instil social values such as family obligations, the rights of the first born, respect for the sacred, condemnation of incest and, in the stratified societies, obedience to chiefs and priests. Although these social myths contained ancient elements and sometimes obsolete language they were constantly reworked and reinterpreted according to the political agenda of those controlling society. Creation myths, far from being the earliest, were often the most recently composed as they contained the guidelines for social interaction. As a general rule one finds that the most stratified societies had the most elaborate creation myths. While in parts of Melanesia and the subcultures of Micronesia and Polynesia there seemed to be little interest in how the world was formed (curiosity being confined to the first human beings) the creation chants elsewhere reached great poetic and philosophic heights. A hymn to Ta'aroa from the Society Islands resembles a hymn from the *Rig Veda* while the 'Kumulipo', the Hawaiian hymn of creation, composed as late as the eighteenth century, provides an evolutional account as opposed to spon-taneous creation.

These hymns provided an introduction to lengthy genealogies connecting the divine with the ruling families.

▲ *A statue to pay homage to the ancestors.*

 **Myths Retold**

THE LEGEND OF TIKI: A CREATION STORY

THE GOD TIKI lived in Havaiipo, the mirror-image world of darkness, where he commanded many spirits. He found that he was lonely so he went to the seashore and created a child in the sand which he then covered over and went away. Three days later he returned and was surprised to find a small hill where he had buried
the child. He scraped the loose sand away and found a beautiful woman whom he named Hinatunaone and who became his wife. A son and daughter were born who were able to procreate. Tiki decided to find them a place to live so he left Havaiipo and found a place in the ocean where he commanded the land of Nukuhiva to appear and placed his grandchildren there. Soon there were too many people and he looked over the water and commanded Uapou to rise. He now left Nukuhiva, where the people made an image of him in stone, but he still created new lands as the population increased: Uahuku in the east; Hivaoa in the south; Tahuata peopled from Uahuku; Mohutani as a resting place; and Fatuhiva peopled from Hivaoa.

ARCHETYPES

BESIDES TRICKSTERS, such as Qat in Melanesia and Maui, most early cults revolved around sea gods (Tinirau known from Japan to the Tuamotus, Tefatumoana and Tangaroa) and land gods (Nafanua). Gods who separated earth from heaven were also archetypal. The cult figures that next emerged were phallic fertility and war gods that were often interchangeable. Thus Rongo presided over agriculture in one group and war in another. Wild women with bulging eyes, bird men, and water monsters were recurring characters. Heroes, clowns, living gods and little people filled the mythic landscape.

◀ *Mask from New Guinea depicting a 'bird man', a typical character in Oceanic mythology.*

Myths Retold

HINA AND TUNA

THE HIGHBORN LADY Hina was a protected virgin living in Samoa, probably a female Tu'i Manu'a or high chief of Manu'a. A god in the form of an eel came to Samoa and lived in Hina's bathing pool. When Hina became pregnant everyone wanted to know who her man was and she replied 'It is the eel, the Shining One'. Her protectors bailed out the pool and cut the eel to pieces. She asked for the head to be buried properly and after five nights it had sprouted into a coconut tree which provided oil and shelter for their child.

The Tahitians and Tuamotuans incorporated the story into the Maui cycle. In the Tuamotuan version, Hina was the daughter-wife of Tiki, who introduced death into the world when she failed to revive him. She then took Tuna of the eternal waters as her lover. When she tired of him all her potential lovers were afraid of Tuna until Maui fought and killed him in an epic battle. Maui cut off the head which Hina planted, to become the coconut palm. The Tahitians told how Hina left the head by a stream while bathing and it sprouted.

SOCIAL MYTHS – NEW INSTITUTIONS

SOCIAL MYTHS WERE invented or completely changed following dramatic historical events. After tribal warfare it was not unusual for a peaceful fertility god to become a war god or a defeated war god to preside over a garden. With the collapse of the Samoan-oriented government of Tonga in the sixteenth or early seventeenth century new myths were invented to justify the use of the psychoactive kava plant as a drug of social control. At the same time the myth of the origin of the Tu'i Tonga was invented or restructured to reinforce the sacredness of the ruling lineage. The first Tu'i Tonga was not only given a divine father but he was also made exceptionally sacred as youngest son of the god reconstructed from shamanic dismemberment.

In the Society Islands when the cult-followers of Tane were defeated sometime early in the eighteenth century the god of dalliance 'Oro replaced his 'father' Ta'aroa as god of the firmament and principal war god. The 'Oro cult created a new priestly caste of players, the 'Arioi society, who acted out the new stories of the gods and served as a cultural guild to ensure mythological conformity.

POST-CHRISTIAN MYTHOLOGY

WITH THE INTRODUCTION of Christianity, first to Micronesia in the seventeenth century, then to Polynesia from the late eighteenth century and from the 1830s in Melanesia, there was rapid nominal conversion to the new religion. The contact experience led to the formation of a number of syncretist cults. In the Society Islands a major cult from 1826, known as Mamaia, was led by 'prophets' claiming to be possessed by Jesus, John the Baptist, Paul and the Virgin Mary. In Tonga and Samoa a shamanistic revival occurred soon after contact and several powerful shamans emerged who were regarded as 'living gods'. A cult named after its chief medium Siovili began in Samoa in the 1830s with transvestite priests possessed by Jesus

▲ *Temple image of the war god, Ku.*

and Samoan spirits. Feather cults occurred in Hawaii and the Gilbert Islands. Throughout Melanesia, there have been numerous millennial and traditional-type cults, many of them linked with expectations of European cargo sent from the heavens. These cults have introduced a number of new god names, from indigenous legendary characters to America's President Johnson.

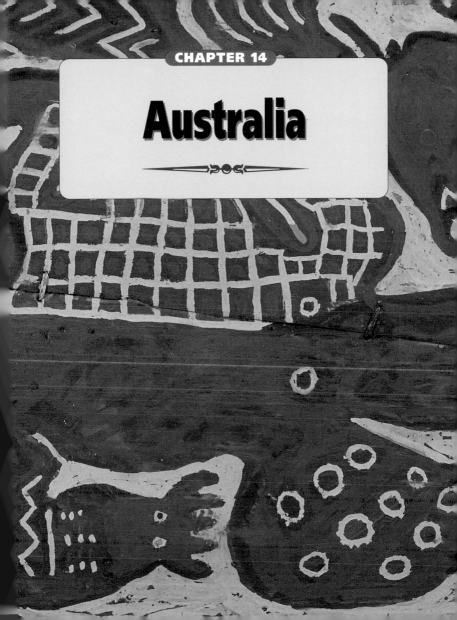

CHAPTER 14

Australia

Australia

HUMANS SETTLED AUSTRALIA during a time when the continent was linked by land to the islands of what is now Indonesia and Papua New Guinea. The earliest recorded evidence of human presence in Australia comes from the Upper Swan River region in Western Australia and dates to almost 40,000 years before the present. It has been estimated that at the time of European contact (1788), there were at least 300,000 people on the continent of Australia. Although difficult to estimate because of the rapid depopulation and dislocation of Aboriginal people that ensued shortly after European settlement, a conservative estimate is that there were 500 distinct tribes or dialect groups in Australia at the end of the eighteenth century.

N TERMS OF HUMAN lifestyle, the continent of Australia at the time of European contact was dominated by the hunting and foraging mode of subsistence (the Torres Strait Islands, though within the national boundaries of Australia, are more appropriately considered culturally to be part of southern Papua, at least traditionally). The climate and terrain in Australia varies markedly, from the arid desert of the major portion of the inland region, to the more fertile and watered valleys and watercourses of the coastal areas. However, even in the coastal areas of, for example, Queensland and South Australia, where abundant fish, vegetable and animal resources afforded the possibility of permanent residency, fixed habitation was rare. Populations moved over considerable distances, not only for the purposes of acquiring food, but to establish and maintain political, marital and ceremonial alliances between groups.

Despite their isolation on an island continent, Aboriginal Australians had regular and important contacts with the people of what is now Papua New Guinea, through the linking Torres Strait Islands, and to the islands of eastern Indonesia. Macassan traders regularly visited the coast of Arnhem Land, and the record and effects of these visits are recorded in the myth, song and painting of the Yolngu people of north-east Arnhem Land.

Anthropologically, the Aboriginal populations throughout Australia first became renowned for the intricacy of their kinship

▲ *Aboriginal bark painting depicting an episode from clan ancestral history.*

◀ *Traditional aboriginal style art showing animals.*

organisation. In all areas, relatives were divided by categories called sections and subsections, based on the intersecting of male and female descent principles. The sections and subsections stipulated what category a person's spouse should fall into and therefore made marriage subject to specific kinship rules. These sections and subsections also fulfilled important ceremonial functions, such as initiation and the transmission of secret religious knowledge.

CREATOR BEINGS

THROUGHOUT AUSTRALIA the subject of the great majority of myths are the wanderings, journeys and actions of certain ancestral creator beings. Characteristically, they moved across the landscape, creating its notable features and distinguishing landmarks, such as waterholes, mountains, specific

rock formations, and also bringing into being the various species – human and non-human – which now populate the earth. For example, in Arnhem Land, the Wagilak Sisters are centrally important creator beings. As they travelled north from their origin in central Australia, they plunged their digging sticks into the ground at various spots. From these spots, waterholes gushed forth.

While they created the landscape and its plant and animal species, these creator beings also named the places they visited and the species they created to inhabit them. Along with the names, the beings also sang songs in which these acts of naming featured. Thus, myth is commonly recited through the medium of song throughout Aboriginal Australia. For example, from a portion of the myth of the two

▲ *Figure believed to have been created by clan ancestral beings who formed the landscape during the Dreamtime.*

Mamandabari heroes among the Walbiri of central Australia: they pass a waterhole named

Wurulyuwanda. On the waterhole they see whistling ducks and galah cockatoos eating grass seeds. They name these creatures by 'singing' them.

TRACKS

THE ROUTES OF THE creator beings are referred to as their 'tracks'. The tracks of important ancestor beings characteristically went across and through the countries of different groups of people. Thus, it is common that no local group, clan or language group owns or knows a complete myth. Usually, a local group knows the segment of the myth that narrates the story of the being while it sojourned through their country. This necessitates different groups coming together periodically in order that the ritual recreation of the entire myth can be accomplished. For example, in central Australia, the two Mamandabari heroes travelled over an enormous area; no one man knew the myth in its entirety. This necessitates custodians from different areas coming together to perform the Gadjari ritual which is based on this myth cycle.

The concept of totemism is integral to Australian Aboriginal mythology. This is broadly speaking the use of a natural species or feature as an emblem of a person or group. Each clan has a variety of different totemic species and items that are specific to it, and which differentiate it from other clans in the same area. Since all totems are associated with a particular place, totem designations are always designations about which locality a person is associated with in specific ways.

▲ *Aboriginal female figure, which represents different sacred beings in different clans.*

Myths Retold

THE WAGILAK MYTH (NORTH-EAST ARNHEM LAND, NORTHERN TERRITORY)

AT THE BEGINNING of time the Wagilak Sisters set off on foot towards the sea, naming places, animals and plants as they went. One of them was pregnant and the other had a child. Before their departure they had both had incestuous relations with men of their own moiety [marriage class]. After the birth of the younger sister's child, they continued their journey and one day stopped near a water hole where the great python Yurlunggor lived.... The older sister polluted the water when her menstrual blood flowed into it. The outraged python came out, caused a deluge of rain and a general flood and then swallowed the women and their children. When the python raised himself the waters covered the surface of the earth and its vegetation. When he lay down again the flood receded.

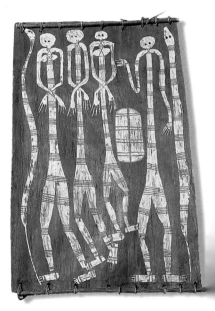

▲ *Male and female figures accompanied by snakes.*

Serpents of all kinds recur in Australian Aboriginal mythology, from the Rainbow Serpent which is found in its archetypal form among the groups of the central desert, to the Carpet Snake, whose dreaming tracks stretch along the coast of eastern Australia. Throughout Australia, the Rainbow Serpent is an important figure and motif in myth. The serpent is usually of immense size and lives in deep waterholes. The Rainbow Serpent appears in many guises throughout Australia. In central Australia, the *wanambi* travelled from Aneri Spring, near the South Australia-Northern Territory border, to the Musgrave Ranges. At times, the *wanambi* made long journeys around the circumference of Mount Connor. The tracks he made at this time are often symbolised in painting by large concentric circles. The path that the *wanambi* travelled became marked with rock formations and sandhills visible today.

The groups near the Proserpine River in North Queensland believed that rain is transformed into quartz crystals at the spot where the rainbow touches the ground. In south-eastern Queensland, the rainbow, or *takkan* among Kabi Kabi speakers,

▲ *A Sacred disc representing ancestors and their weapons.*

THE ALL FATHER

IN SOUTH-EASTERN AUSTRALIA, we can speak of a single male creator being, whom the early anthropologist A. W. Howitt referred to as the 'All Father'. Among the people of the Lower Murray River area of South Australia, he is referred to as Ngurunderi; further up the Murray River, he is called Baiame, Daramulun, and other names. In other parts of Australia, the feminine principle is also important and it is possible to speak of a Great Mother: in north-east Arnhem Land, the two Djanggawul Sisters are called 'daughters of the sun'; they represent the sun and its life-giving properties.

would sometimes reveal the presence of such crystals in the bodies of men. These men would be able to become *gundil*, or sorcery-doctors, capable of healing and other feats of magic.

THE DREAMING

THE CONCEPT OF THE Creation Time, when the ancestral beings made the world in the form in which present-day people encounter it, is widespread in Aboriginal thought. This is commonly called the 'Dreamtime' or 'the

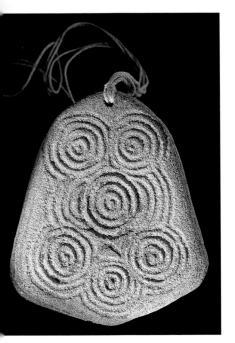

▲ *Sacred discs represent the immortal spirit, the patterns represent a sacred site.*

Dreaming' in Australia. The Walbiri call this period *djugurba* which, strictly speaking, refers to the stories and attendant designs about ancestral actions during this creative time. It means an act of creation which was an actual event in ancestral times but is still ongoing and still exerting creative power in the human present. Access to the significance of ancestral creation is often gained through the power of dreams, which is why the term is used in this way.

The Walbiri say they dream themselves of the designs their ancestors are supposed to have laid down across the country. In other areas of Australia, a woman may, shortly before learning she is pregnant, dream of a species, or of a certain place. This is interpreted as indicating the totemic affiliation of the child and its spiritual progenitor.

 **Myths Retold**

CREATION MYTH: UNAMBAL (NORTH-WEST AUSTRALIA)

IN THE BEGINNING only sky and earth existed. Ungud, the Creator Being, lived under the earth in the form of a great python. Ungud is associated with both the earth and the water. The sky being Wallanganda is associated with the Milky Way. Wallanganda is supposed to have made everything, but it was Ungud who made the water deep and caused the rain to fall, and this is how life began on earth. Together, Wallanganda and Ungud created everything.

However, the acts of creation only occurred at night, when the two beings dreamed. Ungud transformed himself into the beings of which he dreamed, while Wallanganda also dreamed the beings to which he gave birth. By means of a spiritual force, Wallanganda projected these dreamed beings into red, black and white designs, the images of which, according to the Unambal, can still be found in caves and rocks.

In Arnhem Land, the Djanggawul and Wagilak creator beings were responsible for creating and naming all the species and places in the landscape. They also placed sacred emblems, *rangga*, in waterholes. The *rangga* are recreated by living human beings, as adjuncts of ritual re-enactments of these primordial acts of mythic creation.

▲ *An incised wooden sacred board.*

ANCESTORS

ANOTHER ASPECT OF this inscriptive mythic activity is that the bodies of the ancestral creator beings themselves become detached and fixed in the landscape. The ancestor beings, for example, among the Aranda of the central desert, left parts of their bodies in the places they travelled. A married woman could feel a sudden pain inside her body which she recognises as an early sign of pregnancy. Later, she would show her husband the exact spot at which this sensation occurred. After consulting with the leading old men of his own clan, the man learns which original totemic ancestor either dwelt in this locality or visited it on one of his wanderings. It is then concluded that this totemic ancestor has caused the women's pregnancy, either by entering into her body himself, or else by hurling a small bull-roarer at her hips and thus causing the pains. The child will belong to the totem of this ancestor.

The relationship between myth and ritual is central to Australian Aboriginal ceremonial life, and to its graphic representation by way of various visual media, primarily painting and carving. To simplify matters, it can be said that the myths provide the charters or templates for human ritual action, whereby people attempt to keep ancestral creativity and fertility alive and working on behalf of present-day human groups.

MYTH AND RITUAL

THE MYTHS DETAIL important acts of creation and naming. They detail the power of ancestral fertility. In this respect, they demonstrate the importance of gender difference as a general principle of Aboriginal social and cosmological organisation. Throughout Australia, much important sacred lore and ceremonial knowledge is in the hands of men. Women were traditionally forbidden to hear or view anything pertaining to men's knowledge, often on pain of death. In western Arnhem Land myth, for example, after Yirawadbad passed on the *ubar* men's ceremony

▲ *Artwork on bark showing a hunter, a kangaroo and other figures.*

to Nadulmi, Nadulmi asked the bird Djig, 'Shall we show it to the women?' and in response was told, 'No, this is only for older men, we cannot show it to women and children'. More recently, anthropologists have also discovered the previously unreported existence of parallel domains of women's religious knowledge in central and south Australia. This knowledge is described as exclusively the right of women to control, pass on and manage.

MYTH AND ART IN AUSTRALIA

THROUGHOUT AUSTRALIA, but particularly in the Northern Territory, graphic designs are an important adjunct to the public narration of myth for ritual and ceremonial purposes. In central Australia, people such as the Walbiri and Pintupi have become renowned for the iconographic designs they paint on various surfaces – for example, the human body, sand, sacred artefacts such as shields and bull-roarers, and more recently with acrylic paints on canvas – which depict certain mythic episodes. In Arnhem Land, local painters inscribe their designs on bark and wood carvings.

▲ *A bark painting depicting an octopus capturing a fisherman.*

Common motifs in central Australia include the concentric circle, which can stand for a camp, waterhole, person, tree or ceremonial ground, connected by a series of dotted patterns depicting the movement of an ancestral being from place to place. In Arnhem Land, designs tend to be less abstract but are also concerned with the visual representation of certain mythic episodes of ancestral movement and creation.

In both areas, the knowledge of these designs and the rights to paint them are governed by an elaborate social and political system, which distributes access to sacred knowledge unevenly within the community. The strategic revelation of secret-sacred designs in the course of public ritual is a major factor in the social impact of ritual itself.

NGURUNDERI (LOWER MURRAY RIVER, SOUTH AUSTRALIA)

NGURUNDERI TRAVELLED down the Murray River, in search of the great Murray Cod (*pondi*). He speared the fish and it swam away, thrashing its tail and widening the river to its present great size. Ngurunderi sent a signal to his brother-in-law Nepele. Nepele waited for the fish and speared it near Point McLeay (Raukkan). The two men cut the fish up and, throwing bits of fish into Lake Alexandrina, called out the name of every fish species now found there, and each fish was brought into being in this way. With the last piece, they said, 'You keep being Murray Cod' ....

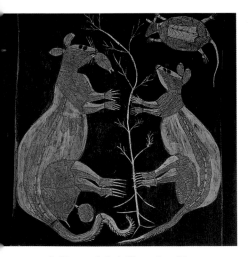

▲ *X-ray style bark illustration of kangaroo.*

Ngurunderi pursued his two wives, who ran away from him after a quarrel. At the place known as Larlangangel, he lifted his canoe and placed it into the sky, where it became the Milky Way.

After pursuing the women further, he came upon them at Encounter Bay. He caused a great storm to appear which drowned the women, who turned into the two small islands called The Pages, off Kangaroo Island. Afterwards, Ngurunderi himself crossed over to Kangaroo Island. Sitting under a casuarina tree, he dived into the water first to cleanse his spirit, and eventually died and went into the sky.

COMPONENTS OF AUSTRALIAN MYTHOLOGY

THERE ARE THREE COMPONENTS to Australian mythology and its religious significance. The first is the body of mythology itself, considered as a set of stories. Second is the system of graphic designs which provide a visual form of the actions of myths. Third there is the country itself, the creation and distinctive features of which the myth and visual art provides an origin account. Thus, as Ronald and Catherine Berndt conclude, myth is always localised: knowledge and control of a mythic episode and its attendant ritual-artistic complex is always restricted to the present-day custodians of the sites to which the myth gives an account in religious and cosmological terms.

The songs, the form through which myths are commonly recited, characteristically focus on key words and references which themselves are connected with specific localities within the country. The songs provide a way to help people remember appropriate details concerning the sacred history of the site in question.

WANDJINA

WANDJINA ARE CLAN SPIRIT beings in the Kimberley region of Western Australia. They are named creator-beings, each of whom is responsible for forming a portion of the landscape, its animals and plants and significant topographical features. The Wandjina were the first people. Each one entered a cave and laid himself down and died when their creative activity was finished. The cave paintings of the Wandjina that are found today are considered to the literal incarnation of these ancestral beings. They are approached by present day Aboriginal inhabitants to aid in increasing the fertility of plants and animals upon which Aboriginal people depend for food.

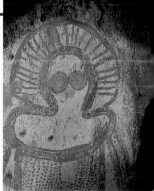

▲ *Wandjina are ancestral beings from the sea and the sky.*

CHAPTER 15

Africa

Africa

IN THE HISTORY OF THE cosmos, there were three ages: the first was a golden time when God, human and animal existed in a perfect harmony. During the second period, the age of creation, the creator god formed the earth, along with humans and animals. It was a period of differentiation, as God originated life by using himself as model, attempting to re-create the golden age on earth. But the perfect age was gone forever, it could not be transferred to the earth, and the earth and humankind were flawed. It was a period of chaos and order, of fear and hope, of the diminishing of the past and the promise of a new future. The chaos-order dualism was sometimes seen as the nature of the creator god.

▲ *Wooden double figure of ancestors.*

IN SOME RELIGIOUS SYSTEMS, this creator was a divine trickster, both a benevolent and creative god, and an unpredictable and frequently destructive trickster. He was a god who had within him both life and death. As time went on, the godly, creative part of the divine trickster and the dualistic god moved further away from humans and earth, and the destructive part of the divine trickster and dualistic god went to the earth, with the echo of perfection and the potential for good remaining. This third age was the contemporary age, a realm in which humans and gods have become remote from each other, in which humans, through their rituals and traditions, seek to duplicate that long lost perfect age.

THE CREATOR GOD

IN AFRICAN RELIGIONS, the creator god takes various forms. God may be a wholly positive being, or a dualistic force composed of both good and evil, order and chaos. The divine trickster is a symbol of the period of transformation that characterises the age of creation: as he moves from the perfect or golden age to the contemporary age, he embodies the changes – the move is from the perfection of God (the creative side of the divine trickster) to the flawed human (the destructive side of the divine trickster).

In the contemporary age, the divine part of this trickster is gone, and what remains is the profane trickster, an unpredictable character whose residual creativeness is seen in the illusions that he establishes, whose amorality is witnessed in his outrageous conduct, often anti-social. From chaos comes order: the struggle between order and chaos, between creativity and destructiveness. That primal cosmological struggle is our struggle writ large. The dualistic god is everyman and everywoman, struggling with the two sides of their nature. The overcoming of chaos and the ordering of the world becomes our promise and our hope, but the divine trickster and the

▲ *Gods were believed to have two sides to their character.*

profane trickster, ever amoral and ever ready to obscure order with chaos, is a part of us as well.

MYTH AND METAPHOR

MYTH BECOMES A constant metaphor for what humans can become, moving from the chaos of their lives to a kind of eternal order. It becomes a

ritualising of their everyday lives, a linkage to their gods. But while they may long for that sense of order, there can be danger in yearning for a oneness with God if that means a loss of free will. The myths often begin with a familiar domestic scene, something the audience can at once relate to: an outrageous human activity; a bride or groom quest; someone under attack. From out of these often anti-social events comes new life. The outrage is purposeful because it represents chaos; the contrasting creation that emerges represents order. Humans long for that original completeness that they have lost. Within them, a battle rages – between the desire for oneness and the demand for independence. This battle they witness as they move closer to the contemporary age, and they see it especially in the trickster character and in the hero, where the struggle between free-willed humanity and God-related unity goes on. That unity is lost as they move closer to their world, and the profane trickster becomes the spectre of what humans could become if they move away from God, toward amorality.

▲ *Male and female statues of ancestors.*

THE AGE OF CREATION

THE MYTHMAKER builds his repertory of stories around an initial sense of oneness that was surrendered, to be followed by an effort to regain the lost accord. Considering the many stories that comprise the African myth systems, a number of common threads can be discerned.

God created the universe, shaped it, and then created life. Two forces contended during the age of creation: forces of chaos and order. In some myths, these forces were extensions of the creator god – his son and daughter, for example – embodying his destructive and creative sides, or a

▲ *Female statue with infant, representing maternity.*

divine trickster, at once life-giving and death-dealing. Such divinities mirror the transformation that characterises the age of creation, a time during which these opposing energies were clashing in the cosmos. So it was that the world and humanity were created, and the struggles writ large in the cosmos became woven into life on the earth and into human nature: in every human being can be found in microcosm the forces that existed in the earliest days when God was in the process of crafting the universe.

KAGGEN

THE CREATOR GOD, when cast in the role of divine trickster, suggests the order-chaos duality of the creator, this character mirroring the duality of the universe. Kaggen (San/Botswana, Namibia, S. Africa), a mantis, is a divine trickster. Revealing his trickster nature, he steals the sheep of some primal ticks, his dispute with the ticks establishing a necessary disjuncture in the mythical world that will lead to its dismantling and reconstruction in earthly terms. The ticks, who possess shelter, clothing and domesticated animals, become the victims of the divine trickster, as he removes them from their world, that world providing the initial infrastructure of early San civilisation.

 **Myths Retold**

THE COSMIC EGG

MEBEGE (Fang, Pahouin/Congo African Republic, Congo, Gabon) was lonely. He pulled some hair from under his right arm, took substance from his brain and lifted a pebble from the sea. He blew on these three items and they formed an egg. Mebege gave the egg to Dibobia, a spider who hung between the sky and the sea. When the egg became hot, Mebege descended and put his sperm on it. The egg cracked and three people emerged. Mebege took a strand of raffia and worked it into a cross, establishing the four directions. He took hair from under his arms, and the lining of his brain, rolled these into a ball, blew on them and created termites and worms. These dispersed in all directions, and with their droppings they built up the earth upon which the three humans stepped.

◄ *A rare Fang (Mebege) mask.*

THE DUALISTIC GOD

TO DRAMATISE AND symbolise the forces active during the early creative period, God is sometimes depicted as a complex, ambiguous figure, both creative and destructive, two contending forces within a single being which becomes a means of revealing the transformational processes at work during this time. Gulu (Ganda/IJganda) is such a creator god. He has a daughter, Nambi, who represents his creative side, and a son, Walumbe, who symbolises his destructive side. Nambi, married to the first man, Kintu, brings life into the world, while her brother, Walumbe, brings death. Kintu and Nambi refuse to share their children with Walumbe, and he therefore begins to take them through death.

GOD'S FOOTPRINTS

WHEN LESA (Lamba/Zambia), the high god and supreme being, visited the earth in the beginning under the name of Luchyele, he came from the east, arranging the countryside – rivers, hills, trees, grass. He came with numbers of people, planting the nations and the communities in their respective places, passing on to the west. On the Itabwa plain can be seen the footprints of Lesa and his people as they passed. The stones were soft like mud, but as soon as Lesa passed the mud hardened, and the marks have been preserved ever since.

▼ *A lone tree dominates the African plain.*

HEAVEN AND EARTH

INITIALLY, THERE WERE connections between God and the mortals he created, between the place where God resided and the earthly home of humans. There was commerce between the heavens and the earth. The daughter of God could visit the earth and there walk among the humans; humans could move to the heavens and visit with and live among the gods. The creator god moved on the face of the earth, bringing new life into being, reshaping and detailing the place he had brought into existence. He met with humans, lived among humans and the humans were his children.

Something occurred to provoke a separation between heaven and earth, between God and his creations – a disobedience, a struggle, an error, fate – and death came into the world. Humans erred and incurred the wrath of God, a message of eternal life sent by God to the earth was somehow tragically intercepted or misconstrued, God became disgusted by the activities of humans; human vanity triumphed over modesty and selflessness. And so a gap was created between heaven and earth, and the gap would yawn into a chasm. And in the end, the break was complete. Humans were on their own.

▼ *Wild beasts, such as the crocodile, were both feared and respected.*

Myths Retold

GOD RETREATS FROM THE EARTH

ABEREWA, THE PRIMORDIAL woman, pounded her mortar with a pestle as she prepared food for her children, and the pestle routinely bumped against the sky. Annoyed, Nyame (Akan, Asante/Ghana), went away. Then Aberewa attempted to re-establish her relationship with him. To do that, she got many mortars, piling them one on top of the other. In the process, she moved closer and closer to the sky. Now, to get to Nyame, she needed just one more mortar. She asked a child to get one for her, but he could find none. In desperation, she told him to take one of the mortars bottom of the pile. He did so, and, when the mortar was removed, the entire tower collapsed.

▲ *A mask of Nimba, the Baga's goddess of fertility.*

HUMANS ENTREAT GOD

LONG AGO, PEOPLE were plagued by wild beasts. And they wondered: if Nguleso, the supreme being (Kakwa/Sudan), exists, why then were they were eaten by these creatures? Some concluded that it was because they were not acting properly; that Nguleso sent the animals to punish them. But when they considered the men who had died, they determined that God had treated them unfairly, because these men had not taken others' property, they had not entered the houses of other men. They therefore called together the spirits, Nguloki, and through them called upon Nguleso in the sky.

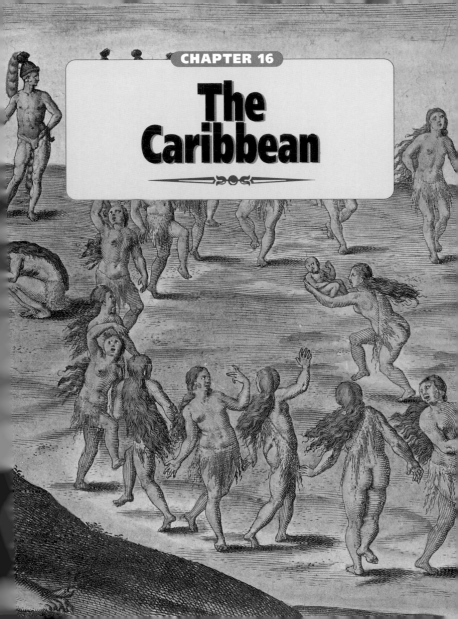

CHAPTER 16

The Caribbean

The Caribbean

THE ISLANDS OF THE Caribbean offered a variety of landscapes to early Amerindian peoples. By 5000 BCE in Trinidad, the first humans had arrived from the tropical rainforests and savannahs of mainland South America. They were hunters and gatherers, and quickly adapted to island life, moving north in sea-going canoes to Tobago, Grenada, Martinique and beyond. These first human settlers must have seen the region as a unique blend of sea, land and sky – quite different from the endless rivers and forests of their homeland.

▲ *The sea plays a fundamental role in the life of the people of the Caribbean.*

AROUND 300 BCE, a new wave of settlers arrived from the mouth of the Orinoco River in Venezuela, bringing with them a settled, village life, agriculture and the kind of shamanic religion and mythic worldview typical of tropical rainforest societies in lowland Amazonia. These people grew manioc (cassava) and sweet potato, and made the first pottery in the Caribbean. With sharp stone axes they felled trees and cleared areas for fields and villages – changing the Caribbean landscape for ever. By 300 CE, they had spread throughout the

▲ *Columbus is greeted by the* caciques.

Caribbean, the sea continuing to play an important role in their everyday and religious lives. Christopher Columbus arrived in the Caribbean in 1492. At this time, the region was occupied by two main Amerindian groups – the Taíno (Arawak) in the Greater Antilles, and the Carib in the Lesser Antilles. Taíno society had evolved out of the previous migrations from South America, and was based on manioc cultivation, which supported large villages ruled by chiefs (*caciques*). In Puerto Rico and Hispaniola they played a rubber ball-game in great stone-lined courts. Taíno religion was based on ancestor worship,

ZEMÍS

THE INDIGENOUS PEOPLES of the Caribbean did not build temples or cities adorned with monumental art. They represented their mythic heroes and gods in carvings of wood, stone and shell. These objects, called *zemís*, possessed supernatural powers, both in their finished form and in the raw material from which they were made. Carved wood *zemís* took the form of birds, human figures and elaborately polished ceremonial benches called *duhos*, on which shamans and chiefs reclined during their narcotic trance journeys to the spirit world. Greenstone frogs, enigmatic faces with staring eyes, spiral decorations and half-human, half-animal beings represented the powers of nature in visual form.

▲ *A zemís stone with its three cardinal points to the sky, the dead and the land of the living.*

with their shamans contacting the spirits by snuffing the hallucinogenic powder *cohoba*.

The Caribs appear to have been late arrivals in the Caribbean, sailing large sea-going canoes from South America around 1000 CE and colonising the Lesser Antilles, especially Dominica, St Vincent and Guadeloupe. Carib society and religion were less sophisticated than that of the Taíno, with villages centred on the mens' meeting house, and their society ruled by war-chiefs. One of the most dramatic and misrepresented aspects of Carib culture was cannibalism. This usually took the form of the ritual consumption of the powdered bones of a relative mixed with liquid in a ceremonial drink. Such practices were misunderstood by Europeans, but played an important role in Carib religion and mythology.

CARIBBEAN MYTHOLOGY

THE MYTHOLOGIES of indigenous Caribbean peoples were similar in many ways to those of their better-known neighbours in Mesoamerica and South America. In particular, they shared ideas of successive creations of the cosmos, and of the spiritual animacy of the physical world. What sets these myths apart is our fragmentary knowledge of them, and the social and physical settings of the Caribbean island landscapes in which they are set. Central to an understanding of Taíno myth is metamorphosis: the ability to change outward appearance from animal to human forms or vice versa.

Behaviour and feelings could also alter, with mythic figures having superhuman animal strength, while animals could possess human sensibilities. Some animals could be tribal ancestors, some trees were the spirits or souls of dead chiefs or *caciques*. The souls of the dead were believed to hide themselves during daylight hours, only to emerge at night to seek out and eat the guava fruit. Taíno myths, like all myths, are philosophical statements of how they regarded and made sense of their uniquely fragmented natural world. The events of Taíno myth take place not in linear, but in mythic time, where movement, nearness and distance have little meaning.

Myths Retold

CREATION OF THE TAÍNO WORLD

CARIBBEAN MYTHOLOGY is less well known than the epics from Mesoamerica and South America. Nevertheless important, if fragmentary, evidence has survived of various creation stories. According to the Taíno chiefs (*caciques*) of Hispaniola, the creation of the universe spanned five eras. The first began when the Supreme Spirit, Yaya, killed his rebellious son, placing the bones in a gourd which he suspended from the rafters of his house.

On examining the gourd one day, Yaya and wife saw that the bones had transformed into fish, which they ate. In a variation of this story, the quadruplet sons of Itiba Cahubaba, 'Bloodied Aged Mother', who had died in childbirth, arrived in Yaya's garden. One of the brothers retrieved the gourd and they all gorged themselves on the fish it contained. Upon hearing Yaya returning they hastily

▲ *Carribean myth tells of how the oceans were created by Yaya.*

replaced the gourd, but it broke, spilling water full of fish which covered the earth and became the ocean. The brothers fled to their grandfather's land but when one of them asked for some cassava bread, the old man became enraged and spat on the boy's back. This spittle transformed into the narcotic *cohoba* which all Taíno shamans used as a gateway to the spirit world.

GUAYAHONA

GUAYAHONA IS ONE OF the most significant archetypal figures in Taíno mythology. As a cult hero, he departs from the cave of origin in Hispaniola and journeys westwards to the island of Guanín – the name given to the alloy of gold and copper revered by the Taíno. Thus, apart from calling the Taíno out from the bowels of the earth, Guayahona undertakes distinctly shamanic journeys in cosmic time to mythic places full of bright spirit power. In such events, the role and identity of human shaman and mythical being are fused with the symbolism of cosmic brilliance which recreates the world through ritual.

▶ *Jamaican with local produce. Cooking signifies civilised life for the Taíno.*

MEANINGS OF TAÍNO MYTHS

TAÍNO CREATION MYTHS are often difficult to explain due to scanty (and often confused) historical material and an almost complete lack of comparative anthropological evidence after the European conquest. What does seem clear, however, is that the god Yaya is a prime mover deity who personifies cosmic time, and that the four brothers who take his gourd full of fish are lesser but more active supernatural beings. Itiba Cahubaba, their mother, is probably Mother Earth from whom all life comes. When one of the brothers asks his grandfather for cassava bread, he is in fact discovering the use of fire used to bake the food. Cooking is the essence of civilised life. The

Taíno used metaphor and allusion in their myth of the creation of people. Caonao is not in fact a province of Hispaniola, but a magical place full of the brilliance of gold and gems. During the third, civilising period of cosmic time, Guahayona travels to various islands, and is given shiny gifts. This has been seen as a mythical account of a rite of passage, during which Guahayona acquires the symbols of tribal leadership and power.

TAÍNO GODS AND SPIRITS

THE TAÍNO PEOPLE WORSHIPPED both ancestors and nature, personifying the supernatural forces of both as powerful gods. Sacred zem' images of stone and wood represented these powerful supernatural beings. The two major Taíno deities were Yúcahu, the 'spirit of cassava' – the staple food of the Taíno – and Atabey, goddess of human fertility. In a world of violently destructive weather, the Taíno also worshipped a female deity, Guabancex, the 'Lady of the Winds', mistress of hurricanes. As with Amerindians elsewhere, the gods and spirits of the Caribbean Taíno symbolised their intimate relationship with the natural forces which shaped the world.

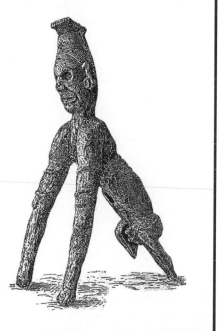

▶ *Opiel Guabiron, the door-keeper to the Underworld.*

Myths Retold

CREATION OF THE FIRST PEOPLE

THE SECOND ERA of Taíno cosmogony was the creation of the first people. According to one account, there were two caves in a land called Caonao on the island of Hispaniola. From one of the caves, the Taíno emerged. When one man neglected his guard duties at the mouth of the cave he was turned to stone by the sun. The others, who had gone fishing, were captured by the sun and turned into trees. One of these called Guahayona washed himself with the *digo* plant and went out before sunrise. But he was caught by the sun, and changed into a bird which sings at dawn. From the second cave, came other, less numerous people of the Caribbean, those who did not share Taíno customs or identity. The second era ends with Guahayona calling to those remaining in the cave to come forth and populate the fertile islands of the Caribbean. In the third era, humans became civilised and women were created as sexual partners for men. During the fourth era, the Taíno spread over the Caribbean, perfected cassava production, lived in well ordered villages and developed a sweet sounding tongue. Columbus' arrival marked the end of the fourth era. The calamitous fifth era saw the disappearance of Taíno society by European maltreatment, disease and assimilation.

▲ *Columbus watches the sacrifice of a baby to the gods.*

THE ORIGINS OF THE WORLD

THE MAIN THEMES OF Caribbean, especially Taíno, mythology, concern the origins of the world and the emergence of people from what appears to be a physical place, but which is actually a golden land located in mythic time. This links the physical and supernatural worlds, providing a mythic charter for the social order of Taíno society. Similarly, the ability to change form, to deceive by physical appearance, is a recurring motif. Taíno myths play on the idea of metamorphosis, integrating everyday and sacred life, acknowledging the presence of death, but infusing spiritual power into the very fabric of their society.

▲ *The physical world is linked with the supernatural in Taíno mythology.*

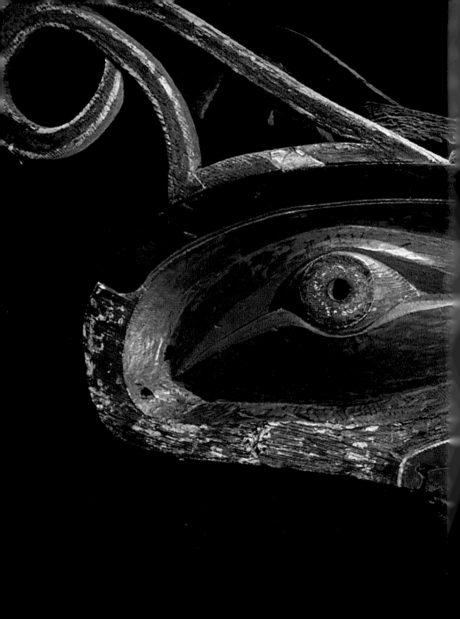

CHAPTER 17

North America

North America

THE ORIGINS OF THE natives of North America may be traced down the ages to a time, as distant as 60,000 years ago, when a colourful horde made its way up from the warm plains of Central Asia, north-eastwards into Siberia. They did not stop at Siberia's boundaries; they crossed from the Chukotka Peninsula into America – for at that time a land or ice bridge connected Chukotka with what is now Alaska.

THEY WERE HUNTERS and gatherers, living on the edge of game herds: hunters of mastodon and mammoth, musk ox and caribou, salmon and trout; gatherers of roots, plants and berries. From Alaska, generations of these people moved down the Columbia River that flowed to the warmer regions in the south, and across the Rocky Mountains.

They met strangers, fought with some and banded together with others. They found bison, then buffalo and followed them south across the plains, eastwards to the Atlantic, all the way south along the Sierra Madre Oriental, over the Mexican Plains, through rain-

▼ *Rivers have helped carve the rugged terrain that is North America.*

forests and into the jungles of
Yucatan. They settled and
moved, learning to use the
bow and bola, chipping
flint, weaving baskets,
making clay pots.

They travelled so far
that today ties of language,
culture and physical
appearance (high
cheekbones, slanted eyes,
darkish skin) still loosely
connect the Indians of Peru
and Bolivia with the Eskimos
of Siberia and Alaska, the Huron
and Iroquois of New York State with
the Chukchi and Koryak of north-
eastern Siberia.

▲ *Hide painting of a post-
hunt buffalo dance.*

There were as many tribes as there were 'stars in the sky', and they spoke at
least 300 languages. But they were always under pressure to move on. A
turning point came in 1492 when Christopher Columbus landed in the New
World. Thinking he had arrived in India, he mistakenly called the peoples
'Indios'; so the English followed suit and called them 'Indians'. Later the
French added *peaux rouges*, 'redskins'. Over the next four centuries, from 1492
to 1890, the native Americans found their lands invaded by several million
Europeans. During that time, particularly in the terrible 30-year span 1860–90,
much of the culture and civilisation of the native Americans was destroyed.

All the same, the Old Ones remembered stories told before the white man
came, stories of their tribes' own special creation and of the beginnings of
things in their own culture, when the people and the gods and the animals all
walked the hunting grounds and talked together.

ORAL TRADITION

THE NATIVE AMERICAN oral tradition does not easily divide into myths and other forms of storytelling (e.g. legends or folktales). The peoples themselves mostly use the term 'stories', distinguishing 'true stories' about the present world, and 'mythic stories' that describe events which happened in an earlier time before human beings appeared.

All myths represent a true account of tribal origins and, in many instances, they sanction institutions and rites. They are therefore sacred, helping to explain the cosmic and social order, as well as relations between humans and gods. Because the peoples had no written language, their stories were not set down on paper until white men travelling among the tribes from the 1830s recorded them. Each village had at least one old man who knew the tales and acted them out, imitating the various characters with a growl, squeal, roar or groan. And the hearers would respond in kind at certain points.

▲ 'Hole-in-the-Sky' pole, decorated with mythical and historical events.

In the days before the US government confined native peoples to reservations, the tribes had extensive inter-tribal contacts, as a result of which tales were exchanged, so the same stories may be found, albeit in different variants, all over the continent.

 **Myths Retold**

THE STORYTELLING STONE

THERE WAS ONCE an orphan who grew up strong and wise. One day, his aunt gave him a bow and arrows, saying, 'It is time for you to learn to hunt. Go to the forest and bring back food.' He set off early next morning and shot three birds. At about midday, the sinew that held the feathers of his arrow came loose, and he sat down upon a flat-topped stone to mend it.

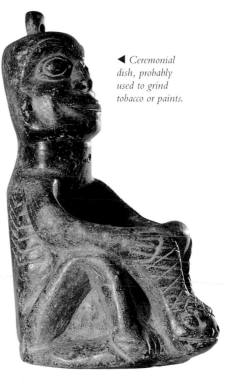

◀ *Ceremonial dish, probably used to grind tobacco or paints.*

Suddenly he heard a deep voice, 'Shall I tell you a story?'

He looked up, but there was no one there. 'Shall I tell you a story?' came the voice again.

The boy began to feel afraid. He looked in every direction, yet still could see nobody. When the voice called out again, he realised that it was coming from the stone on which was sitting.

'Shall I tell you a story?' 'What are stories?' asked the boy.

'Stories are what happened in the long-ago time. My stories are like the stars that never fade.'

When the stone had finished one story, it began another.

All the while the boy sat, head bowed, listening. Towards sundown, the stone suddenly said, 'We will rest now. Come again tomorrow and bring the people of your camp to listen to my stories. Tell each to bring a gift.'

That evening the boy told the whole camp about the story-telling stone. And so it was, next morning, the people followed him into the forest. Each person put meat or bread or tobacco on the stone before sitting down. When all was quiet the stone spoke.

'Now I shall tell you stories of the long ago. Some of you will remember every word I say, some only part, others none at all. Now listen closely.'

The people bent their heads and listened. By the time the stone had finished, the sun was almost down. The stone then said, 'My stories are all told. Keep them safe in your heads and tell them to your children and your children's children, and so on down the ages. And when you ask someone for a story always give a gift.'

And so it was. All the stories we know come from the stone, and from the stone came all the wisdom we have.

TRICKSTERS AND MISCHIEF-MAKERS

THE MOST POPULAR personage of North American mythology is the trickster. This being combines human and animal features and is, at once, a figure of fun, a joker, a fool and creator of the universe. The trickster-god is best shown in the Raven stories of the North Pacific coast and the Coyote cycles of the Great Plains.

The trickster takes many forms. He is the Great Hare for the Winnabago people of Wisconsin, Nanabush or Glooskap in northern and eastern North America (the Woodlands), Rabbit in the south-east, Spider in parts of the Great Plains and Mink or Blue Jay on the north-east coast.

In the Raven cycle, Raven is a transformer: part god and part clown. His insatiable appetite has him searching for something to eat, tricking animals out of their food supply. He is also an incurable womaniser, though he is often thwarted in his quest. Like Coyote, however, he is often creative and invaluable to the tribe. Hence the Haida name for Raven is He-Who-Must-Be-Obeyed.

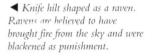

◄ *Knife hilt shaped as a raven. Ravens are believed to have brought fire from the sky and were blackened as punishment.*

 **Myths Retold**

COYOTE AND THE SALMON

COYOTE CAN CHANGE shape whenever he wants. One day, while crossing a river, he fell into the water. To escape drowning he changed himself into a wooden board and was swept downstream until he ran into a dam.

Soon an old woman noticed the board and decided it would make a good food dish. So she took it home and put salmon in it for her dinner. Imagine her surprise when the salmon disappeared so quickly she hardly got a bite to eat. She grew so angry that she threw the board into the fire.

At once Coyote, finding himself in the fire, changed himself into a baby which cried in pain. Quickly, the woman grabbed him from the fire and brought the baby up as her own.

Time passed and the baby grew up, but it was always naughty and disobedient. One day the woman was going on a journey, but before leaving she told the coyote-child, 'While I'm gone, do not open any of the boxes in my barn.'

Coyote promised, but being disobedient he had no intention of keeping the promise. He was curious to know what was inside.

First of all, however, he wanted to get rid of the dam that had stopped him being swept out to sea. There were no salmon in Coyote's country and he wanted his people upstream to enjoy the tasty salmon. So he had first to destroy the dam so that the salmon could swim upstream.

▼ *A shaman's rattle in the form of a salmon.*

No sooner had the old woman gone than Coyote smashed the dam with an axe, letting the salmon swim upstream.

Then, to satisfy his curiosity he began to open the four boxes. To his dismay, out of the first box poured a horde of angry smoke wasps; out of the second a black cloud of salmon flies; out of the third a cloud of blow-flies; and out of the fourth an army of meat beetles.

From that day on, Coyote was able to provide his people with as much tasty salmon as they wanted. However, because he was so disobedient, his people are tormented by smoke wasps, salmon flies, blow flies and meat beetles. Every year these insects reach their peak in the spring, at the very time the salmon begin their run upstream.

ANIMALS

MOST TALES ARE ABOUT animals who have a close kinship with people. Indeed, there was a time when the two were indistinguishable and could change shape at will. Bears, in particular, are closest to humans: they sometimes walk on two legs and have a skeleton much like that of humans. Bears and other animals are an important source of spirit power, and it is necessary to observe certain rituals before going out to hunt them. Each animal also personifies certain traits. The rabbit or coyote is often a trickster and mischief maker; the turtle or tortoise is slow but sure; the fox and deer represent speed; the moose and buffalo strength.

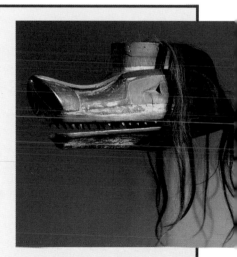

▲ *A wooden head-dress used by the Wolf Society.*

CREATION MYTHS

THE MOST WIDESPREAD creation myth concerns an animal which dives to the bottom of the sea for mud. The duck (or other bird) brings up the mud in its beak and it grows to form the earth. In a Cheyenne myth, the earth is said to rest on the back of Grandmother Turtle.

In most myths humankind is created out of clay (Hopi), or grass, feathers, sticks or ears of corn. Humans also emerge from the bones of the dead, the Earthmaker's sweat or merely by making a wish.

Some tribes have the gods mating: Mother Earth with Father Sky; the Sun with the Moon; Morning Star with Evening Star. According to the Iroquois and Huron in the north-east and the Navaho in the south-west, the first being was a woman.

The Micmac of eastern Canada see creation as in a constant state of flux. Their universe consists of six worlds: the World Beneath the Earth; the World Beneath the Water; Earth World; Ghost World; the World Above the Earth; and the World Above the Sky. But reality is never set forever; it changes according to people's will.

◀ *Burial bowl, punctured at the base to let the spirits out, painted with a male and female figure.*

SUPREME BEINGS, GODS AND HEROES

MOST NATIVE AMERICANS have a supreme god or spirit. It is Awonawilona (The-One-Who-Contains-All) for the Pueblo peoples, in what is now Arizona and New Mexico; Tirawa (Heavenly Arch) for the Pawnee of Oklahoma; Sagalie Tyee for the Coast Salish in British Columbia; Gitchi

▲ *A head-dress in the form of the Thunderbird, identified by its hook beak and feathered horns.*

Manitou for the Algonquians of north-east Canada; and the twin brothers Tobats and Shinoh to the Pahutes of Utah.

Whoever the supreme god is, he normally leaves the everyday affairs of the world to other gods to manage.

Stars are personified heroes who hunt through the sky. The thunder, wind and storm, for example, live in human form and can take the shape also of an animal. Thus, it is the beating of the Thunderbird's wings that creates the noise of thunder as well as the storm below, as it flies through the sky. Anything struck by the Thunderbird's lightning exerts a spiritual power which is to be either avoided or venerated.

Heroes who overcome seemingly impossible obstacles may be demi-gods, or ordinary mortals who have to go through certain ordeals, like going to the sky world or down to the land of the dead to rescue a maiden who has died. The demi-gods rid the earth of primeval monsters in mythical times.

THE FOUR AGES

THE NAVAHO AND THEIR cousins the Apache are the largest group of surviving North American native peoples, with a population of some 160,000. Their traditions contain the most complete account of the creation myth, which consists of four stages. The first, the Beginning, tells of the ascent of the first people from the Underworld to earth. The second, the Animal Hero Age, describes how the earth was set in order and the adventures of the early inhabitants. The third, the God Age, tells of the slaying of monsters. The fourth age portrays the growth of the Navaho nation in its early wanderings.

 **Myths Retold**

LITTLE STAR

EARLY ONE MORNING as the Sun rose from his bed, his handsome son, Morning Star, told him, 'I have fallen in love with a maid of the Blackfoot tribe and want her for my wife.'

Despite his father's warnings, Morning Star painted his bronze body, stuck an eagle's feather in his hair, put on his scarlet cloak and shining black moccasins, and appeared before the maid he loved.

She fell in love at once and agreed to be his wife, leaving her home on the plains and flying up to his home in the skies. The Sun warned her she must never look down on her earthly home, and she gave her word.

After a while, a son, Little Star, was born. One day, as she sat in her mother-in-law's, the Moon's, tepee, Morning Star's wife asked why the big iron pot in the centre always boiled without a fire.

▼ *Shield decorated with a turtle, a thunderbird, stars and the milky way.*

'It has a source to fuel it,' said the Moon. 'But heed my words: you must never move the pot. If you do, misfortune will befall you.'

At midday, when the Moon was asleep, the wife could not restrain her curiosity. She approached the pot and pulled it aside.

To her surprise, she could see right through the hole beneath the pot.

And there was her former home, the green prairie, the blossoming wolf willow and dog rose. And she was filled with a longing to see Her kinsfolk again.

As soon as Morning Star's father, the Sun, heard of her disobedience, he ordered her to return to earth with her child. 'No more will you see your husband,' he said. 'That will be your punishment for disobedience.'

The maid and her son were wrapped tightly in a caribou skin and lowered on a leather thong through the hole beneath the iron pot. But before they reached the earth, the little boy forced his head out of the skin and was cut along the side of his face by the thong. Ever afterwards he was known by the tribe as Poia, Scarface.

He grew up ugly and scarred, and one day decided to journey to his father to have the scar removed. After many moons, he came to a rocky shore and saw a path of light stretching before him across the waters to the sky.

When he reached his father, he did indeed have the scar removed; he returned to earth and married the chief's daughter whom he loved.

SHAMANS AND MEDICINE MEN

ONLY THE SHAMAN has the power to commune with the gods or spirits, to mediate between them and ordinary mortals, to talk with the souls of the dead on behalf of the living. He would be a mystic, poet, sage, healer of the sick, guardian of the tribe and repository of stories.

▲ *Carved figure of a medicine man.*

To become a shaman, a person had to 'receive the call', to suffer a religious experience and be initiated into the mysteries of the art. By symbolic death and resurrection, he acquired a new mode of being, his physical and mental frame underwent a thorough change. During this period of initiation, the novice would see the spirits of the universe and leave his body like a spirit, soaring through the heavens and the Underworld. There he would be introduced to the different spirits and taught which one to address in future trances.

Those who do not possess the full range of shamanistic attributes become only 'medicine men'. Since sickness was thought to be caused by an evil spirit entering the victim's body, the shaman could call it out and cure the patient. He would do so by a special ritual, beating a rhythm on his drum, swaying and chanting, steadily increasing the sound and interspersing it with long-drawn out sighs, groans and hysterical laughter.

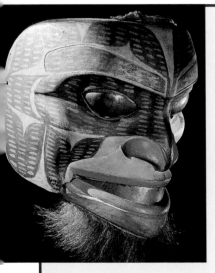

▲ *Mask with articulated eyes and jaw to convey different emotions.*

MASKS

IN MANY CEREMONIES the actors wear masks representing various supernatural beings who possess great healing powers. The Yei masks of the Navaho are made of buckskin from deer that have been ceremonially killed. The spilling of blood must be avoided, so the deer is suffocated by having sacred meal or corn pollen stuffed into its nostrils. These masks are worn during the Yeibichai winter curing ritual or Night Chant; it can only be held at night, when snakes are asleep. The rite is performed to cure patients of madness or fits. During the last two nights of the nine-day ceremony, however, the Yeibichais initiate young boys and girls into the secrets of the masked gods.

ANIMISM

NORTH AMERICAN NATIVES are animists – they believe that everything that moves (clouds, water, leaves, wind) is alive. They therefore live in harmony with Nature and give a story to each part of it: trees and flowers; birds and animals; moon and stars. Thus, the water lily which looks up as we paddle past is really a star fallen from heaven. The Milky Way is the snow shaken from the cloak of Wakinu; the bear, as he crosses the Bridge of Dead Souls on his way to the Eternal Hunting Grounds. The Pleiades are seven poor boys who, forever cold and hungry in this world, were changed into stars.

THE OTHER WORLD

THE afterworld is generally described as a place of peace and happiness, and especially of plentiful game for hunting – hence the name 'Happy Hunting Grounds'. Because of the absence among many tribes of an Under-world or hell, death appears to present little fear. After death, the person merely travels to the spirit land and remains there, living as he or she did on earth.

The Other World may be reached by the living through various means. Some cross the rainbow or a swirling river or sea. With help from demi–gods, mortals may tread over a magic chain of arrows or a tree that is stretched into the world above. Some people may just shut their eyes and wish themselves there.

Numerous tales exist of men of the Afterworld looking down and falling in love with an earthly maiden, then coming down to earth, having a child and taking his family back home. The earth wife usually breaks a taboo, after which she must depart with her child by descending a rope or leather thong. In a Blackfoot story where the marriage is successful, the tepees of their many children may be seen in the evening sky as the Milky Way.

▲ *Ritual robes and equipment of a shaman: staff, rattle, necklace and bear claw crown.*

CHAPTER 18

Central and South America

Central and South America

THE FIRST HUMANS MADE their way to the Americas between 30,000 and 20,000 years ago across a land bridge which connected Siberia and Alaska. By 15,000 years ago, humans were living in the southernmost part of South America, at the site of Monte Verde in Chile. For some 15 millennia, until Christopher Columbus landed in the Bahamas in 1492 CE, Amerindian peoples developed in cultural and geographical isolation from the rest of the world. This had profound consequences for the course of Pre-Columbian civilisation and the shape of its mythologies and religions. Untouched by the political, religious, military or cultural upheavals in the rest of the world, and Mediterranean Europe in particular, the Americas were insulated also from the ravages of many Old World diseases. The Amerindian's lack of immunity turned even the common cold and smallpox into killers, bringing about a cataclysmic decline in indigenous populations as they came

into contact with Europeans. However, this same isolation had produced a unique blend of religion, worldview and mythology – one which, broadly speaking, was shared throughout the Americas by tribe and empire alike.

◀ *The pyramid of the Magician at Uxmal.*

WHAT EUROPEANS DISCOVERED in the Americas from the late fifteenth century onwards was a pristine world, where the power of myth was a concrete reality, the natural world infused with spirit power and the spark of divinity visible in every rock, plant and animal. Mesoamerican and South American peoples lived in a variety of contrasting natural surroundings. In both their areas, volcanoes, mountain chains, arid deserts and humid tropical rainforests made up a

▲ *Page from the* Codex Fejervary-Mayer *showing the fire god at the centre of the universe being fed on sacrificial blood.*

landscape of dramatic contrasts. In South America in particular, the twin rivers of the Amazon and Orinoco flowed through Amazonian lowlands, producing the world's most diverse plant-life, and supporting a startling variety of animals.

The close physical relationships between Amerindians and their surroundings influenced their views of the natural world and the spirits they believed inhabited it. Civilisation developed to varying degrees in each of these environmental areas. The great Pre-Columbian societies arose in Mesoamerica and in the central part of Andes in South America. The gradual move away from hunting and gathering in these areas and the development of agriculture formed the basis for civilised life, increasing populations, and the rise of villages, cities, and eventually imperial states. The mythologies of Mesoamerica and South America were as varied as the people, but they shared a unity of purpose and a coherence in a typically Amerindian worldview where physical and spiritual matters were indissolubly linked.

Mesoamerica Defined

MESOAMERICA IS THE term used to describe that part of Central America whose inhabitants shared important cultural features from around 1000 BCE until the Spanish conquest of 1519–21. It encompasses most of modern Mexico, Guatemala and Belize, as well as parts of Honduras, El Salvador, Nicaragua and Costa Rica. For almost 3,000 years, a variety of civilisations flourished in the contrasting landscapes – from arid high plateaux to lowland tropical rainforests.

Despite underlying differences in language, politics and styles of art, the peoples of Mesoamerica displayed a surprising unity in their religious beliefs and mythologies, in their use of hieroglyphic writing, a 260-day sacred calendar and in playing a rubber ball-game. Mesoamerica's distinctive combination of agriculture, village life, and religious ritual, had appeared by 2000 BCE. Around 1200 BCE, the Olmec emerged as the region's first civilisation, introducing a pantheon of half-human, half-animal gods, monumental architecture, human sacrifice and bloodletting. Together with pyramid building, trading in exotic goods, ancestor worship and the divine status of dynastic rulers, these were ideas and practices emulated by all subsequent Mesoamerican cultures.

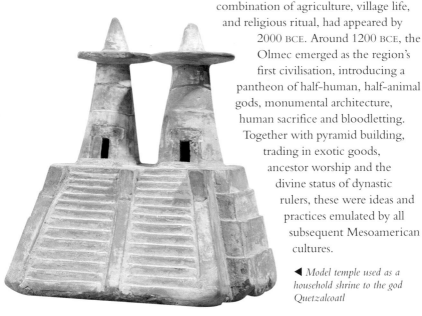

◀ *Model temple used as a household shrine to the god Quetzalcoatl*

 **Myths Retold**

AZTEC CREATIONS AND THE MYTH OF THE SUNS

THE AZTECS, LIKE MANY Mesoamerican peoples, believed that the universe was conceived in a struggle between the powers of light and darkness. In the beginning were Ometeotl and Omecihuatl, the male and female lords of duality. Their cosmic offspring were the four Tezcatlipocas: Red Tezcatlipoca or Xipe Totec associated with the east; Blue Tezcatlipoca or Huitzilopochtli with the south; White Tezcatlipoca or Quetzalcoatl with the west; and Black Tezcatlipoca with the north. These were joined by the lords of fertility, Tlaloc the rain god, and Chalchiuhtlicue, his consort, goddess of water. It was a series of cosmic struggle between these sibling gods that led to the creation and destruction of successive worlds that is such a feature of Mesomerican creation myths. In

▲ *Lady Precious Green,
Chalchuitlicue, the fertility goddess.*

Aztec belief, there were five creations or 'Suns' – each identified by the cataclysm which engulfed it.

The first creation, presided over by Tezcatlipoca, was called 'Four-Jaguar', and was a time when giants walked the earth. After 676 years, Quetzalcoatl knocked Tezcatlipoca into the water and the earth was consumed by jaguars. This initiated the second creation, 'Four-Wind', ruled by Quetzalcoatl, and brought to an end when Tezcatlipoca took his revenge by casting Quetzalcoatl off his throne, turning people into monkeys and destroying the world with hurricane winds. The third creation was called 'Four-Rain', and was dominated by fire. Governed by the rain god Tlaloc, it was destroyed by fiery rain sent by Quetzalcoatl. Then came the fourth creation, known as 'Four-Water', which was identified with Chalchiuhtlicue, the water goddess. This world ended when the earth was engulfed by flood, and its human inhabitants turned into fish.

▲ *The Two Lord Ometecuhtli was both male and female and the supreme creative deity.*

With the passing of these imperfect worlds, Tezcatlipoca and Quetzalcoatl transform into two great trees and raise the sky above the earth. Quetzalcoatl then descends to the Underworld and retrieves the bones of people drowned in the flood. Human flesh is created when the bones are ground into powder and mixed with the penitential blood of the gods. Although the earth is now inhabited by people, it remains in darkness. The gods gather at Teotihuacan determined to bring about the fifth creation – the Aztec world. The god Nanahuatzin hurls himself into a blazing fire and is magically transformed into the rising sun. When he remains motionless, the other gods sacrifice their blood to give him the energy required for his daily journey across the heavens. This fifth world era is called 'Four-Movement'.

QUETZALCOATL

THE UNITY OF MESOAMERICAN religions and myths is illustrated by recurring figures who play crucial roles in the epic encounters of the supernatural world. One of the most frequently depicted characters is Quetzalcoatl, whose name means 'feathered serpent'. Sometimes a god, and other times a king or priest, images of Quetzalcoatl appear most graphically on the Temple of Quetzalcoatl at Teotihuacan. In later epochs, the deity is confused with the historical figure Ce Acatl Topiltzin Quetzalcoatl, ruler of the Toltecs of Tula. During Aztec times, he was the patron of rulership, venerated at the city of Cholula. The Spanish conquistador Hernan Cortes was closely identified with the deity.

THE NATURE OF MESOAMERICAN MYTH

THROUGHOUT MESOAMERICA, individual myths and groups of related myths, served to integrate and make sense of the political, spiritual and natural worlds of their creators. This they did by placing their society at the centre of the universe, and by bestowing a sacred legitimacy on the social hierarchy and the activities of the élite. The ideologies of dynastic Maya kings or Aztec emperors were presented in mythical terms as the will of divine rulers who were at one with the supernatural world. In the Mesoamerican worldview, the spiritual boundaries between life and death were indistinct, and humans, animals, ancestors and gods could mingle in spirit form, changing their outward appearance. Time itself was cyclical, and events repeated themselves according to patterns established in mythic eras. Births, deaths, marriages, war and sacrifice were not unique to the physical world, but re-enactments of momentous events enshrined in myth. This explains the widespread Mesoamerican obsession with time, and the sacred and secular calendars which measured its passing and predicted the future. At an everyday level, myths illustrated ideas of life and death, the fertility of people, animals and plants, and the fundamental unity of life. Myths were powerful things – they swayed nations, gave societies their sacred identities and accounted for the rise and fall of cities and empires.

Animals here represent blocks of time, while the profiles of the gods represent numbers. ▶

THE JAGUAR

IN MESOAMERICA, Olmec jaguar gods were the earliest deities. Their associations with royalty and fertility influenced many later civilisations. Among the Maya, the supreme creator was Itzamna, lord of all gods and patron of writing. Closely related to him was the jaguar-eared Sun God, Kinich Ahau, who travelled through the Underworld at night from west to east. Among the Aztecs, the foremost deity was Tezcatlipoca, 'Lord of the Smoking Mirror', the omnipotent patron of royalty and sorcerers. Uniquely Aztec was Huitzilopochtli, 'Hummingbird of the South',

▲ *Shield Jaguar stands here with a torch whilst his wife, Lady Xoc draws a rope through her tongue as a blood sacrifice.*

the tribal war god to whom human sacrifices were made.

HIGHLAND MYTHS

IN HIGHLAND MESOAMERICA, myths reflected the physical and cultural realities of life beyond the tropical rainforests. Creation myths in particular were linked to a changing and unstable landscape, whose rainfall was unpredictable, and where flash floods and volcanic activity presented a constant threat to civilised life. These physical realities played an active part in shaping understandings of the world and also appeared in myths which embodied this knowledge. The third Aztec creation was characterised by fire and destroyed by fiery rain – a reference, some authorities believe, to the devastating effects of volcanic explosions. Similarly, the Aztec glyphic name for the fifth creation – the Aztec era itself – was 'Four-Movement', suggesting a link between powerful spirit forces which animated the universe, and unpredictable earthquake tremors which shook the Valley of Mexico. In this landscape, heat contended with cold, downpour with drought, and plenty with famine – realities personified as gods of water, sun and unpredictable fate in creation myths. Highland Mexico during Aztec times was also a mosaic of different peoples, dynasties and traditions – most of whom had long preceded the Aztec people. The Aztec myth of the 'Five Suns' put the Aztecs centre stage, describing the past as a series of failures, and the present as the gift of Aztec rule based on regular and bloody human sacrifices to nourish the gods that gave birth to the world.

▲ *Mayan figurine of a mythological character.*

 **Myths Retold**

MAYA CREATIONS IN THE POPOL VUH

THE *POPOL VUH*, or 'book of counsel', is a unique masterpiece of Maya literature, preserving ancient myths relating the creation of the world of the Quiché Maya of Guatemala. The *Popol Vuh* tells how, in the beginning, in total silence, the creator gods Gugumatz and Huracan shaped the earth, dividing the mountains from the water, separating sky from earth. After making the trees and bushes, they created a world of animals – jaguars, deer, birds and serpents. But the creatures were unable to speak, and could not praise their makers nor call out their illustrious names. So dissatisfied were the two gods that they condemned the animals to offer their flesh to any who would eat it, then set their minds to a second creation. This time the deities fashioned humans in the hope that they would immortalise their creators names in prayer. But they were made of mud, and crumbled away, dissolving in the swirling waters. Disappointed again, *Gugumatz* and *Huracan* tried a third time, calling for help on ancestral diviners, sorcerers and spirit animals. On this occasion, humans were carved from wood, and they spoke and looked like real people. Yet, as they populated the earth, the manikins had no memories of their makers and failed to speak their names. The gods wreaked their revenge by turning the world

▲ *Jade plaque showing a Mayan ruler in full regalia standing on a bench supported by two prisoners.*

THE CALENDAR STONE

AZTEC CREATION MYTHS are vividly portrayed in the impressive Calendar Stone. Discovered in 1790 nearby the Great Aztec Temple in Mexico City, the 4 m (12 ft) wide disc is less a true calendar than a monumental vision of Aztec creations carved in stone. At the centre is the face of the sun god Tonatiuh, flanked by two giant claws and four boxed figures representing the four previous suns – dedicated to the jaguar, wind, fire and water. Surrounding these are day signs from the sacred calendar and symbolic representations of Tezcatlipoca, Quetzalcoatl and Tlaloc. The Calendar Stone is a reminder of how entwined art and myth are in ancient Mesoamerica.

▲ *The Calendar Stone.*

upside down, making the pots, grinding stones and even dogs rebel against the people of wood until this third creation was also destroyed.

In the fourth and final attempt at making creatures who would honour their creators, the gods discovered that to fashion human flesh, they had to use maize. The fox, coyote, parrot and crow brought ears of white and yellow maize to the deities who transformed it into the first four men – the mythic founders of the four lineages of the Quiché Maya. The men of maize were handsome and good, they saw and understood everything, and they praised and nourished their creators. Gugumatz and Huracan, however, were jealous of the perfection of their creations, worried that the men would become as great as the gods themselves. So they subtly changed the nature and powers of the four – limiting their understanding of the world, diluting their uniqueness by creating women and enabling them to procreate. Most of all they clouded their vision, so that now they could see only what was close by. With this creation, the founding of the Quiché nation was assured, and in the east the world's first dawn broke, and light spread over the earth.

LOWLAND MYTHS

ALTHOUGH LOWLAND PEOPLES shared many features of their mythology with their highland neighbours, they were inspired and also constrained by the tropical rainforests and swampy rivers of their environment. These areas had an excess not a shortage of water, possessed lush vegetation and abounded in plant and animal foods as well as innumerable dangerous animals. They experienced dramatic shifts in climate, from burning sun to hurricane-force winds and electrical storms, to tropical downpours and consequent floods. Maya mythology and art, and their creation stories especially, embodied these natural forces in the successive world eras so typical of Mesoamerican cosmogony. In the *Popol Vuh* of the Quiché Maya, Hurricane or Huracan, was one of the cosmic pair of creator gods who

shaped the world, and the power of his storm winds turned the world upside down, ending the third world era. The luxuriance of the tropical rainforest and its animal life is a feature of the first world era, and acknowledged in the fashioning of wooden people in the third creation. Unlike the multi-ethnic highlands, the Maya lowlands were inhabited only by Maya-speaking peoples. A deep ethnic unity underlay broader Mesoamerican similarities, bestowing a uniquely Maya character to their epic myths.

◀ *Sculpture of the personification of the maize god.*

ANDEAN CIVILISATION DEFINED

IN SOUTH AMERICA, the central Andes of modern Peru and Bolivia were home to the great Pre-Columbian civilisations. From before 1000 BCE until the Spanish conquest in 1532 CE, a diversity of cultures flourished in this region of contrasting landscapes. Geography stimulated cultural development.

The proximity of three distinct environments – high mountains, Pacific coast, and Amazonian tropical rainforests – encouraged craft specialisation and facilitated trade.

Although there was never the underlying unity in religion and myth that characterised Mesoamerica, many cultural traits were shared by Andean civilisations over 3,000 years. These included the common view of a natural world animated by spirits and ancestors, pilgrimage, human sacrifice, and the artistic

▲ *Ceramic plate depicting a dancing jaguar, crocodile or supernatural creature.*

representation of religious and mythological ideas in gold, silver, textiles and pottery. Yet no Andean civilisation developed a writing system and so ideas and beliefs were transmitted orally. Chav'n (800–200 BCE) was the region's first major civilisation, creating a distinctive art style in which ferocious supernatural jaguars and eagles decorated architecture, pottery and goldwork. Along with sophisticated stone-built temples and elaborate textiles, these features became the hallmarks of all subsequent Andean civilisations, from the coastal cultures of the Mochica and Nazca, to the highland empires of Tiwanaku, Huari and Inca.

Myths Retold

ANDEAN AND INCA CREATION MYTHS

THE DOMINANT FEATURE of Andean creation myths was the multiple attempts at shaping not just the natural world, but the varied nations who inhabited it. Imperial Inca civilisation saw its place of origin not in Cuzco its capital, but in and around Lake Titicaca to the south. As in Mesoamerica, creations were seen in terms of the relationships between light and dark, and successive endeavours by deities to perfect their handiwork. In one Inca version, the god Viracocha had first created a world of darkness, inhabited by a race of giants fashioned in stone. When these first people ignored their creator's wishes, Viracocha punished them by sending a great flood to destroy the world. All perished with the exception of one man and one woman who were transported by magic to the god's abode at Tiwanaku. Viracocha tried a second time, making people out of clay, painting on them the clothes whose varied designs and

▲ *Golden bird, probably of supernatural origin, holding mythological significance.*

colours distinguished one nation from another. He also endowed each group with its own customs, language, and way of life. With his divine breath, Viracocha animated his creations, sending them to earth and commanding them to emerge from natural features of the landscape – such as caves, lakes and mountains. At each place of emergence they were to honour their maker by building shrines for his worship. Pleased with his success, Viracocha then created light from the darkness – order from chaos – so that his people could see and live in an orderly world. He caused the sun, moon and stars to rise up to the heavens from the Island of the Sun in Lake Titicaca.

As the sun ascended in the first dawn, Viracocha cried out to the Inca people and their leader Manco Capac, foretelling that they would be great conquerors and the lords of many nations. As a divine blessing, the god gave Manco Capac a beautiful headdress and a great battle-axe as signs of his royal status amongst men. Manco led his brothers and sisters into the heart of the earth from where they emerged into the daylight at the place of three caves known as Pacariqtambo. This account of the magical and transforming activities of Viracocha is only one Inca version of an ancient and pan-Andean cycle of creation myths. At its heart lies the idea of the spiritual unity of people and landscape, of sacred places, journeys, and the appearance of humans at the dawning of first light.

▲ *Terracotta statue of the goddess of childbirth giving birth.*

GODS OF THE ANDES

THE ANDEAN WORLD, and the Inca pantheon in particular, was ruled by powerful sky gods, who presided over the heavens or dwelt atop snow-capped mountain peaks. They sent rain, hail, lightning and drought to afflict the earth, and had to be appeased if disaster was to be averted. Among the most powerful Inca deities was Inti, the sun god – divine ancestor of Inca royalty, represented as a golden disc surrounded by sun-rays. Mama Kilya, his consort, was the moon goddess, whose duty it was to regulate the Inca ritual calendar. Ilyap'a, god of thunder, sent the rains by smashing a great jar of celestial water.

ONE OF THE COMMON motifs in Pre-Columbian South American art is a supernatural feline being, variations of which appear in almost all Andean civilisations from Chav'n to Inca. Carved in stone, cast in gold, or painted onto pottery or textiles, this being can appear naturalistically – as a jaguar or puma – or as a fanged half-human, half-animal creature. More recently, shamans are recorded as saying they shape-shift into ferocious jaguars under the influence of narcotic drugs, and so much of this prehistoric imagery may be visual excerpts from ancient myths concerning human-animal transformation.

THE NATURE OF ANDEAN MYTHOLOGY

ANDEAN MYTHOLOGY was characterised by a concern with origins, ancestors and fertility, and influenced by the dramatic landscapes of the region. Despite local and regional differences, myths tended to focus on deities and events which symbolised the realities of living in a volcanically active region, rocked by earthquakes, and dominated by high snow-capped peaks which themselves created dramatic local weather patterns. Throughout the Andean cultural area, myths incorporated landscape and climate, telling of how founding ancestors had emerged from caves or lakes, how rocks turned into people and back again, and how the social order was bestowed on

▲ *The lost city of Machu Picchu, never found by the invading Spanish.*

humans by the gods. They explained how, in order to maintain the cosmic status quo, sacrifices, rituals and pilgrimages had to be observed. As in Mesoamerica, Andean myths served to legitimate the ruling élite by creating genealogies to primordial times, establishing the divine status of kings and emperors, and blending the natural and social worlds. Andean mythology provided a framework for living, and a sacred charter for ethnic identity. For imperial civilisations, mythology was an integral part of the ideology of military expansion, and a method by which the rituals of society and empire were integrated with state religion and social obligations.

VIRACOCHA

IN ANDEAN MYTHOLOGY, Viracocha was widely regarded as the source of all divine power – an omnipresent, primordial being. Unlike other gods, he had no name – Viracocha was merely a term of respect. The Inca Viracocha seems to have been a distant being who set the wheels of cosmic creation in motion, but who left day-to-day matters to more active deities. Similar prime-mover figures exist in non-Inca mythologies. They are culture-heroes, who make long pilgrimages, measure the world, and organise cosmic and earthly space. In this respect, Viracocha was an archetypal figure rather than a uniquely Inca god.

▲ *Viracocha, a creator deity, god of rain who is believed to have created the sun and the moon.*

CIVILISATION IN AMAZONIA AND THE LOWLANDS

THE TROPICAL LOWLANDS of the Amazon never reached the heights of
civilisation attained in the Andes. Although there were no great cities or empires
to compare with Chav'n, Moche or the Inca, parts of Amazonia were densely
populated in prehistoric times. By 2000 BCE, pottery making was widespread, and
between 400–1300 CE, a sophisticated culture developed on the island of Maraj –
at the mouth of the Amazon. These people cultivated maize and manioc (cassava),

built large housemounds and crafted colourful
anthropomorphic burial urns whose female forms suggest
the importance of women in everyday life and mythology.

Knowledge of lowland prehistory is limited however.
More abundant and better documented is the seemingly
infinite variety of small-scale Amerindian societies
occupying this region from the time of European arrival
to the present. From the Amazon and Orinoco rivers of
northern South America to the Mato Grosso grasslands to
the south, groups of Amerindians lived a life of hunting,
gathering and horticulture in a diversity of surroundings.
Language, customs, religion, art and houses differed, but
all shared a basic Amerindian view of a world animated by
spirits and controlled by ancestors. In these kinds of
societies, there was often little room for an elaborate social
hierarchy. Chiefs and shamans rather than emperors held
sway over these societies, and in some parts still do.

◀ *Two pronged-silver diadem, originally part of a
elaborate head-dress worn by chiefs and shamans.*

MYTHIC WORLDS OF THE AMAZON

LOWLAND AMERINDIAN peoples are often described as technologically
inferior to the great Pre-Columbian civilisations of the Andes. Yet their
societies, rituals and religious beliefs reveal a spirituality and mythic imagination

which recalls the most sophisticated intellectual achievements of the Incas and their predecessors. In many ways, the diversity of Amazonian peoples inhabit a world of myth and magic, where otherwise local myths display an underlying unity. This similarity is produced partly by different groups sharing common concerns and dealing with them with a common logic. It is reinforced by an intimate knowledge of plants and animals, the weather and an abiding belief in the transformative powers of the shaman. Created in mythic time, the Amerindian universe can be replicated in the design of a house, and the shape of the human body. It is ruled by powerful spirits whose capricious actions are tempered only by the shaman confronting them in trance in the shape of a spirit bird or jaguar. The shaman is often a society's most important figure. As keeper of the tribes' mythic traditions, he knows more myths than anybody else, and is able to interpret them more meaningfully. In the shamans hands, myths are powerful tools and weapons, for with them he speaks to the ancestors, and accounts for every aspect of life and death.

▲ *Gold bead in the form of a snarling jaguar, signifies chiefs association with spirits.*

THE MASTER OF ANIMALS

A RECURRING FIGURE in Lowland Amazonian mythology is the 'Master of Animals'. Created in primordial times, these supernatural beings have responsibility for the fertility of the animal kingdom and have to be appeased by the shaman if hunting is to be successful. Every animal has its master, which is often the largest member of its species. It is usually the multicoloured jaguar, as the largest lowland predator, which is regarded as the master of all animal species. Jaguars eat all animals but are prey to none, and thus are a natural prototype for an all-powerful guardian of animal spirits.

 **Myths Retold**

THE ORIGINS OF FIRE

IN AMAZONIA, FIRE symbolises creation and civilised life. In Brazilian Kayapo mythology, the first people possessed no fire and ate their food raw like wild beasts. One day, a young boy, Botoque, was abandoned by his elder brother-in-law while gathering macaw eggs in the jungle. After several days eating his own excrement, Botoque saw a jaguar carrying a bow and arrow and various kinds of game. The jaguar promised not to eat him, offering instead to adopt him as a son and a hunting companion. Botoque climbed on the jaguar's back and returned to the great cat's house. Here, the boy saw fire and ate cooked meat for the first time. Due to the hostility of the jaguar's wife, the jaguar showed Botoque how to make a bow and arrow. When the jaguar's wife threatened him, he killed her with an arrow, gathered up some cooked meat, his weapons and a burning ember, and returned to his own village. On seeing these wondrous gifts, the men returned to the jaguar's house, stealing fire, cooked meat, and bows and arrows. Incensed at his adopted son's behaviour, the jaguar now eats its food raw, while humans eat theirs cooked.

MEANING OF AMAZONIAN MYTHS

AMAZONIAN MYTHS deal mainly with explaining and ordering human relationships both within society itself, and the wider natural and supernatural worlds. In a universe where myth and history converge, social life is seen as the result of a careful fusing of antagonistic and spiritually dangerous things, such as men and women, kin and in-laws, or wild beasts and humans. In order for a group to endure, its members must observe social rules and ritual obligations first created by the ancestors and enshrined in myth. If these are transgressed chaos and disaster quickly follow. Many of these myths, which seek also to explain civilised life in opposition to nature, take the form of creation stories and variations of the origins of fire. Thus, many creation

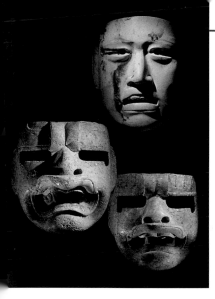

▲ *Trilogy of masks representing man, the earth and the sky.*

myths are concerned with a number of overlapping issues – the origins of hunting, the secret of cooking food and the relationships between humans and animals and different human groups. Reversal is also a common theme, where animals once were armed but now hunt unaided, or where women once ruled the world until men took over. In the tropical lowlands, processes of creation and decay are magnified by lush conditions of jungle life, by sudden death and cannibalism – Amazonian myths reflect these dramatic conditions, providing a structure for understanding the jungle world.

THEMES IN AMAZONIAN MYTHOLOGY

THE MAIN THEMES of Lowland mythology are those concerned with the regulation of human society and its relationship with the natural world. These issues are often entwined, found together in creation myths which relate how light and order was brough into being, how animals and sometimes women were the earth's original masters, and how men usurped their position. Defining human culture in opposition to the untamed world of beasts is also a dominant theme. Reversals, transformations and balance are key features of Amazonian myth.

▶ *Jars decorated with skeletal figures, linked to shamanistic ideas on music, death and fertility.*

SUPERNATURAL IMAGES and designs are revealed to the shaman in drug-induced trance. Powerful narcotics, like ayahuasca, create vivid, multi-coloured visions in which natural forms can be recombined, made larger, or smaller. Many are held to be sacred. Imbued with protective power, these designs are painted onto communal longhouses, applied to the skin for ritual festivities, and used as a basis for the making and decoration of baskets, textiles and pottery. Such designs are symbolic representations of myth-ological events and cult heroes, and they link the objects and architecture of everyday life with the sacred realm of the ancestors.

▲ *Gold statue thought to represent a supernatural being or a shaman.*

AMAZONIAN CREATION

AMONG THE DESANA of the Colombian Amazon, creation occurs when an inscrutable and invisible Creator Sun explodes yellow light into the void. The Sun Father, Pagë Abé, sets about creating the natural world in all its details – animals, plants and forests, each with their own identity, habits and places. The Sun lays down the principles of existence, spreading brilliance and understanding like solar semen throughout the universe. He then delegates further creativity to a host of supernatural beings – masters of individual realms such as the sky, rivers and animal kingdom. In the Desana cosmogony, dramatic acts of transformative creation are carried out by females such as the Daughter of *Aracú* Fish. To these culture heroes falls the responsibility of inventing many of the details of existence and cultural life – the shapes and colours of animals, the techniques of human hunting and food production, and the symbolic domains of ritual and art. The Sun now takes two forms. By day he resides in the sky, providing heat, light and fertility for the life which he and his female protagonists have created. On earth he is the protective supernatural jaguar. The Sun then commands another supernatural, Pamurí-mahsë, to transport the first people to the earth in a large canoe.

▼ *The maize cobs on this effigy jar are gods associated with fertility and food.*

Glossary

AETIOLOGY
Today the study of natural phenomena, but primitive people employed naturally occurring events in initiations, religious practices and rituals.

AFTERLIFE
Believed to be where the spirit went after bodily death; also known as paradise, Underworld, Hades, Heaven, Elysian fields, Netherworld.

ALLEGORY
Storytelling device where one thing is described as another in order to convey a moral or practical lesson.

ANCESTOR VENERATION
Ancestor worship – where people deify their ancestors, and trace descent to a common ancestor who watch over their progeny.

ANIMAL MYTHS
Hunter-gatherer tribes often saw close connections between man and animal, believing both capable of transformation.

ANIMISM
Those living closely with nature often attached stories to it, believing spirits inhabited anything that moved, such as sticks, trees and stones.

ANTHROPOLOGY
Academic pursuit following Darwin's theories to study human evolution, differences in lifestyles, cultures and societies across the world.

ANTHROPOMORPHISM
Part of myth or literature where human traits or characteristics are attributed to animals, inanimate objects or deities.

ARYAN
Believed to be the language of ancient peoples living between central Asia and Europe which developed into Indo-European languages.

ASCETICISM
Where a people may express themselves through art for its own sake rather than for moral, religious or educational purposes.

ASTRAL DEITIES
As explanations for the planets, people or deities were believed to have transformed into the moon, stars or sun.

AUTOCHTHONY
Relating to native or aboriginal people, suggesting ancestry and close connection with the earth, possibly on a spiritual level.

BABYLONIA
Ancient civilisation on the Euphrates River, now Iraq, and site of the Hanging Gardens of Babylon.

BARDS
In Celtic and Eastern European cultures Bards were storytellers passing on stories through generations.

BATTLE MYTHS
Battle myths and heroics reinforce cultural identity whilst the favours of gods of war can be prayed for or used to explain losses.

BRONZE AGE
Describes the period after 2000 BC when people began using metal-making technology based on copper and its alloys.

BUDDHISM
Buddha's sixth-century teachings were that by following virtuous paths one could attain the destruction of mortal desires and anguishes.

BYZANTIUM
Ancient Greek city at the centre of a Mediterranean empire, with a distinctive architecture and orthodox religious art.

CAULDRONS
Often magical, cauldrons were seen as life-restoring, brewers of wisdom, holders of visions and ultimately the Holy Grail.

CHRISTIANITY
World religion derived from the life of Christ, the son of God, who came to earth, suffered persecution for his teachings, was crucified and rose from the dead.

CLANS
Social grouping based on kinship theoretically descended from a single ancestor, sometimes represented as a spirit being.

CONFUCIANISM
Chinese beliefs and practices, from Confucius, relating to nature gods, imperial ancestors and the balancing of yin and yang.

COSMOGONIC MYTHS
Common creation myth where primeval earth is separated from the sky, and stars and planets created by gods or humans.

CREATION MYTHS
Most cultures have an origin of the world myth, often where the world and order were created out of chaos.

CYCLE OF LIFE
Cycle of birth, death and afterlife or reincarnation, depending on specific religions or beliefs.

DEGENERATION
Where myths are infiltrated by the influence of the different world religions that they resemble, leading to eventual loss of the original.

DRAVIDIAN
Non-Indo-European peoples from southern India and Sri Lanka with around 20 languages and a 2,000-year literary history.

DRUIDISM
Pre-Christian pagan religion of the Celtic people where priests were learned, artistic and important members of the social order.

DUALISM
Belief that reality is dual in nature, made up of material objects and how these are perceived by our minds.

ECOGEOGRAPHICAL SYSTEMS
A people's geographical positioning, climate, environment and resources often determine myths and beliefs.

ENLIGHTENMENT
Awakening to reality in Buddhist belief is followed by the soul's departure from the cycle of death and reincarnation.

ETHNIC IDENTITY
Ethnicity is where an ethnic group feels a common sense of identity based on shared culture, language, customs and religion.

EVIL EYE
Some superstitious cultures attributed magical powers to certain individuals believing they could inflict harm with a glance.

EVOLUTION
Process of change in animal and plant forms as they adapt to environments or learn to manage them as humans have.

FERTILITY DEITIES
Most primitive cultures were phallocentric, concerned with reproductive powers and believed certain deities governed fertility.

FETISHES
Belief in the supernatural powers of an inanimate object, the fetish, which has religious or magical importance.

FOUNDATION MYTHS
Common to most cultures and religions are myths concerning the creation of people and their environment or state.

GRAIL LEGEND
Celtic legends of King Arthur's quest for the supernatural powers held by the cup used by Jesus at the Last Supper.

GUARDIAN SPIRIT
Widely held belief in protecting spirits or angels, either an animal, the free soul of a sleeping person, or an ancestor.

HEADS
For some cultures heads contained the soul, and enemies were beheaded to take possession of their soul.

HELLENISTIC
Classic period in Greek civilisation from 323 BC, when Greek culture and myths spread throughout the Mediterranean.

HERETICS
Christian churches turned pagan myths of vampires, witchcraft and sorcery against heretics – those accused of non-conformity.

HEROES
A hero's ability to overcome seemingly invincible enemies and forces of nature is a universal theme in world mythology.

HINDUISM
The dominant religion of India, Hinduism's complex system of customs and beliefs include numerous gods, reincarnation and a caste system.

ICE AGE
Up to 20 periods of widescale glaciation have occurred in the earth's history – the last immediately preceding historic times.

ICONOGRAPHY
The worshipping of symbolic objects or icons, which have specific significance to certain cultures or religions – such as crucifixes.

IDEOLOGY
Set of ideas and beliefs a people hold about themselves offering a framework for how they should order their lives.

INCANTATION
In magical or religious rituals certain words or sounds are repeated, often by a group, and sometimes to cast spells.

INITIATION
Ceremony or rights of passage whereby young men (generally) are tested or taught the fundamentals of survival and adulthood.

ISLAM
Founded in the seventh century by the prophet Muhammad, messenger of Allah, Islam emphasises God's omnipotence and inscrutability.

JAINISM
Ancient ascetic Indian religion emphasising non-violence and compassion for all forms of life, but not a belief in deities.

KINSHIP
Human relationships based on blood or marriage, grouped as family, clan or tribe often with strict rules, customs and taboos.

MASKS
Symbols worn in worship rituals to represent supernatural healing beings, gods, ancestors or to re-enact or retell significant events.

MATRIARCHAL SOCIETIES
Certain cultures known to have been dominated by worship of female gods and female fertility before phallocentricism.

MEDIEVAL
The cultures and beliefs of the Middle Ages; after the Roman Empire's fifth-century decline to the fifteenth-century Renaissance.

MEDITATION
Individual act of spiritual contemplation or where a shaman might commune with spirit gods as part of a ritual.

MESOPOTAMIA
Site of powerful ancient civilisations of Sumer and Babylon, now Iraq, 3500 BC with a wealth of art, particularly sculpture.

MOTHER GODDESSES
Some ancient cultures saw goddesses in an overall cosmology with mother goddesses as the earth and the father as the sky.

MUSE
In Greek mythology, the nine daughters of the god Zeus each inspire a form of human artistic expression or endeavour.

MYTHIC NARRATIVE
Narratives are stories and these were the means to convey myths and keep them alive either orally, in writing or song.

NATURE SPIRITS
Animist cultures believed that spirits, sometimes ancestors, inhabited trees, rocks or rivers; this explained their changing appearance.

NEOLITHIC
Final part of the Stone Age period marked by the development of agriculture and forest clearance around 8000–3000 BC.

ORAL TRADITIONS
Where a culture has no written tradition myths are passed down through generations by bards, elders, shamans and storytellers.

PAGANISM
From the fourteenth century, worshippers following religions other than Christianity were regarded as pagans and associated with superstition and sorcery.

PASTORALISM
Belief or ideology in the power and importance of the land, where stories will incorporate man and the environment.

PHALLIC SYMBOL
In patriarchal societies male fertility was prayed for and worshipped using symbols in the form of or representing the penis.

PILGRIMAGES
A journey to worship at a sacred place or shrine particularly, but not only, associated with the major organised religions.

PREHISTORIC
From the beginning of life on earth 3.5 billion years ago, to 3500 BC when humans began to keep records.

PRIMEVAL
Relates to the earliest period of the world, in mythical terms perhaps the period after creation and before foundation.

PROPHECY
Sometimes regarded as a gift where a soothsayer, prophet or seer can foretell the future either magically or in visions.

REINCARNATION
Depending on cultural variant, part or all of a soul departs after death and inhabits the body of a newborn child.

RELIGIOUS CULTS
Many ancient cultures worshipped numerous gods, but those following one of these or an ancestor god were called cults.

RENAISSANCE
Fourteenth to seventeenth century European intellectual and artistic movement, ending the Middle Ages with its emphasis on science and exploration.

RESURRECTION
Rebirth myths widely held throughout the ancient world often symbolised by snakes which are able to shed their skins.

RITUALS
Religious ceremony with certain set patterns, incantations, dances and singing, to mark particular events such as initiations, births or deaths.

SACRIFICE AND OFFERINGS
Ancient peoples believed either human or animal sacrifices or votive offerings would appease gods.

SAGAS
Traditional Scandinavian prose narratives concerning kings, families and adventures; part of oral traditions but written down in the eleventh century.

SAGES
Profoundly wise men who educated and advised, sometimes foretold the future and were generally honoured by their society.

SANSKRIT
Sacred classical language of Hinduism, the language of law, medicine and epic stories, it has influenced many Indo-European languages.

SCARAB BEETLES
Often brilliantly coloured and industrious, scarab beetles were revered as divine and depicted in their art by Ancient Egyptians.

SEMITIC
Peoples of ancient cultures in the Middle East, speakers of Semitic languages and founders of Islam, Judaism and Christianity.

SHAMAN
Ancient priests believed to be both of the spirit and material world and possess supernatural powers of healing and transformation.

SHAMANISM
Oldest-known form of organised religion, belief in the power of shamans who transact between the human and spiritual worlds.

SHINTO
Ancient Japanese religion combining oneness with the mysterious forces of nature and devotion to royal descendants of the sun goddess.

SHRINE
Religious places of worship marked by statues, rocks, buildings, crosses or gifts to be offered to or signifying the deity.

SOCIAL MYTHS
Used to instill social values, family obligations, taboos against incest, obedience to social hierarchies and guidelines on behaviour.

SOLAR BODIES
Stars and planets, the presence of which were explained as deities as part of many foundation or creation myths.

SORCERY
Magical practices that control the forces of nature by supernatural means, perhaps as part of religious rituals.

STONE AGE
The earliest period of human culture marked by the use of stone implements and covering Paleolithic, Mesolithic and Neolithic times.

SUPREME BEING
Where a culture believes in a life-giving being who personifies the life force that animates human and animal worlds.

SYMBOLIC RELATIONSHIPS
Where important aspects of a culture's life, such as food, water and animals are embodied in their myths and worship.

TABOOS
Social group and religious prohibitions or restrictions to behaviour, such as incest or desecrating sacred objects.

THERIOMORPHIC
Where a god or deity takes the shape of an animal and may be depicted in carvings or paintings.

TOTEMS
Sacred clan or individual totems may be animal, plant or carved objects and represent the kinship with the totem.

TRANCES
Shamans in certain cultures experienced drug-induced hallucinogenic trances to converse with gods or spirits.

TRANSFORMATION
Metamorphosis of one animate of inanimate object into another – animals into humans and vice versa, part of animism and shamanism.

VAMPIRES
Evil Slavic and Eastern European mythic creature believed to be dead, yet animated and capable of making others into vampires.

WATER NYMPHS
A life-giving and destructive force; some cultures believed it was alive or contained creatures they wished to please.

Author Biographies

Arthur Cotterell: General Editor and Introduction

Arthur Cotterell is Principal of Kingston College in Surrey. He is a world-renowned authority on the mythologies of the world, and has written, contributed to and edited many volumes on the subject.

Loren Auerbach: Northern Europe

Loren Auerbach gained her Masters degree at King's College (University of London) specialising in Old English and Old Icelandic. She has taught and given lectures at both London University and Oxford University. Her most recent work is *Sagas of the Norsemen* in the Time Life Books series 'Myth and Mankind'.

Professor Anne M. Birrell: China

Anne M. Birrell is a widely published world authority on Chinese mythology. Her introductory book for Penguin has become a standard work on the subject.

Rev Dr Martin Boord: Tibet and Mongolia

Prior to attaining his doctoral degree at the School of Oriental & African Studies at the University of London, Martin Boord spent eight years in India training in Buddhist philosophy and practice under some of the most eminent Tibetan lamas of the modern age. Author of *The Cult of the Deity Vajrakila* (Tring 1993), his published translations include *Overview of the Buddhist Tantra* (Dharamsala 1996). He currently resides in Oxford as an independent scholar and translator.

Miranda Bruce-Mitford: Sri Lanka; Southeast Asia

Miranda Bruce-Mitford is an art historian and author who has written and contributed to many publications on the art and culture of southern Asia.

Peter A. Clayton: Egypt

Peter A. Clayton is an Egyptologist and author of many books on ancient Egypt, notably *Chronicle of the Pharaohs* (1994, repr. 1996, 1998) that have been translated into six languages. For the last 25 years, every year, he has been a guest lecturer in Egypt and in many universities and museums in Europe and Australia.

Dr Ray Dunning: Celtic

Dr Ray Dunning was born in 1947 in Brecon, South Wales. He has taught art and art history in schools and colleges for many years and his illustrations appear in books on mythology and the ancient world. He is currently Head of the Department of Design Studies at Kingston College.

Dr James H. Grayson: Korea

James Huntley Grayson is Reader in Modern Korean Studies and Director of the Centre for Korean Studies, School of East Asian Studies, University of Sheffield. An anthropologist and former Methodist missionary to Korea (1971–87), he has written widely on Korean religion and folklore. His books include *Korea: A Religious History* and *Myths and Legends from Korea*.

Dr Niel Gunson: Oceania

Niel Gunson is an historian at the Australian National University. His recently published works include contributions to the *Atlas of World Religions* and the *Encyclopedia of the Pacific Islands*.

Stephen Hodge: Japan

Stephen Hodge is a linguist in Japanese and an author with a specialist knowledge of Japanese culture.

World Mythology

Dr Gwendolyn Leick: Ancient Near East

Gwendolyn Leick is a historian of the Ancient Near East. She is widely published in the field and her works include the *Dictionary of Near Eastern Mythology* (Routledge).

Dr Helen Morales: Greece and Rome

Dr Helen Morales is a lecturer in Classics at the University of Reading, having been educated at New Hall and Newnham College, Cambridge. She has published on later Greek literature and Roman art. She is co-editor of the Classical Studies journal *Omnibus*, published for schools and anyone else with a passion for the ancient world.

Mark Nuttall: Siberia and the Arctic

Mark Nuttall is a social anthropologist specialising in the cultures of the Arctic and North Atlantic. He has researched and travelled extensively in Greenland, Alaska and other northern regions. His most recent book is *Protecting the Arctic: Indigenous Peoples and Cultural Survival* (Harwood Academic Publishers), and he is currently Lecturer in Anthropology and Sociology at the University of Aberdeen.

Richard Prime: India

Richard Prime studied architecture before spending 15 years studying and teaching Krishna Consciousness. He works as a freelance writer and broadcaster, and as adviser on religion and conservation to WWF and to the Alliance on Religions and Conservation. His books include *Hinduism and Ecology* (1992) and *Ramayana, A Journey* (1997).

Professor James Riordan: Central and Eastern Europe; North America

James Riordan was born in Portsmouth, England. He has travelled extensively in Central and Eastern Europe, lived in Russia for five years and has published several books on the myths and folklore of the area. He is currently Professor of Russian Studies in the Department of Linguistic and International Studies at the University of Surrey.

Dr Nicholas J. Saunders: Caribbean; Central and South America

Nicholas J. Saunders studied archeology at Sheffield and Southampton Universities, and anthropology at Cambridge University. He has specialised in pre-Columbian America for over 20 years, holding teaching and research positions in Mexico, Trinidad, Jamaica, the USA and the UK. He is currently a lecturer in archeology and anthropology at University College, London.

Professor Harold Scheub: Africa

Harold Scheub is Professor of African Languages and Literature at the University of Wisconsin. He has recently completed his *Dictionary of African Mythology* for Oxford University Press.

Bruce Wannell: Persia

Bruce Wannell was born in Melbourne and educated at Oxford; he taught at Isfahan University and worked with Afghan refugees in Peshawar; he has contributed programs to the Persian and Pushtu service of the BBC World Service, had translated Persian mystical poetry and written on Islamic art and travel.

Professor James Weiner: Australia

James Weiner is a senior anthropologist at the Australian National University. His writings include contributions to *World Mythology* (Simon & Schuster).

Picture Credits

Picture Credits

Academy for Korean Studies: 198, 201, 202

AKG Photo: 17, 34, 100, 196, 203, 214.

Christie's Images: 132 (b), 186, 245, 248.

Circa Photo Library: 136, 173, 175.

Chief Pedro Guanikeyu Torres: 255, 259

Clayton, Peter A.: 42, 43, 44, 45, 46, 47, 49.

Collection Kharbine-Tapabor: 102, 109.

Courtesy of Kojiki Nikonshoki (Shinchosha, 1991): 197

e.t.archive: 18, 195.

Foundry Arts: 183. David Banfield: 48. Lucinda Hawksley 249.

Gunson, Niel: 222

Image Select/Chris Fairclough: 106, 131, 191, 225.

Image Select/Girandon: 14, 29, 35, 90, 101, 107, 139, 194, 255, 260.

Mary Evans Picture Library: 22, 23, 25, 27, 71, 82, 85, 89.

Palekh Art, Courtesy of Professor J. Riordan: 103, 105.

Robiou, Sebastian: 261

Saunders, N. J.: 294.

Scandibild: 117, 121, 122, 126.

Still Pictures: 138.

Topham Picturepoint: 12, 16, 19, 26, 28, 32, 38, 132 (t), 134, 135, 170, 190.

Travel Photo International: 254, 257, 258.

Visual Arts Library: 150 (t)

Visual Arts Library/Artephot: 97. Artephot/Brumaire: 166. Artephot/Nimatallah: 52, 53, 54, 56, 58, 61, 62, 73. Artephot/Faillet: 171, 293. Artephot/S. Fiore: 118. Artephot/Held: 59, 66, 216, 224, 230, 244, 250. Artephot/Kumasegawa: 162, 167. Artephot/Lavaud: 158, 164, 179, 185, 187. Artephot/G. Mandel: 182 (t). Artephot/Ogawa: 192. Artephot/M. Pietri: 147, 153. Artephot/R. Roland: 287. Artephot/Ru Sui Chu: 181, 198. Artephot/Scandibild: 115. Artephot/Varga: 63, 251.

Visual Arts Library/Bridgeman Art Library: 13, 15, 21, 24, 30, 36, 37, 39, 43, 55, 60, 65, 67, 68, 69, 70, 72, 77, 84, 93, 169, 178, 182 (b), 220. Bridgeman Art Library/Girandon: 137.

Visual Arts Library/Edimedia: 81, 83, 142, 143, 146, 148, 150 (b), 152 (t), 152 (b), 155 (t), 155 (br), 156, 163, 217, 219, 224, 226, 246, 247, 299 (t).

Visual Arts Library/Werner Forman Archive: 78 (l), 296, 172, 174, 209 (t), 264, 266, 281 (b). Dorset Natural History and Archaeological Society: 76. Musee de Rennes. 78 (r). National Museum of Ireland: 87. National Museum of Wales: 91. National Museum, Copenhagen: 94. British Museum, London: 95, 211 (t), 211 (b), 275, 283, 286, 290, 301. Univer sitetets Oldoksamling, Oslo: 112. Universitetetsbibliteket, Uppsala, Sweden: 113. Statens Historiska Museum, Stockholm: 116, 123, 114, 125, 119. Arhus Kunstmuseum, Denmark: 120. Manx Museum, Isle of Man: 124. Viking Ship Museum, Byg- doy: 127. National Gallery, Prague: 145. Victoria and Albert Museum, London: 155 (bl). Schatzkammer der Residenz, Munich: 157, 159. Philip Goldman Collection, London: 165, 168, 208. Private Collection: 206, 207, 234, 292. Denpasar Museum, Bali: 209, 210 (b). Art Gallery of NSW, Sydney: 231, 238. Aboriginal: 232. Private Collection New York: 233, 241, 288. Tara Collection, New York: 235, 236, 237. Private Col- lection, Prague: 239, 240. H W Read Collection, Plains Indian Museum, Wyoming: 265. Centennial Museum, Vancouver, Canada: 267. James Hooper Collection, England: 269. Mr and Mrs John A. Putman: 270. Denver Art Museum, Colorado: 271. Maxwell Museum of Anthropology, Alburquerque: 272. Museum of Anthropology, Vancouver Canada: 273. Smithsonian Institute, Washington: 274. Provincial Museum, Victoria, Canada: 276. National Museum of Man, Ottawa, Canada: 277. Liverpool Muse- um, Liverpool: 281 (t). Museum für Völkerkunde, Berlin: 282, 299 (b), 295. Museum für Völkerkunde, Basel: 284. National Museum of Anthropology, Mexico: 285, 289. Toni Ralph Collection, New York: 291. David Bernstein Fine Art, New York: 297, 300.

Index